JUNK
"SOME SAY"

A JOKESMITH'S HARDEST DAY
WHEN A DIOLOGUE IS WANTED WHICH HAS NEITHER HUMOR NOR SUGGESTION OF AN IDEA

RELATIVITY

HE HANDS OVER THE FRUIT OF HIS TOIL ON A SILVER PLATTER,
AND THEN GETS ABOUT ONE EIGHTH OF THE JUICE

THE GALLEY
DEDICATED TO THE STATESWHERE CHILD LABOR IS STILL PERMITTED

# TO LAUGH THAT WE MAY NOT WEEP

## The
## LIFE & TIMES
## Of
## ART YOUNG

EDITED BY GLENN BRAY & FRANK M. YOUNG
INTRODUCTION BY ART SPIEGELMAN

Fantagraphics Books
SEATTLE

Publisher and Executive Editor: **Gary Groth**
Senior Editor: **J. Michael Catron**
Designer: **Sean David Williams**
Proofreader: **Conrad Groth**
Production: **Paul Baresh**
Associate Publisher: **Eric Reynolds**

Fantagraphics Books, Inc.
7563 Lake City Way NE
Seattle, WA 98115
(800) 657-1100

Fantagraphics.com. • Twitter: @fantagraphics •
facebook.com/fantagraphics.

First edition: September 2017

ISBN 978-1-60699-994-3

Library of Congress Control Number: 2016947863

Printed in China

# To Laugh

## The Life

### That

#### & Times of

# We May

##### Art Young

# Not Weep

# CONTENTS

ABOVE: Art Young in his studio, c. 1915–1920

**01** P. 8

**INTRODUCTION**
art spiegelman

**02** P. 16

**THE LIFE & TIMES**
Frank M. Young

**03** P. 40

**POLITICS & PERSONALITIES**
Anthony Mourek
Valerie Higgins

**04** P. 62

**SOCIAL COMMENTARIES**

**05** P. 114

**THE MASSES**
Marc Moorash

**06** P. 132

**GAGS**

**07** p. 154

FANTASY & MUSINGS

**08** p. 198

COMPLEXES

**09** p. 204

GOOD MORNING
Marc Moorash

**10** p. 232

QUOTATION CARTOONS

**11** p. 244

EPHEMERA

**12** p. 262

ART YOUNG ON ART

**13** p. 270

ON RELIGION

**14** p. 282

TYPES & PORTRAITS

**15** p. 306

APPROACHING YOUNG'S
TREESCAPES
Justin Green

**16** p. 324

ART YOUNG'S INFERNOS
Glenn Bray

**17** p. 338

POLITICAL MISCELLANEOUS

**18** p. 356

ART YOUNG ON ART YOUNG

**19** p. 370

ARGOSY ESSAY & IMAGES
Judith Lowry

**20** p. 376

EPILOGUE & THANK YOU
Laura Ten Eyck

**21** p. 378

CONTRIBUTOR BIOGRAPHIES

**22** p. 380

EDITOR BIOGRAPHIES

**23** p. 381

A SELECTED
ART YOUNG
BIBLIOGRAPHY
Marc Moorash

FOLLOWING SPREAD: **In a World of Plenty**
*Life*, October 10, 1912
From Art Young's personal tear sheet file

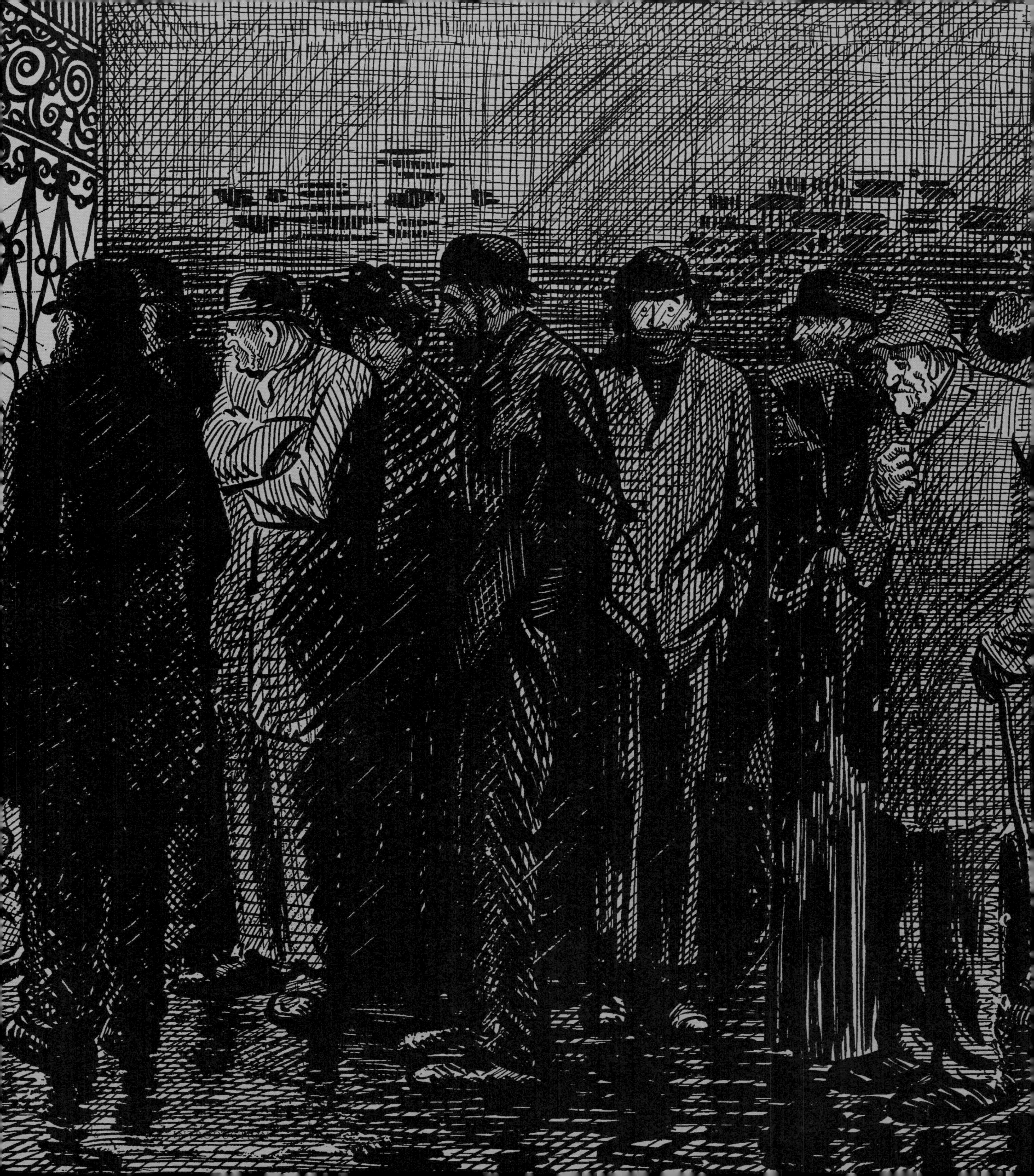

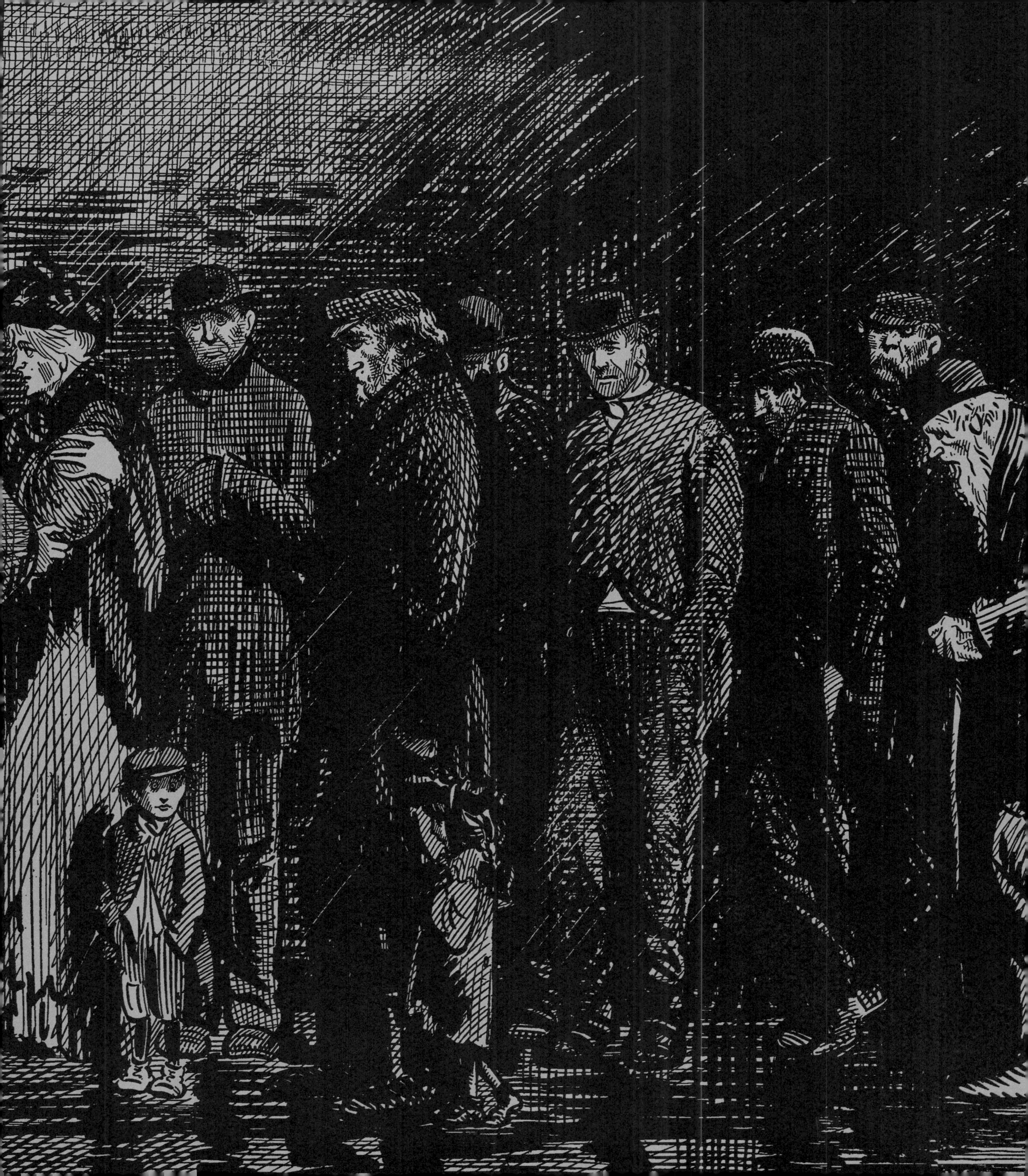

# ART YOUNG: AN INTRODUCTION

Let the
Thinking
People
Rule

# 01

OPPOSITE: **Let the Thinking People Rule**
*Metropolitan Magazine,* November 1917
8.5" x 11"

## @%&#!! I don't understand. Why would Art Young — the greatest radical political cartoonist in our history — need any introduction???

Never mind, I remember now: Art Young was a Radical! Political!! Cartoonist!!!

1.   *Radical.* We Americans, poor fish, have a perpetually recurring case of amnesia, trying to wriggle off the hook when it comes to facing our history as a Rapacious Capitalist Empire. We prefer to think of ourselves as wide-eyed innocents with perpetually renewing hymens. Just reading this far has made some of you twitch at the threat of an inconvenient truth and slam the book shut. (What on Earth were you doing, looking at a book anyway?) Others have already rolled over, and gone back to sleep because …

2.   *Political.* The word conjures up either boredom or futile contention. The only concept less inviting is "political radical" — Anarchist bomb-throwing troublemakers — sounds dangerous, so what could be worse? Oh, I know the answer to that rhetorical question too …

3.   *Cartoonist!* A creator of trivial diversions, only worth the time more fruitfully spent dozing if the creator is (a) hilarious, (b) salacious, or preferably (c) both. In fact, one of the few phrases more snooze-worthy than "political" may be "political cartoonist," especially in its current, demeaned American form. As newspapers disappear and circulations dwindle, the political cartoonist has become an endangered species that, in order to survive, has usually been reduced to making tepid gag cartoons about current events with no whiff of controversy since one canceled subscription or lost advertiser can spell death for yet one more paper. So, Art Young — the greatest Radical Political Cartoonist in our history — with three strikes against him, won the Oblivion trifecta.

Of course, Art Young's profession is not always and everywhere dismissed as trivial — just ask the murdered *Charlie Hebdo* artists. And it's not all about Mohammad: tinpot despots — in countries that include Malaysia, Venezuela, India, Syria, and Iran to name a very few recent offenders — have acknowledged how potent cartoons can be by offering tribute to the cartoonists in the form of police harassment, massive fines, long prison terms, and torture.

# · L I F E ·

If it is a picture called "Afterglow," and if it looks like an explosion in a tomato cannery, it is: "Above the heads of the people."

If it is a scene in the slums, and the people resemble idiots and comic supplement types: "The artist is in sympathy with the suffering poor and paints a scathing rebuke to our social system."

If it is "A girl holding her hat" (note the title), it is: "An intellectual interpretation of childhood and shows this original artist at his best."

If it is a mussy portrait that shows very little resemblance to the sitter: "It is more than a mere portrait. The artist has caught the soul of his subject."

PUZZLE EXPERT

If the paint is laid on so thick you can hang your umbrella on it: "It stands out in virile contrast to the anæmic productions of the older masters, and is an artistic triumph."

If it is a symbolic spasm, called "The Heel of Destiny," and about as good in color and drawing as a four-year-old child would do, it is: "The work of a genius whose note of defiance for conventional methods and unbridled love of life augurs well for the future of American art."

If it is a picture that you like and others like, why, of course, it is no good at all.

OPPOSITE: How to Judge a Picture
According to Modern Criticism
*Life*, June 3, 1913

ABOVE: The Uprising of the Proletariat
*Good Morning*, July 15, 1920

In the 19th and the early 20th century the power of the political cartoon to shape thought and mobilize opinion was a given. Young first understood the power for positive change that he wielded when one of his drawings in a 1909 *Puck* (p. 27) shamed New York's wealthy Trinity Church into eventually tearing down and replacing the pestilent slum buildings it profited from. He happily embraced the term "propaganda," seeing it simply as propagating his own ideas. His contempt was reserved for the editorial prostitution involved in drawing for an editor's convictions rather than one's own. (Young confessed he didn't *have* convictions until he was about 40; then he put his mouth where his money wasn't — refusing stunningly lucrative staff contracts to take the vow of poverty that comes with *working* for the radical press.) I'm glad to report that he was never quite convicted for his convictions, though he was sued for libel twice by the Associated Press after accurately accusing them of covering up the bloody details of a West Virginia coal miners' strike; and his

anti-war cartoons for *The Masses* during World War I literally got him tried for treason.

Art Young's ability to clearly identify and enrage powerful enemies matches the standards set by George Grosz, who was variously tried for blasphemy, slander, and obscenity by the Nazis before fleeing to America for his life (an uprooting that mostly destroyed Grosz as an artist since he needed to be near his enemies to thrive). Young didn't have Grosz's talent for hatred. His indignation was visceral, but his generous soul and empathic heart put him in the same Olympian league as Daumier. Grosz and Daumier were painters as well as cartoonists, and that helped keep them from slipping into the cultural memory hole that swallowed Art Young.

Political cartoons usually have a very short half-life — comments on the passing parade are just confetti to be tossed out after the parade has gone by, salvaged mostly by historians or other political cartoonists looking to recycle them. Even Art Young's boyhood hero, Thomas

Capitalism
*Life*, February 23, 1911
Collection of Marc Moorash

Nast — who gave us our contemporary image of Santa Claus and its antonym, the Republican Elephant — is only remembered for his cartoons of the Tweed Ring's political corruption because they're useful for spicing up the gray monotony of American history textbooks. Discussing his selection process for work in his 1936 collection of *The Best of Art Young* (the only major retrospective of his work 'til right now) he wrote:

I did not spend many years of my life cartooning the trivial turns in current politics. Although a few of these are related to the topical issues of other days, it will be noted that practically all of them are generalizations on the one important issue of this era the world over: Plutocracy versus the principles of Socialism.

Art Young might be a bit disheartened to find out that the grand Soviet experiment kinda fizzled. But by having kept his eye on the fundamentals, his cartoons are rarely musty artifacts from yesterday's papers and seem like urgent dispatches from tomorrow's news. His classic 1911 *Life* cartoon, "Capitalism," (amusingly subtitled "The Last Supper"), depicts terminal gluttony. It could be an accurate Facebook avatar for any of today's one-percenters heedlessly destroying the lives of the 99 percent of us who share the planet they're making unbreathable — even for their own privileged progeny.

I love that drawing, one of the artist's clearest and most straightforwardly angry indictments, damning the greedy beast to plummet directly into Art Young's Inferno; but there is somehow an elusive touch of compassion even for this monster, heedlessly guzzling swill from his bejeweled cauldron. Young finds a way to hate the sin but not the sinner that arises from his deeply ingrained sense of humor, manifested in masterful exaggeration — one can't draw that creature's body gesture without inhabiting the pose. It is built on the artist's recognition of his own — and Everyman's — capacity for gluttony, an understanding that we are all closer to animals than gods.

Man and Beast
*The Best of Art Young*, 1936

It's a theme he visits often in his work (see, for example, *Man and Beast*, *"There's a divinity that shapes our ends"*). The artist's Lightness of Being made the audience able to bear the unbearable and it separates his work from the shrill, self-righteous sentimentality of many of his radical, political cartoon comrades. It's the quality that forced even the prosecuting attorney in Young's trial for treason to acknowledge, in his summation, "Everybody likes Art Young"; and it's why thousands from across the political spectrum came out to mourn him when he died.

If Young hasn't been sufficiently remembered, it is not because his pictures aren't memorable. He'd studied to be a painter, but said he preferred a large audience to being displayed on a rich man's walls, and he was impatient with pictures that didn't make a clear point. (This need for content is personified by his landscape drawings, *Trees at Night* (p. 306). He reclaims the landscape — usually the painter's domain — as ground for a cartoonist's imposed

meanings by anthropomorphizing his silhouetted willows with painterly washes so they literally weep.

Young told Max Eastman, his fellow conspirator at *The Masses*, that he was as totally devoted to the aesthetic elements of his work as any painter. "I worry over composition, drawing, light and shade, elimination — above all elimination — from breakfast time to dinner." I'm pretty sure that he wasn't just referring to his digestive tract, but to the cartoonist's craft of making an efficient, stripped-down image. One can see the progression from his youthful drawings that emulate the wood engravings of Gustave Doré's *Inferno* and Thomas Nast's tight crosshatching to his signature, mature style of streamlined ink lines echoing early 20th century modern woodcuts (that had themselves been influenced by Japanese prints). Some of his drawings are reminiscent of the graphic rigor of his younger contemporary and friend, Rockwell Kent, but without the bombast. Though comfortable in various black-and-white media, including

"Chee, Annie, look at de stars — thick as bed-bugs!"
*The Best of Art Young*, 1936

crayon drawing and painted washes, it's Young's boldly composed later line work that fully embodies the paradox of humble virtuosity.

Young was searching for images that were coherent intellectually as well as formally. Saul Steinberg defined the elusive goal as making an image that, once seen, can never be unseen — and Young was a world-class master at distilling his thoughts about the class war down to memorable symbolic representations. His work was understandable to all classes, and miraculously managed to avoid the sectarian infighting that traditionally defines and eviscerates the radical left.

But I would be doing Young a great disservice if I left you with the impression that he was "just" a political cartoonist. Many of his cartoons have no overt political agenda, except insofar as *everything* is political. They are intentionally and genuinely amusing (though, astonishingly, never cruel or condescending), and often appeared in "general interest" magazines ranging from *The New Yorker* to *The Saturday Evening Post*. While many of Art Young's political cartoons were direct lessons on America's rigged economic con game, *all* of his work was also a lesson in empathy. We have never needed more of both.

— *art spiegelman*

ABOVE: **The Freedom of the Presses**
*The Masses*, December 1912

RIGHT: art spiegelman (left) and Glenn Bray (right) at Argosy Bookstore with Art Young's archives. New York City, January 2013. Photo by Laura Ten Eyck.

# THE LIFE & TIMES

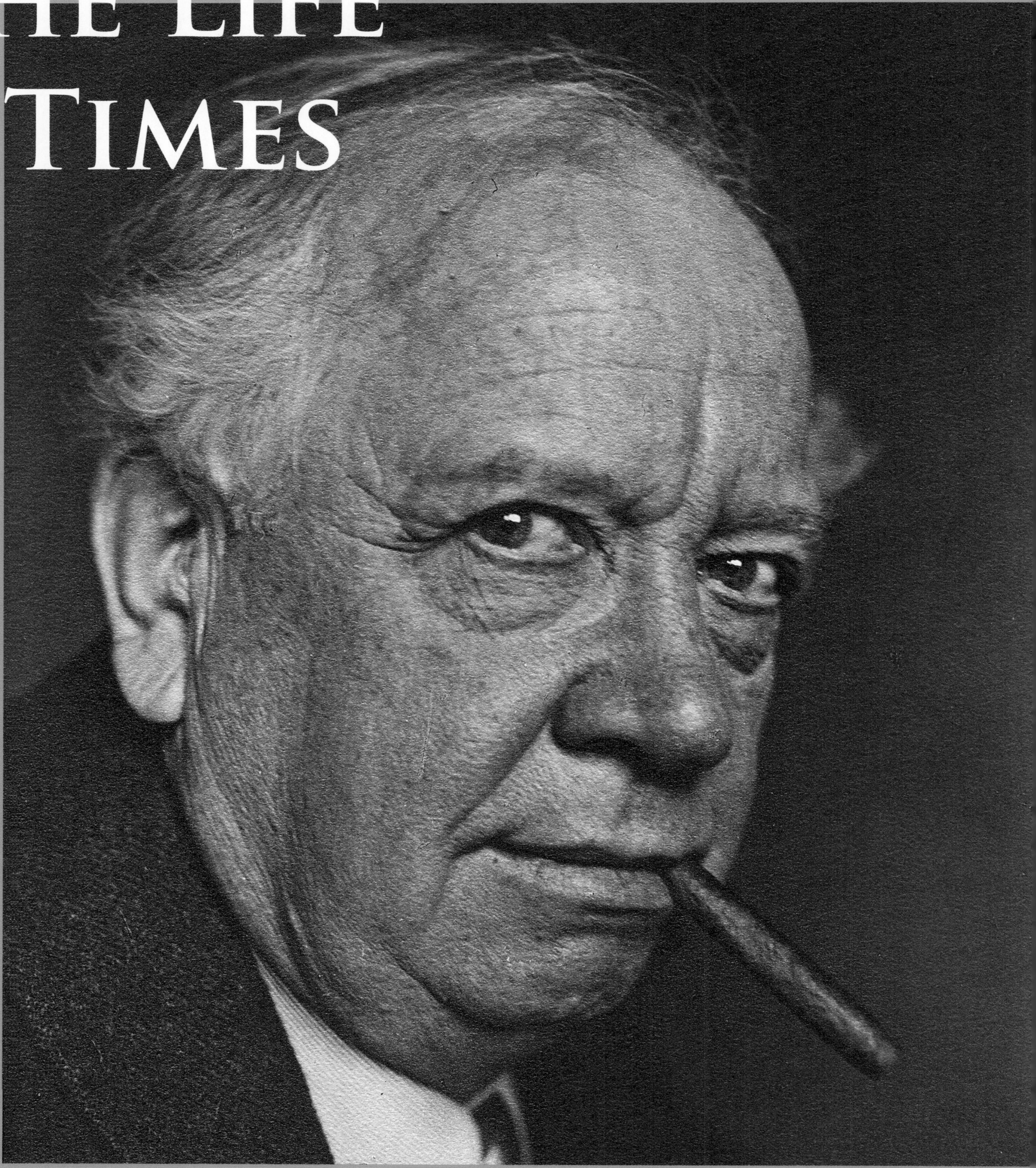

## 02

**FRANK M. YOUNG**

## Art Young's name, and work, have been off the beaten path of comics and cartooning history in the last 50 years. He has by no means been forgotten. His work, still highly regarded by cartoonists and devotees of the graphic arts, has been hidden from the public eye.

At the peak of his powers, Young was a highly articulate voice in American arts and letters. His instantly recognizable style — which spanned the baroque detail of Victorian America and the streamlined, modernistic look of Art Deco — decorated a passionate humanist worldview.

Speaking for the dispossessed, the neglected, and the exploited, Art Young's voice expressed a truth that cut through layers of civility and smug entitlement. His satiric eye, which saw (through) politicians, the wealthy, the middle class, glad-handers, con artists, and the fads and foibles of his day, never disemboweled its targets. It said what it saw, and called into question the fallacy of each subject.

Humor and humanity are the leavening agents in his work. Young saw the best — and worst — of mankind, and celebrated its humanity as he castigated its inhumanity. His most biting, effective pieces always find the humor in their situations. This humor is sometimes dark, but at all times accurate and exquisite. Few cartoonists — or authors — have addressed the insanity of war, or the inequity of the American class system, with greater eloquence.

Many of Young's cartoons are strikingly relevant to 21st-century America. We still have a schism between the haves and the have-nots; the tools of warfare have become smarter and faster, but the threat of war still hangs over our heads. Workers have gradually lost much of the ground gained in labor reforms of the 20th century — as corporations, now considered people, merge and submerge the world around us.

History, indeed, repeats itself. Our modern world of unemployment, homelessness, and the working poor — where a one-percent elite prospers while 99 percent fight to survive — looks a lot like an Art Young cartoon.

ABOVE: **April Fool**
*The Masses,* April 1913

OPPOSITE: **Art Young**, c. 1920

DANIEL S. YOUNG          AMANDA W. YOUNG

— 4 —

#6        Remembrance of my father and Mother

*The leading citizens of Monroe — town of my boyhood — were the subjects for my first cartoons. The announcement held in my hand refers to a previous cartoon, which had aroused the anger of our district attorney. It reads: "Ladies and Gents, P.K. Clawson is not on exhibition — he's dangerous."*

*— Art Young*

**TOP:** Remembrance of my Father and Mother
14" x 10"

**ABOVE:** Art Young's First Published Illustration
*His Life and Times*

**OPPOSITE:** Leading Citizens of Monroe
*On My Way*, 1928

Art Young's life story is one of struggle, individuality, celebrity, persecution, and fortitude. His political conversion — from Republican to an ardent voice for socialism and labor reform — helped others see the light of a complex, often brutal world around them. That voice cost him financial stability. Through his life, brief periods of prosperity were bookended with times of poverty, of working *pro bono* for causes he believed in, such as the magazines *Good Morning* and *The Masses*, rather than prosper via more conservative, crowd-pleasing work.

Young was admired by colleagues, publishers, and the American public. His cartoons are not all politically themed. He was capable of devastatingly funny portraits of his fellow man (as in his delightful series *Types of the Old Home Town*) and of elegant flights of fancy (his haunting cartoons for the book *Trees at Night*).

Young might have sought the comfortably short leash of a mainstream syndicated comic strip, or created neutral gag cartoons for high-circulation slick magazines. Instead, he chose to work for publications that had the guts to print his contrary views on a world of constant change.

Born a year after the end of the Civil War, Art Young lived to see the darkest days of World War II. The America of his lifetime — 1866 to 1943 — grew from a mostly agrarian society to a chaos of developing technology.

As the Industrial Revolution encompassed America in the latter decades of the 19th century, cities became meccas for those who wished to pursue a career, make money, and get away from small-town or farm life.

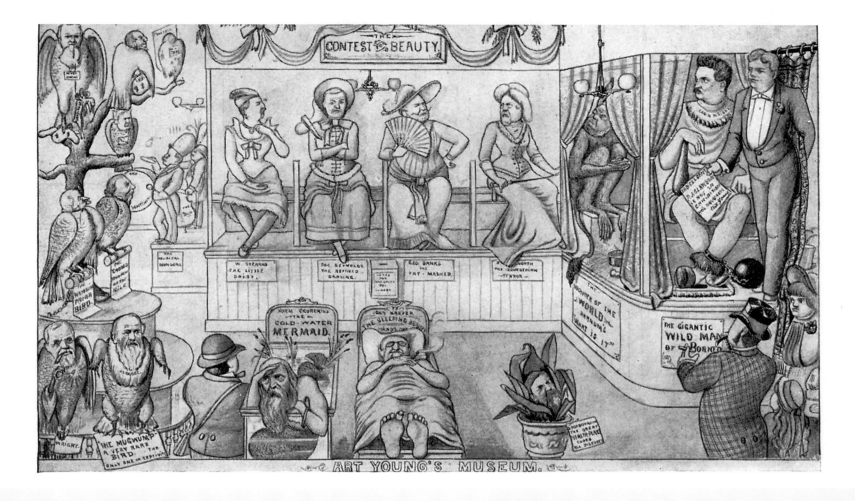

## DREAM-DAYS BACK ON THE FARM

ARTHUR HENRY YOUNG was born on January 14, 1866, in Orangeville, Illinois, "a few miles south of the Wisconsin line." Young's family relocated to Monroe, Wisconsin, in 1867. His father, Daniel S. Young, ran a general store, which, due to its closeness to the town courthouse and square, also functioned as a social hub for the community.

One of four children, Art was doted upon by his parents, and encouraged to develop an interest in drawing. An early and abiding influence was Gustave Doré, whose engravings in Dante's *Inferno* enthralled the curious child. By his teenage years, Art was, in his words, Monroe's "prodigy in art." His compulsion to draw overrode a traditional education. Young never finished high school, but his calling was evident.

Young Art gained local notoriety with his caricatures of Monroe citizens, including political figures — some of whom quailed at the youthful lampoons posted in Dan Young's store and in the local post office. Those not subject to his scrutiny guffawed at his topical cartoons.

Monroe would remain dear to Art Young's heart, but it was understood he wouldn't spend his life there. A sale to *Judge* magazine — an illustrated humor weekly — netted Young seven dollars and further encouraged his ambition.

At 17, Young moved to Chicago. He studied at the Chicago Academy of Design under John H. Vanderpoel, best known for his classic text *The Human Figure*. Young admired Vanderpoel's attentive, frank criticisms and feedback.

While at the academy, Young published a few freelance cartoons and soon found regular work with the Chicago *Evening Mail*. For the newspaper, Young captured street scenes, which he transferred from pencil sketches to chalk plate engravings. "I didn't like this roundabout way of making a picture," Young recalled, but the newsroom and publishing experience excited and engaged him.

Via Chicago's public library, Young discovered other influences, including R. Caton Woodville, the British illustrator noted for his energetic battle scenes, F. Barnard's illustrations in Charles Dickens's books, and the eminent cartoonists George Cruikshank, Sir John Tenniel, and John Leech.

Young found the publishing mainstream preferable to the strictures of art school. Nicknamed "Nosey" by journalist Eugene Wood, Young explored Chicago, attending lectures, the theater, and mass meetings.

In 1885, Art Young began the education of his social conscience. Via mass meetings and street speeches, Young first learned of the growing dissatisfaction between America's work force and the capitalist businessmen who employed them. Wage cuts and strikes caused many workers to lose their jobs and fomented a mutual distrust — and contempt — of workers and businesses.

With its ties to industry, Chicago was an inevitable center for the labor movement. Advocates fought to instill an eight-hour workday, end starvation wages, and ensure the safety and welfare of the American worker.

Although Young didn't realize it at first, nor change from his

Chicago, or about the "best mayor" it ever had that the sultan and his ministers do not know now, trust Carter H. Harrison to tell it to them.

ABOVE: Carter Harrison Abroad
*Chicago Evening Mail*
Early chalk engraving

OPPOSITE ABOVE: A Tempting Impulse
Early cartoon as published in color in *Puck*

OPPOSITE BELOW: Joseph Keppler signed portrait print
Collection of Art Young

Republican political views, he became more open to the plight of the American worker. The Haymarket riots of May 1886, in which a mass meeting in protest of police violence and unfair work conditions literally exploded into violence and death, galvanized the labor movement. Seven policemen and several civilians were killed and wounded. Eight men were, perhaps, unfairly tried and found guilty for planting and exploding a bomb at the assembly. Four of the eight were hanged; another took his life rather than face public execution.

Assigned to cover the trials as a sketch artist, Young found himself at first "swayed by ... detailed reports of the black-heartedness of the defendants," via biased, sensational news accounts. Upon hearing the voluntary testimony of Albert Parsons, who emerged from safe hiding to appear in court, Young noted: "My sympathies began to lean in the other direction ... [i]f Parsons were guilty, I reasoned ... he would not have come back ..."

Young moved to the Chicago *Daily News* in the wake of the trial. For that paper, he interviewed and sketched the eight condemned men, two days before four of them met the gallows. Young was relieved when another artist was assigned their execution.

After a quick stint at the *Tribune*, Young moved to New York City and became a freelancer. This unfocused life soon palled, and Young enrolled in the Art Students' League. Despite this serious study, Young's attention increasingly turned to the weekly humor magazines *Life*, *Judge*, and *Puck*.

Young admired *Puck* in particular. Dominated by the skillful but staid work of Joseph Keppler, the magazine epitomized the state of late-19th-century cartooning. In the tradition of Thomas Nast, *Puck* cartoons stress baroque, painterly detail, quasi-realistic figures, and occur in a single-scene tableau. They are not cartoons, or comics, as we would come to know them in the 20th century. Frederick Opper, one of newspaper comics' early talents, and Eugene "Zim" Zimmerman, whose how-to books on cartooning influenced a generation of artists, were also *Puck* mainstays.

Young most admired Nast. His political cartoons fearlessly attacked corrupt politicians, unfair conditions, and other plights of urban life. As Young noted, "the darts of his satire were sharp."

At loose ends in 1889 New York, Young was contacted by writer/humorist Clarence Webster with an irresistible offer. Webster planned a trip of Europe, financed by the Chicago *Inter Ocean*. Webster asked Young to illustrate his articles. After a brief visit to Monroe, Young met Webster in New York, where the two sailed for Liverpool, England.

A TEMPTING IMPULSE.

UNCLE JOE PLUGG—"Woman's Exchange, eh? If it won't be so blamed wicked, I'd almost feel like exchangin' Mandy fer a woman with more 'get up' to her an' not so allfired humly."

After some innocents-abroad misadventures, Young and Webster settled in Paris. There, Young studied at the Académie Julian and the Colarossi School. "I was deadly earnest about developing my talent," he recalled. Amidst his hard work, Young had a life-changing epiphany:

> I became more and more convinced that graphic art was my road to recognition … [i]f one painted a portrait, or a landscape, or whatever, for a rich man to own in his private gallery, what was the use … [A] cartoon could be reproduced by simple mechanical processes and easily made available to hundreds of thousands. I wanted a large audience …

A near-fatal attack of pleurisy ended Young's Paris studies. His father traveled to his bedside — a heroic trip for the small-town storekeeper — and saw him through fits of delirium. By May 1890, Young was well enough to return to Monroe, where he convalesced and reconnected with his family and friends.

Among the latter was Elizabeth North, who would become Young's wife. A five-year courtship began as the bashful Young struggled to make a name as a cartoonist.

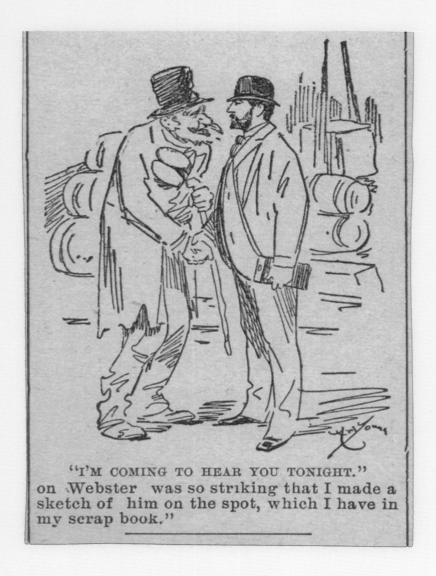

"I'M COMING TO HEAR YOU TONIGHT."
on Webster was so striking that I made a
sketch of him on the spot, which I have in
my scrap book."

ABOVE: Art Young sketch of author-humorist Clarence Webster

ABOVE RIGHT: Elizabeth North (Young)
1893

## A HELL OF AN IDEA

WHILE IN MONROE, at loose ends, Young conceived of a book inspired by a formative influence:

> I began toying … with the writing and illustrating of a book dealing with the intimate affairs in the Hell of my own time … I figured that Hades must have changed a good deal through the centuries … just as the upper world had changed for better or for worse.

The book, which was published as *Hell Up to Date*, was no mere imitation of Dante and Doré. Young satirized high and low figures of modern society with a wit worthy of Gilbert and Sullivan's comic operas. Fitting punishments were devised for everyone from "small town gossips" to "the monopolists and snobbish rich sitting in frying pans over fires."

While Young created the book, he headlined a traveling revue organized by Chicago entrepreneur Wyllys Abbot. With much promotional ballyhoo, Young drew portraits and cartoons to musical accompaniment. The act was well received and played its final show in Young's hometown, where Clarence Webster joined the troupe.

ABOVE: **A Dentist's Fate**
*Through Hell With Hiprah Hunt*, 1901
7.5" x 8.5"

RIGHT: **Camel Riding on the Plaisance**
Cover to *The Inter Ocean Illustrated Supplement* (Chicago), June 21, 1893
(Original art, p. 183)

Anxious to revive his career, Young returned to Chicago in late 1891. He was hired as editorial cartoonist for the *Inter Ocean*, a widely circulated Midwestern newspaper. Young was published daily, which was a first for Midwestern papers. Walt McDougall, as Young notes in his memoir, had been doing a daily cartoon for the New York *World* "as early as 1884."

Young attended the 1892 Republican convention, where he met McDougall and Thomas Nast. Young still aligned himself with the Republican Party, although he continued to question this allegiance.

Nast stayed in Chicago, and worked with Young at the *Inter Ocean*. The newspaper bought a color printing press, and, in the fall of 1892, published the country's first color Sunday supplement. Nast and Young did full-page cartoons for this circulation-boosting innovation. Young was thrilled to work with one of his graphic heroes: "[I]t was gratifying to see my name featured in advertisements with that of the artist I had admired so much in the dream-days back on the farm."

While Nast did mostly political cartoons, Young addressed current events, including the World's Columbian Exposition (a.k.a. the Chicago World's Fair), sporting events, and the expansion of Chicago.

*Hell Up to Date* was published at the end of 1892. Young was pleased by praise from cartoonist A.B. Frost — another of his longstanding favorites. According to Art Young's biographer, Marc Moorash, the book had more than 15 printings, although the creator never saw much money from its sales.

In 1893, Young illustrated another, more ephemeral book written by his colleague and traveling companion, Clarence Webster, in his guise of "Conflagration Jones." *Hawaii: A Snap Shot*, a 64-page comedic essay, is a trifle in Young's bibliography, but remains the most visible remnant of his collaborations with Webster.

Young covered the Chicago World's Fair, among other highlights of 1893 and 1894. As he covered Chicago for the *Inter Ocean*, he saw, first hand, the corruption and deliberate suppression of evidence in the city's politics. Young felt increasing inner conflict over the anti-Democrat cartoons he wrote and drew — in particular, a series that attacked Grover Cleveland's presidential administration.

After the closing of the World's Fair, an economic slump hit Chicago. Young continued in his capacity as daily cartoonist through 1894.

Home for the holidays that December, Young and Elizabeth North decided to tie the knot. They were wed on New Year's Day 1895 — the start of a complex, problematic marriage.

**ABOVE: Keir Hardie**
*Art Young: His Life and Times*, 1939

**OPPOSITE: E.V. Debs**
Eugene V. Debs portrait, c. 1920
7" x 5"
Collection of Marc Moorash

Young moved, without his wife, to Denver, Colorado, where he worked as cartoonist for the city's *Times*.

In Denver, Young heard Scottish workers' advocate Keir Hardie speak. Young was deeply moved by Hardie's descriptions of the plights of Welsh miners. Mistreatment of labor, he learned, was not uniquely American.

Young missed city life. He and Elizabeth reunited and moved to New York in early 1896. Young freelanced, selling cartoons to *Puck*, *Life*, and *Judge*. In 1897, he completed a second book, *Authors' Readings*. An illustrated celebration of Young's favorite writers, it sold poorly. A planned sequel was scuttled.

The sinking of the USS *Maine*, in February 1898, lit the fuse for the Spanish-American War. New York's yellow press had a field day with the conflict. Young, at first, fell for the distorted jingoism — until reports of American troops' deaths from dysentery broke through the patriotic front. Though still Republican, Young questioned his affiliation, and the purpose of this — or any — war.

Though Young loved his wife, he still chafed at his lack of freedom. He and Elizabeth separated, and Young lived solo in New York. There, he drew cartoons for the *Evening Journal*, under editor Arthur Brisbane. Young worked alongside Fred Opper and T.S. Sullivant.

Pressured by friends, Young gave married life with Elizabeth another go. He became a father. Despite the birth of his first son, North, Young again felt at odds with the demands of matrimony. He often avoided his wife by attending lectures.

During this period, Young created a sequel to his first Hell book, *Through Hell With Hiprah Hunt* (1901).

As well, Young first met Eugene V. Debs, then America's strongest personal voice for socialism. Debs's speeches jarred Young. "I was living in a world that was morally and spiritually diseased," he wrote in his memoirs, "and I was learning some of the reasons why."

The insight made Young realize he could no longer kowtow to the biased views of his employers. Young took his family (which, in 1904, included a second son, Donald) and retreated to rural Bethel, Connecticut. At first, the family liked this rustic environment. Young soon realized he could not cope with marriage, and he again separated from Elizabeth. The couple was never officially divorced, but this break marked the end of their many attempts at cohabitation.

E.V. Debs

## ON HIS WAY, ON HIS OWN

YOUNG WOULD REMAIN connected to Bethel for the rest of his life, but he now returned to New York. Six months later, Elizabeth and the two children relocated to California. On his own, Young steeped himself in socialist literature and attended more forums and lectures. He was determined to see both sides of the struggle, and to understand it without bias.

Young's social conscience still cost him work. As he said in *His Life and Times*: "I was now developing a hatred for all bourgeois institutions … and trying hard to live up to my own ideas of right and wrong … no one could hire me to draw a cartoon that I did not believe in …"

Young returned a $100 check to *Life* magazine, payment for a cartoon he had done to order, and which he felt slandered the Jewish community. Though the editor was peeved, he allowed Young to draw a cartoon of his own creation that showed Jesus criticized by businessmen for "not being practical." *Life* paid him for the cartoon, but it never ran. As the editor confessed, according to

Young, "we're trying to get up nerve enough around here to publish your Christ picture."

Young officially joined the Socialist Party in 1910. Now committed to espousing this cause via cartoons, he found few takers. *Life* printed some of Young's socialist pieces, including "The Last Supper," a powerful allegory on greed, entitlement, and selfishness.

When Dutch socialist Piet Vlag launched *The Masses*, in 1911, Young found a new home for his work. *The Masses* remains among the finest American magazines — impressive for contributions by an early 20th century Who's Who of arts, letters, and politics. Young enjoyed a freedom of expression he'd not found before as a cartoonist.

Editor Max Eastman and radical journalist John Reed soon joined *The Masses'* inner circle. Despite financial struggles, the magazine survived and improved with each new issue. "Nice people didn't want it around," Young famously said of *The Masses*, which questioned the tenets of American society, morality, and industry.

Young realized that his cartoons had the power to make positive change. His cartoon "Holy Trinity," published in *Puck*'s first issue

## THE FORTUNES OF AMERICA.

CAPITALIST: 'IT TAKES BRAINS TO BUILD THEM.'

WAGE-WORKER: 'YES, BUT DON'T YOU FORGET THAT IT TAKES A FEW BACKS'

The Fortunes of America
28.25" x 16.5"

of 1909, denounced New York's Trinity Church for its ownership of disease-ridden tenement slums. Though the church publicly dismissed the cartoon, it quietly bulldozed those wretched buildings in 1911. Its actions were attributed, by journalist Charles Edward Russell, to the persuasive power of Young's image.

A comparison of this printed color version with the piece's original art (seen on p. 280) attests to the persuasive power of Art Young's line. His is an earthy, sinuous, firmly rooted hand. By the time of "Holy Trinity" he had shed most of the baroque influence of the Joseph Keppler era of cartooning. His bold, decisive brushwork anticipates future cartoonists of note, including Roy Crane and Harvey Kurtzman.

Young had a painter's eye for composition and control of the viewer's focus. His bold areas of black and white, seasoned with vigorous crosshatching and other tonal effects, leads the viewer to the heart of each cartoon.

The shift from light to dark in "Holy Trinity" is masterful cartoon art. The wispy pen lines in the upper third of the piece create a tranquil, meditative mood. This feel is interrupted by the dark

brush lines of the preacher's pulpit — our gateway to the dark, messy reality behind this virginal façade.

Young's anguished brush lines, which gradually thicken and darken, lead us to see the real-world issues of poverty, famine, crime, and disease that lie just beneath the surface. He shows human figures in suffering — boldly drawn in light and shadow and finally reduced to anonymous silhouettes. The woodcut-like line work reinforces our feeling that this lower world is rotting, contaminated, and helpless.

Young's artistic eye only improves from "Holy Trinity" onward, but his idiosyncrasy — the elements that distinguish his work from the hundreds of others at his level — is fully evident here. Our eyes are still seduced by his soulful command of dark and light.

"Holy Trinity" is a precursor to Young's work for *The Masses*, in which he was free to tackle any subject, from slum children musing that the stars in the night sky above them are "thick as bed-bugs!" to commentaries on organized labor, the penal system, and, most famously, World War I.

ABOVE: Cover print: "Special Christmas Number"
*The Masses*, December 1913
10.5" x 13.5"

RIGHT: **Holy Trinity**
The Wealthy Church and Its Real Estate Holdings
*Puck*, January 6, 1909, centerfold (printed sideways in the magazine)
(Original art, p. 280)

Young's *Masses* work didn't alienate him from the main-stream. In 1912, the *Metropolitan Magazine* hired Young to do a monthly survey of the Washington, D.C. political parade in words and images. With the editors' agreement that his *Masses* work would continue, the *Metropolitan* brought Young to a national audience, and made him one of America's earliest national cartoon commentators on the political scene.

Young relished this opportunity:

I had been drawing cartoons … for an audience which in the main was already converted, but now I could appeal to those who were "sitting in darkness."

Young's monthly illustrated column appeared in the *Metropolitan* for the next six years. Meanwhile, his *Masses* work brought him — and the magazine — great controversy.

GARRISON

*nice weather for war*

TRYING TO LOOK DIGNIFIED

SUGGESTING EASE

Art Young

Detail from Art Young column in *Metropolitan Magazine*

## THE MASSES ON TRIAL

YOUNG'S CARTOON "POISONED at the Source," which accompanied Eastman's editorial "The Worst Monopoly" in the July 1913 issue of *The Masses*, criticized the Associated Press for suppressing and skewing its coverage of the mistreatment of coal miners in Kanawha County, West Virginia.

The strike, which lasted from April 1912 through July 1913, centered on a list of eight demands by coal workers through their union, the United Mine Workers of America, including the rights of free speech and lawful assembly, lawful and accurate weighing of coal, and the miners being forced to buy goods from company-owned retail stores. The workers also requested a salary increase of 15 cents per day. The strike brought death and discord, as the coal companies hired armed private security forces — the Blackwater of their day — to stifle the striking workers.

Edward M. Steel Jr., in *The Court-Martial of Mother Jones*, determined that the conflict was responsible for around 50 deaths by violence and many more by starvation. Banker Fred Stanton estimated the cost of the strike at $100 million.

That this story was not covered in the national news — and was seemingly buried by the AP — incensed Young and Eastman, as did the coal companies' request that the U.S. government declare martial law in West Virginia and hold a military tribunal to convict the striking workers.

As Eastman wrote in his editorial: "so long as the substance of current history continues to be held in cold storage, adulterated, colored with poisonous intentions, and sold to the highest bidder to suit his private purposes, there is small hope that even the free and the intelligent will take the side of justice in the struggle that is before us."

In November 1913, based on a complaint by the Associated Press, Young and Eastman were indicted in New York state court on the first of two charges of criminal libel. The two were not arrested but had to post bail of $1,000.

The press rallied around Young and Eastman, including the *New York Call*, which blasted the AP for picking on such a small magazine as *The Masses*. The paper also warned that "Socialist and radical magazine men" were investigating the strike and compiling information that could prove damning to the AP. It soon became evident that the AP had done exactly what Young and Eastman had accused it of. As Marc Moorash of the Bethel Historical Society has noted, Young and his comrades were among the first Americans to question the mass media and its treatment of news events.

The second libel indictment was filed in January 1914 in response to an editorial that same month about the first libel trial. The editorial was written by radical Floyd Dell, who had been hired as associate editor of *The Masses*. Young and Eastman were accused of libeling AP president Frank Noyes. It seemed clear that the charges were more about Noyes's wounded pride than the suppression of strike news.

After Young and Eastman, through their lawyer, asked to subpoena the AP's records, the second case was quietly dropped. The AP feared that *The Masses'* potential exposé of the AP would offer

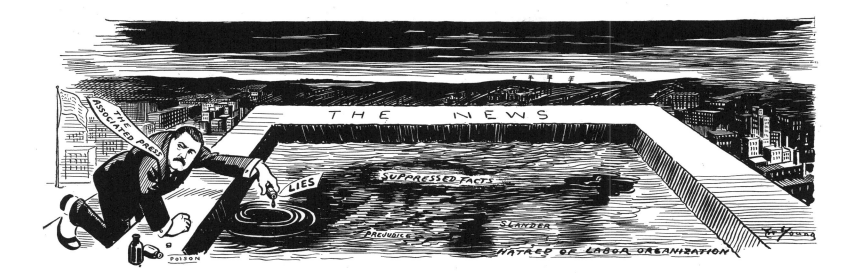

damaging proof that the wire service had suppressed the story of the bloody strike.

Still facing the original libel charge, Young and Eastman again found themselves surrounded by sympathetic colleagues. Friends of the two arranged a mass meeting at Cooper Union Hall in New York. More than 2,500 people attended the event, which featured lawyer and reformist Amos Pinchot, who accused the AP of being "a monopolistic corporation, not only in constraint of news, but in constraint of truth."

The remaining libel case was not pursued in court, and, a year after its inception, newspapers reported that the indictments had been dismissed. Young and Eastman's bail was returned without explanation. As Young wrote in his 1939 memoir, *Art Young: His Life and Times*, "the AP was in the position of the hunter who had a bear by the tail and didn't know how to let go of it."

Young and Eastman returned to their work. Young's work kept him in the Washington, D.C. area, although he maintained a New York City address.

Young and John Reed covered the 1916 national political conventions as World War I was being fought in Europe. President Woodrow Wilson, an avowed isolationist, was re-elected to a second term by assuring the public that America would stay out of the conflict.

Despite Reed's faith that Wilson would keep the U.S. out of the war, Young was suspicious of the president's agenda:

> I didn't believe it, and had said so over and over again. I felt he would like to, but I said, "They won't let him."… I knew, as everyone handling news did, how the propaganda factories were working ceaselessly to force us into the slaughter.

President Wilson was inaugurated into his new term March 4, 1917. On April 2, he declared war against Germany. By April 6, both houses of Congress had authorized the U.S. entry into the World War.

As the press fanned the flames of war, *The Masses* suffered. The magazine was banned from many newsstands and libraries and was deliberately delayed — or banned outright — from the U.S. mails.

On July 10, 1917, *The New York Times* reported that William H. Lamar, assistant attorney general and solicitor for the U.S. Post Office, utilizing

ABOVE: **Poisoned at the Source**
*The Masses*, July 1913

BELOW: Art Young and Max Eastman, c. 1913

**ABOVE:** Having Their Fling
*The Masses,* September 1917

**OPPOSITE:** Art Young's handwritten note about "Having Their Fling."

This particular copy of Young's cartoon printed in that issue of *The Masses* was submitted as evidence in his trial (as indicated by the clerk of the court's exhibit stamp), which Young references in his note opposite.

his authority under the recently passed Espionage Act of June 1917, had "barred from the mails issues of *The Appeal to Reason, The American Socialist, The International Socialist Review, The Four Lights,* and *The Masses.*"

The Espionage Act, a distant forerunner of the Homeland Security Act of 2002, was born of war hysteria and was used to suppress military insubordination and actions that cast aspersions on military recruitment and operations. The Espionage Act was later augmented by the Sedition Act of 1918. While the Sedition Act was overturned in 1921, elements of the Espionage Act remain in federal law today.

Eastman's anti-jingoism editorials in *The Masses* caused the magazine's August 1917 issue to be deemed "unmailable" under the Espionage Act. The suppression of *The Masses* was contested by Young and Eastman's attorney, Gilbert Roe, who had represented them in the AP libel cases. Judge Billings Learned Hand ruled in favor of the magazine, stating his belief that the Post Office had no valid basis to suppress *The Masses* and that political and social criticism were "the privilege of the individual in countries dependent upon the free expression of opinion as the ultimate source of authority."

Perhaps bolstered by Judge Hand's ruling, *The Masses* attacked the war frenzy with even greater vigor. Its September 1917 issue ran Young's brilliant "Having Their Fling." A century hasn't taken the edge off the cartoon's biting satire, which shows the clergy, the press, big business, and politics dancing gleefully to the death march of a devil's orchestra.

This was Young's bravest moment as a social satirist. The powers that be were outraged. In October 1917, Young, Eastman, and other *Masses* contributors were charged under the Espionage Act with "conspiracy to obstruct the recruiting and enlistment service of the U.S." for the publication of "seditious articles, cartoons and poems." If convicted, they each faced sentences of up to 20 years and fines of up to $10,000. The magazine's second-class mailing permit was also revoked.

THE *METROPOLITAN,* ONCE supportive of the Socialist cause, adopted a pro-war tone and dismissed Young in the fall of 1917. Fearing further

One of the drawings for which the artist was indicted in 1918 (note the official stamp of disapproval) upper right hand corner

backlash, Eastman began *The Liberator*, a new magazine that soft-pedaled *The Masses'* fierce viewpoint.

The trial, which began in federal court in New York City in April 1918, served up a display of hysterical "patriotism" and grandstanding by the prosecuting attorneys. In his memoir, Young recalls "patriotic music … being played lustily by an army band" in the park next to the court building, where it was set up to promote the sale of Liberty Bonds. The music continued throughout the eight-day trial, to depressing effect for the artist:

> To me, who considered myself quite as patriotic in a real sense as those who had to prove it by emotional excess, this music sounded sad, not to say ominous, like the relentless beat of a funeral march.

Young felt that the trial judge, Augustus Hand (a cousin of Judge Billings Learned Hand) was "a conscientious judge … [he] had not been stampeded by the war mania, and he consistently tried to be fair …"

The trial often veered into cheap theatrics, some of which confounded the judge. Prosecutor Earl Barnes spouted melodramatic rhetoric, and, in Young's words, "read from the exhibits in awe-inspiring tones, and held up the offending cartoons with a gesture of horror as if he were displaying the pistol with which Booth shot Abraham Lincoln."

The trial's sensational aspects wearied Young, who famously fell asleep during the proceedings. After witnessing much accusation and chest thumping in the courtroom, the jury was unable to reach a verdict. Young recalled that the jury's final tally was 10 to 2 for conviction. Other sources say it was 11-to-1. But the decision had to be unanimous. Judge Hand declared a mistrial.

Though a free man, Young found himself socially and professionally ostracized in the trial's wake.

A re-trial, in September 1918, with prosecutor Barnes again playing his role to the hilt, attempted to redress the prior mistrial. In Young's words, "the same evidence was set forth, and with much the same kind of argument on both sides." Once again, the jury could not agree. Another mistrial was declared, and that brought an end to the matter.

As Eugene V. Debs and other pro-union, pro-labor activists were imprisoned, and war hysteria frustrated the exercise of free expression, Young felt nervous and exhausted.

Art Young at one of the two *The Masses* trials in 1918

## NEW VENTURES, NEW PROSPERITY

IN EARLY 1919, Young founded *Good Morning* with former *Life* editor Ellis O. Jones. *Good Morning* was intended to be a lighter, more amusing mix of commentary and satire. Young felt that forthright comedy was the best way to get the socialist message across.

*Good Morning* sold out of its first issue. Within five months, Young was its sole editor. Young worked *pro bono*, and invested much time and energy in the project.

Its most popular feature was "The Poor Fish," a satire of just-folks philosophy that reveals the shortcomings of its speaker rather than any real wisdom. By 1921, Young had run out of capital, and ended *Good Morning*. "Poor Fish" was fondly remembered. In a touching letter to Young dated November 10, 1923, Helen Keller references the feature: "How would the 'Poor Fish' solve my dilemma?"

The trials' impact had since faded. Young did cartoons for *The Nation* magazine, starting in 1922. Later, *The Saturday Evening Post* invited Young to contribute. For the mainstream *Post*, Young created two of his most charming works, *Trees at Night* and *Types of the Old Home-Town*. *Trees at Night* saw book publication in 1927. (*Types of the Old Home-Town* would have to wait until 2015 to be collected in book form, in a handcrafted limited edition.) After a decade of struggle, Young was back on top, earning good pay and finding new avenues of artistic expression.

Much of this new income was channeled into one of Young's longtime dreams: to create a public gallery of his artwork in Bethel. Amidst the quixotic mishaps of the gallery's creation, Young wrote his first prose book. *On My Way*, published in 1928, has the intimacy of a journal and offers gentle, often poetic musings on the artist's life, friends, and artistic convictions.

*Trees at Night* and *On My Way* were well received by critics and the public. At age 62, Young was newly beloved, and had a wide, receptive audience for his work. This sweet spot was short-lived.

After the stock market crash of 1929, Young's work dried up. As he scrounged for new

ABOVE: "Gee Bill, you look like Hell"
*Good Morning*, May 22, 1919, cover
14.75" x 15.75"

ABOVE RIGHT: Poor Fish Family
*Good Morning*, April 1, 1921
6" x 6"

venues, Young was asked by the *Encyclopedia Britannica* to write an entry on cartooning for their 1930 edition. Young eloquently summed up the cartoonist's art and practice.

Now a senior citizen, Young was plagued by health problems. Diagnosed with dangerously high blood pressure and a leaky heart valve, he was told to rest and avoid exertion. Young fell into a funk and feared his best days were over.

*Hell Up to Date* had its 40th anniversary in 1932. Young was inspired to revisit this satiric world with the best of his three "Hell" volumes, 1934's *Art Young's Inferno*. With its dazzling streamlined drawings, which convey motion, emotion, and humor in a way that anticipates Harvey Kurtzman's work, *Art Young's Inferno* was an artistic triumph, and Young's peak work as a cartoonist. The boldness and vigor of these drawings has few equals in cartoon art. Saleswise, *Art Young's Inferno* fizzled — as did many noteworthy books from the worst throes of the Great Depression.

He was getting old and known to be wealthy, as wealth was rated in those days of long ago. Still he was not what you would call contented. Something lacking, — for life hardly seemed worthwhile. Perhaps some cultural activity would take the boredom out of the hours, and naturally he harked back to the days of his youth when he liked to paint pictures and enjoyed life.

At sixty-five he had a studio fixed up in his home where he tried to rejuvenate his artistic talent. The high spot of this period occurred when a well-known art critic looked at some of his oil paintings and said that they were 'not so bad.'

## IT'S A LONG ROAD ...

YOUNG'S WAS NOW a life of struggle, with sparse work and little money. His many friends still loved him and worried about his well-being. As a result of a 1934 testimonial benefit arranged in his honor by the League for Mutual Aid, Young was given enough money to live for the next four to five years without worry.

Vanguard Press published the most widely known Art Young book, *The Best Of*, in late 1936. By that time, writer John Nicholas Beffel, a prominent columnist for *The Nation* and *The New Republic*, was at work with Young on a volume of traditional memoirs. The collaboration began as early as 1933, via their correspondence, and transitioned into more formal prose.

Written in fits and starts as Young's morale and health allowed, the book was published in 1939 as *His Life and Times*. The quotations by Young used in this essay come from that memoir.

Beffel wrote about his collaboration with Young in the April-May 1944 issue of *Direction* magazine, published as a posthumous tribute. He found Young a charming, if occasionally distracted, presence. Beffel's hand in shaping *His Life and Times* allowed Young to present his version of the events in his life with candor, wit, and accuracy.

Young's health problems worsened after the book's publication. Beffel retained his friendship with Young, who now largely lived off the charity of friends, and occasionally published cartoons as his well-being — and the market — permitted. After a stay in a sanitarium, and a stringent diet, Young emerged 55 pounds lighter. Back in New York, he spent his time reminiscing with old friends, seeing Broadway comedies (he was delighted by the anarchic show *Hellzapoppin*), and watching the world go by.

Young eschewed further involvement in the socialist scene. Beffel reported Young "observing sadly how much time and energy

P. 98 (52)

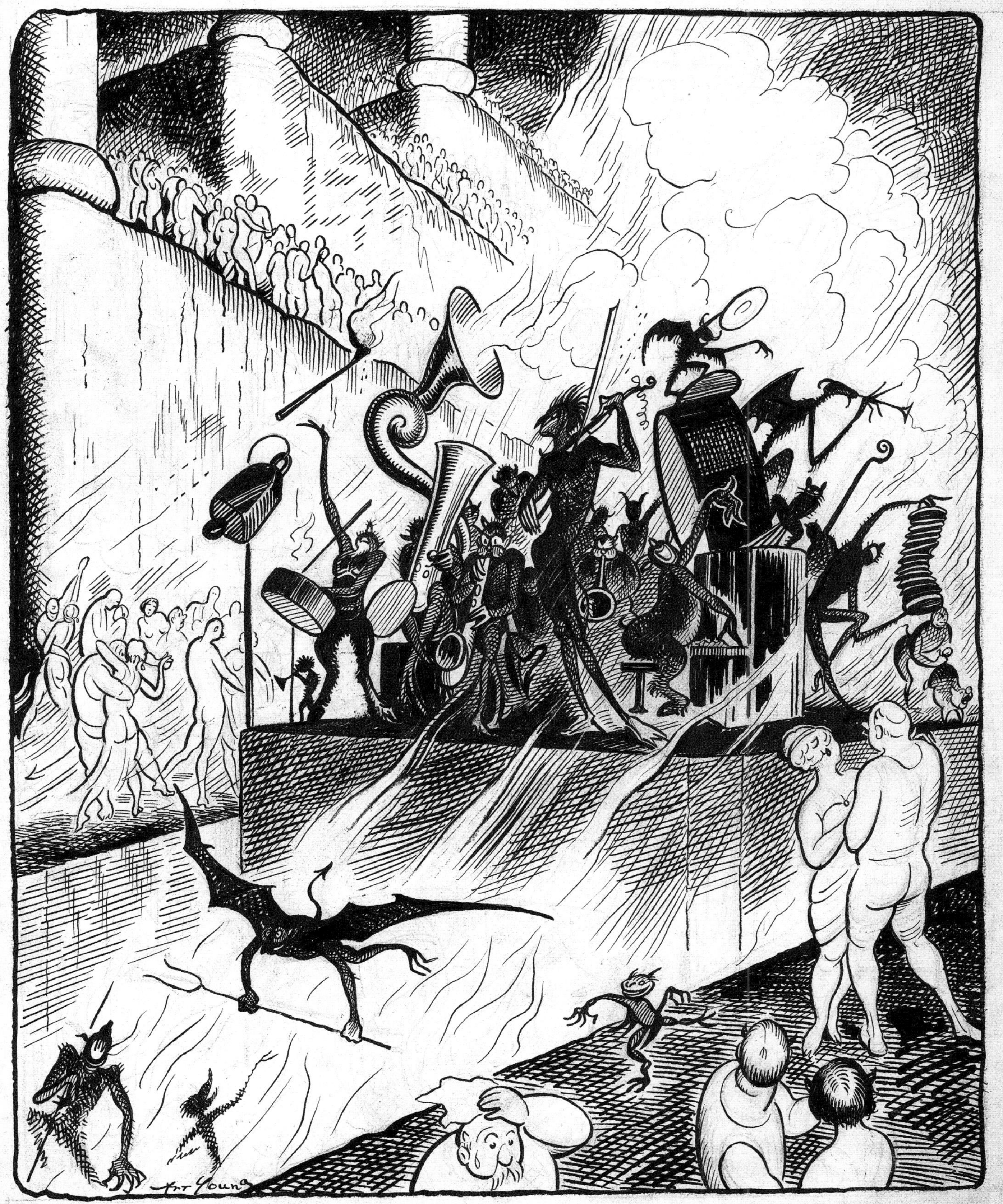
Art Young

6 1/2"

The music

*The Best of Art Young,* dust jacket front, 1936

were wasted by internal fighting … which might better have been turned against the common enemy, Capitalism."

Young drafted his will in 1939, and sold his Connecticut property in 1942. He disassembled his museum, and left all his artworks and manuscripts to be, in Beffel's words, "sold or otherwise disposed of by a designated committee."

Young's estate was willed to his wife and two sons. He died in his room at the Hotel Irving, in New York, on December 29, 1943. He was 77.

Art Young drew to the end of his life. Among his last cartoons are a series that exquisitely lampoons Adolf Hitler and a 1944 New Year's greeting with a poignant last line: "It's a long road, but now we are getting somewhere."

Over 500 people attended a memorial in his honor, held in January of 1944. *The New York Times*, in a New Year's Eve, 1943, editorial piece, said of Art Young:

Art Young, who died in this city Wednesday night at the age of 77, wouldn't have liked to have it said that he was a lovable soul in spite of his sometimes heterodox opinions. He valued his opinions. He had worked them out for himself, and for them he had sacrificed the chance to accumulate a fair share of this world's goods.

He happened to be a man who couldn't hate any one, and whom no one could hate, but that was something he couldn't help. He was born that way … he would have liked to be remembered for his selfless sincerity, and he will be by people who followed him every step of the way and people who didn't.

Right or wrong, or partly right and partly wrong like the rest of us, he was a good American …

ABOVE: *Direction*, April-May 1944, cover

RIGHT: **Four Freedoms**
For Art Young's New Year's card, 1944
11" x 17"

Vaulting Ambition that Overleaps Itself
9.5" x 13.5"

YOUNG'S WORK QUIETLY fell out of circulation, hidden in the pages of decades-old magazines and newspapers. More often encountered were his two volumes of autobiography and tattering copies of his *Best of*, which grabbed the attention of younger cartoonists who happened upon it, hidden in plain sight among the pitiful retinue of cartooning and comics-related books tolerated on library shelves.

Though some of the political figures in his work may no longer be significant, Young's humanist wit and gentle-but-accurate satire speaks to us through the years — sometimes with a surprising power. It is a pleasure to bring Art Young and his work back into the public eye.

ABOVE: **Rounding Up the Memories**
*New Masses*, April 1939
Reprinted in *Art Young: His Life and Times*, 1939
13″ x 9″

RIGHT: **Art Young in a Gale**
*On My Way*, 1928
7.5″ x 9.5″

# POLITICS & PERSONALITIES

## 03

**ANTHONY J. MOUREK AND VALERIE HIGGINS**

**Political cartoons are drawings that attack, defend, or comment on individuals or issues of the day. They are drawn from the point of view of the artist, often with significant input from an editor, and are intended to influence a contemporary readership. Good cartoons can communicate their messages with few or no words. Yet outside of their own time and place, they are often unintelligible without extensive explanation.**

Art Young was a political cartoonist for over half a century and a contemporary of both Thomas Nast (1840–1902) and Herblock (1909–2001). He considered his political cartoons his most significant work, writing in *The Best of Art Young* that his cartoons on politics and government "occupied most of [his] time since boyhood" and "may prove to have been the most worth while, if not my best work."[1] Young noted that the bulk of his political cartoons did not focus on the "trivial turns in current politics,"[2] but were rather "generalizations on the one important issue of this era the world over: Plutocracy versus the principles of Socialism."[3] This chapter, however, will highlight some of Young's cartoons that do comment on specific individuals and events. These works, examined roughly chronologically, serve as useful snapshots of how Young's attitudes toward the political and social world around him developed over time. As he moved from Chicago to New York, from Republican to Socialist, from the presidency of Benjamin Harrison to that of Franklin Roosevelt, his art and beliefs changed. Following are a few examples of that change put in historic context.

## 1. PROTECTING THE AMERICAN HOME

IN 1892 A cholera epidemic raged in Europe, which made some of the ships arriving in the United States from European ports a public health hazard. This epidemic was part of what has come to be called the fifth cholera pandemic, which originated in India and spread through Asia, Africa, South America, and portions of Europe, and lasted from 1881 to 1896.[4] Hamburg, Germany was particularly hard hit, and on August 31, 1892, the steamship *Moravia* of the American-Hamburg Packet Line arrived in New

**Protecting the American Home**
*The Inter Ocean Illustrated Supplement*
(Chicago), 1892
26" x 19"
Collection of Anthony J. Mourek

York having lost 22 of its passengers to cholera on the voyage.[5] The arrival of this ship prompted President Benjamin Harrison to approve an order issued by the Surgeon General of the Marine Hospital Service the next day, which stated that "no vessel from any foreign port carrying immigrants shall be admitted to enter any port of the United States until such vessel shall have undergone quarantine detention of twenty days, and such greater number of days as may be fixed in each special case by the State authorities."[6]

Two more steamships from the Hamburg-American Packet Line, both of which had lost passengers to cholera on the voyage, arrived on September 3 and were quarantined with the *Moravia* off Swinburne Island to prevent the disease from spreading to New York City.[7] In his December 6, 1892 State of the Union message, President Harrison said, "The subject of quarantine regulations, inspection, and control was brought suddenly to my attention by the

arrival at our ports in August last of vessels infected with cholera … We are peculiarly subject in our great ports to the spread of infectious diseases by reason of the fact that unrestricted immigration brings to us out of European cities, in the overcrowded steerages of great steamships, a large number of persons whose surroundings make them the easy victims of the plague. This consideration … leads me to renew the suggestion that admission to our country and to the high privileges of its citizenship should be more restricted and more careful."[8]

In this cartoon from early in his career, Young depicts Republican President Benjamin Harrison as a heroic figure, holding the three American-Hamburg Packet Line ships at bay behind a quarantine chain and shielding a vulnerable American family. This cartoon was published during an election year while Young was still "a Republican employed by a Republican paper."[9] He would rarely depict any person in power so uncritically in his later years. Also, any depiction of the suffering of the cholera-stricken immigrants on the quarantined ships is notably absent. Young's cartoon does, however, attack the steamship companies for their greed and includes early versions of the villainous, corpulent capitalists that would feature so prominently in many of his later cartoons about the conflict between socialism and capitalism.

## 2. THEY WON'T BE HAPPY TILL THEY GET IT

JUST BEFORE CHRISTMAS, 1892, Young made use of themes that had been popularized by the cartoonist Thomas Nast, whose Christmas illustrations of Santa Claus and children had become iconic images of the holiday.[10] In Young's drawing, the children with stockings hung by the fire are hardened Chicago politicians seeking the mayoralty at a time when the city was undertaking the largest public expenditure in its short history.[11] The World's Columbian Exposition, organized in honor of the 400th anniversary of Columbus's discovery of America, put Chicago in the nation's spotlight and would have a significant impact on the culture of the United States as it approached the 20th century.[12]

Sleeping in the bed is the incumbent mayor, Republican Hempstead Washburne, who had attended the October 21, 1892 dedication of The World's Columbian Exposition.[13] The only problem was that after nearly three years of preparation, the fairgrounds were not completed and the fair was not going to open in 1892.[14] Believing he would not be reelected, Mayor Washburne chose not to seek another term in 1893,[15] and the Republican nomination instead went to Samuel Allerton.[16]

Sitting on the bed expectantly are two politicians vying for the Democratic nomination: Carter Harrison Sr., the former mayor, and Washington Hesing, the owner of the German-language newspaper *Illinois Staats-Zeitung*[17]. Harrison would win the nomination, become mayor in April 1893,[18] and open the Columbian Exposition on May 1, 1893.[19] President Grover Cleveland would appoint Hesing as Chicago Postmaster for delivering the German vote to him in the 1892 presidential election.[20]

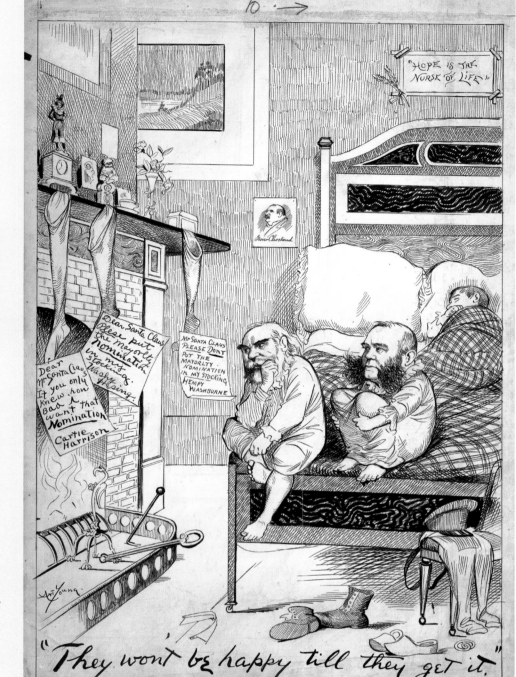

They Won't Be Happy Till They Get It
*The Inter Ocean Illustrated Supplement* (Chicago), 1892
16" x 23"
Collection of Anthony J. Mourek

**Carter Harrison Bluster**
*The Inter Ocean Illustrated Supplement* (Chicago), 1893
Ink drawing
18″ x 21″
Collection of Anthony J. Mourek

## 3. CARTER HARRISON BLUSTER

IN THIS CARTOON, published in the Republican *Inter Ocean*, Young once again shows partisan leanings, entering the fray of the hotly contested 1893 Chicago mayoral election, held during the Columbian Exposition. Carter Harrison Sr. had served as Chicago's mayor from 1879 to 1887,[21] and he was once again nominated as the Democratic candidate for mayor in 1893. Young depicts him emerging from a rotten egg emblazoned with charges like "reckless rule during anarchist troubles" (likely an allusion to what many saw as his poor handling of the events surrounding the Haymarket Square Riot in 1886),[22] "catering to dangerous classes," and "in nationality all things to all men." Behind Harrison, men at the Citizens Headquarters, Republican Headquarters, and Labor Headquarters all gag at his smell. Two signs in the background name Samuel W. Allerton, the joint Republican Party and Citizens' Party candidate for mayor.[23][24] Allerton was particularly popular among the German-Americans of Chicago,[25] a fact which Young notes with a "Mass Meetings German" sign in his image. Harrison won the election in spite of the efforts of the Republican and Citizens' parties, but he was assassinated in his home later that year by a man who felt Harrison owed him a city job.[26]

With this cartoon, Young delves deeply into the "turns in current politics" he would later eschew. It is especially interesting that Young attacks Harrison for appealing to different nationalities, coddling dangerous elements in the city, and mishandling the Haymarket Square Riot. Harrison was known at the time for being pro-labor and even attended the May 4, 1886 labor protest meeting in Haymarket Square before a bombing turned the event into a riot.[27]

Young seems to be taking the side of those who believed Harrison had allowed the riot to occur by being too lenient on the labor activists, a position much at odds with his later views. Young himself would say of the trial and execution of four men arrested for the Haymarket bombing that "not until several years later did I discover that there was another side to the story" and of a cartoon he drew for an anti-Anarchist book, "if the dead can hear, I ask forgiveness now for that act. I was young and I had been misled by the clamor of many voices raised to justify a dark and shameful deed."[28]

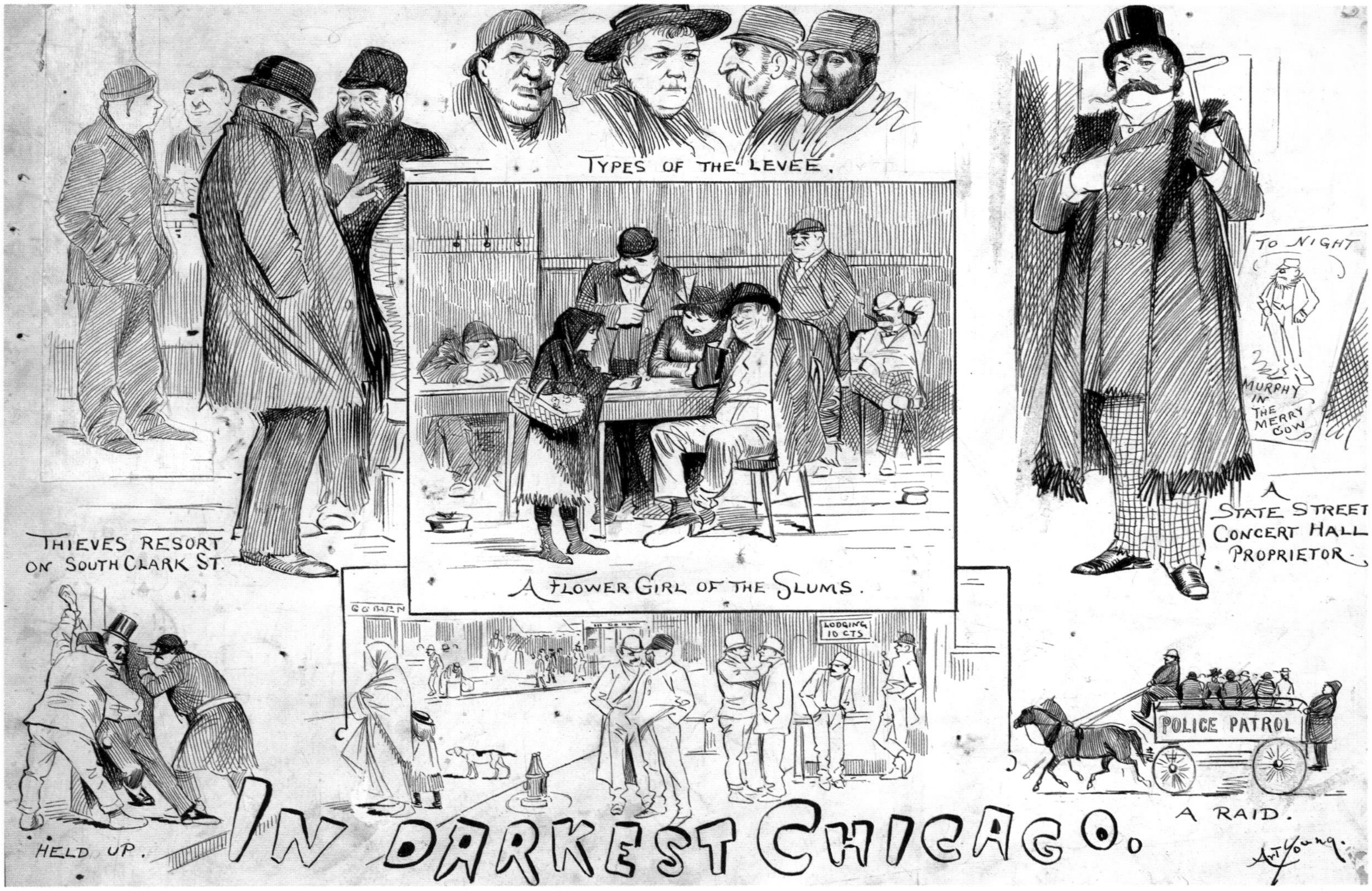
TYPES OF THE LEVEE.
THIEVES RESORT ON SOUTH CLARK ST.
A FLOWER GIRL OF THE SLUMS.
TO NIGHT
MURPHY IN THE MERRY COW
A STATE STREET CONCERT HALL PROPRIETOR.
LODGING 10 CTS
POLICE PATROL
HELD UP.
IN DARKEST CHICAGO.
A RAID.

In Darkest Chicago
*The Inter Ocean Illustrated Supplement* (Chicago), c. 1893
Ink drawing
22.625" x 15.375"
Collection of Anthony J. Mourek

## 4. IN DARKEST CHICAGO

THIS NON-POLITICAL CARTOON from the days of Chicago's Columbian Exposition serves as an interesting counterpoint to Young's political cartoons on the 1893 Chicago mayoral elections. Many fair visitors spent money in the "Levee," a notable vice district in Chicago, and many politicians got a cut of that money.[29] The Levee's location between the fairgrounds and the hotels in Chicago's Loop helped it draw tourists leaving the fair to its nighttime, illegal entertainments.[30] This cartoon, also published in *Inter Ocean Magazine*, depicts "types of the Levee."

Vice districts were havens for crime, but the city tolerated that crime with the intention of keeping it confined to a distinct, manageable area. The cartoon shows thieves congregating and preying upon passers-by, an impoverished girl selling flowers on the street, a disreputable concert hall, and a police raid. Several of the sinister Levee types have facial features that are meant to suggest they are foreigners, including several Irish figures. It is interesting that, in his early days, Young was willing to use such hints of foreignness to evoke feelings of distrust in his audience. He would later write of his conversion to socialism that "it never occurred to me to be against Socialism or any other theory because it originated in Europe. I felt that such an objection was just plain silly; that 'alien theory,' 'imported doctrine,' and such phrases of contempt were deliberately coined to discredit a growing cause."

**Stealing Thunder**
*The Coming Nation* (Cave Mills, Tennessee), c. 1901–1909
Ink drawing
13.5" x 20"
Collection of Anthony J. Mourek

## 5. STEALING THUNDER

HERE YOUNG SHOWS President Theodore Roosevelt stealing thunder from the socialist cause by providing temporary relief measures, supporting laws that benefit labor, and giving in to some of the socialists' immediate demands. This is a reference to policies Roosevelt pursued as part of his "Square Deal" platform. Roosevelt's position was that the interests of labor and capital had to be balanced and that both should receive fair treatment. To this end, Roosevelt advocated for the government to take an active role in ensuring that each side dealt fairly with the other. In 1902, Roosevelt mediated the United Mine Workers' strike, which resulted in the workers receiving increased wages and shorter working hours. This was the first time a U.S. president treated both sides in a labor dispute as equals. His administration also filed over 40 lawsuits in an attempt to break up trusts, supported the establishment of the Department of Commerce and Labor, and set limits on the rates railroads could charge.[31]

By this point Young's sympathies were with the socialists and this cartoon was published in a socialist periodical. Roosevelt's position was more moderate than Young probably would have liked, so Young has shown him weakening the socialist position by supporting reforms to address some of the issues that angered the socialists while leaving the basic structure of capitalism intact. While this cartoon deals with the political issues of the day, Young's broader focus on the conflict between socialism and capitalism is increasingly visible.

## 6. "YOU'RE A LIAR — I DIDN'T EAT NO WAHTERMELON — DEED I DIDN'T"

WHILE ART YOUNG was progressive in many things, cartoons like this one show that, whatever his personal attitudes toward African Americans, he was willing to play to the racist attitudes of his audience. Young depicts former President Theodore Roosevelt as an African American man and uses the stereotype that African Americans are fond of watermelon[32] as a metaphor for Roosevelt's behavior.

In 1912, Roosevelt, who was unhappy with President William Howard Taft's administration, split from the Republican Party and founded the Progressive, or Bull Moose, Party. When Young drew this cartoon, Roosevelt was running for president as a third party candidate.[33] This cartoon probably refers to the controversy that emerged in 1912 over campaign funds Roosevelt had received in 1904. Senator Boies Penrose, who was a member of the Republican National Executive Committee and chairman of the New York Republican State Committee, had received a $25,000 check from John D. Archbold of the Standard Oil Company. In August of 1912, when Penrose was under investigation, he stated that the money went toward Roosevelt's campaign in New York, and that it assisted Roosevelt in carrying New York in the 1904 election.[34] Ultimately, it emerged that both Standard Oil and J.P. Morgan had contributed to Roosevelt's 1904 campaign. In testimony before a Senate investigating committee on October 4, 1912, Roosevelt denied that he had any knowledge of these contributions. He also denied that anyone received favors for contributing to his campaign.[35]

Young is clearly skeptical of Roosevelt's innocence. The fact that he has used a racial stereotype of African Americans to comment on Roosevelt's behavior reveals how pervasive and unquestioned these stereotypes were at the time. Young is also echoing the image, common at the time, of African Americans stealing watermelons from watermelon patches. Additionally, he is drawing on racist notions that African Americans were simple-minded or childlike[36] by depicting Roosevelt as a black man denying that he has eaten any watermelon when he is obviously surrounded by rinds.

"You're a liar — I didn't eat no wahtermelon — deed I didn't."
*Puck,* September 10, 1912
Ink and crayon drawing
12″ x 13″
Collection of Anthony J. Mourek

That a cartoonist like Art Young, who considered himself open-minded and identified as a socialist,[37] would use a racial stereotype in this way is particularly revealing of how entrenched racism was in the United States at this time. In his autobiography, Young describes a trip to Alabama some time around the turn of the century, on which he observed "happy-go-lucky Negroes (thus I thought of them then, not knowing of the hard lives of which their apparently care-free attitude gave me no hint),"[38] showing that he may have later come to some awareness of the uncritical way in which he accepted racist stereotypes in his earlier years.

### 7. [UNTITLED: TAFT AS ABANDONED WOMAN]

SITTING PRESIDENT THEODORE Roosevelt refused to run for re-election in 1909, instead selecting William Howard Taft as his successor for the Republican nomination.[39] Taft served as president from 1908 to 1912, but his presidency was marred by impressions that he was indecisive and weak-willed.[40] Unhappy with Taft's administration, Roosevelt tried to obtain the Republican nomination in 1912. Despite Roosevelt's strong showing in the primaries, at the Republican National Convention in Chicago he obtained only 187 votes from the delegates. Senator Robert M. La Follette of Wisconsin won 41, and Taft won 561.[41] While this was enough to give Taft the nomination, it created a deep rift in the Republican

Party. It prompted Roosevelt to start the "Bull Moose Party" and run for president as a Progressive, drawing many of the more progressive Republicans with him.[42] This ultimately split Republican voters and allowed Woodrow Wilson to win the election.[43]

To illustrate the split, Young depicts Taft as an abandoned woman. Taft is surrounded by photographs of the people who once supported him, including Roosevelt and La Follette, and holds notes from radical Republicans who have deserted him for being too conservative and conservative Republicans who have deserted him for being too radical. Much like Young used racist imagery to criticize Roosevelt in the previous cartoon, here he plays into gender stereotypes of the time by depicting Taft as a woman in order to show Taft's indecisiveness and passivity.

## 8. [UNTITLED: TWO-FACED WOODROW WILSON]

TODAY, PRESIDENT WOODROW Wilson is largely remembered as an advocate for peace. His Fourteen Points speech, his support of the League of Nations, and his receipt of the Nobel Peace Prize are some of the most familiar facts about the 28th president.[44] In 1917, when Young went to the White House to meet Wilson on the day he signed the Jones Act, he too had a rosier view of the president than he would have in later years. Young observed to Wilson, "you may have noticed, Mr. President … that I've never drawn any especially harsh cartoons of you."[45]

In this cartoon from *Good Morning*, however, Young shows that his attitude toward Wilson seems to have changed. While the left side depicts the peace-loving, progressive Wilson, the right side shows him as a tyrannical ruler. The paper reading "Barbaric rule by 'law'" and "suppressed speech" likely refers to several pieces of unpopular legislation. These included the Selective Service Act of 1917, which instituted the draft; the Espionage Act of 1917, which, in addition to prohibiting the sharing of military information with enemies of the United States, also prohibited any hindering of military recruitment; and the Sedition Act of 1918, which prohibited the publishing of any material calling for an end to the war or any protests against the government which might hinder the war effort. More than 1,000 Americans were jailed under the Espionage Act and the Sedition Act.[46]

Young also comments on Wilson's actions in Latin America. On the horizon of the cartoon are islands labeled "San Domingo" and "Porto Rico" with the word "Tyranny" above them. This refers to the eight-year occupation of the Dominican Republic by United States troops that began in 1916 under Wilson's orders, ostensibly to bring stability to the country,[47] and the United States' ongoing relationship with Puerto Rico, which was an unincorporated territory of the United States and was treated as a colony. Tensions between the United States and Puerto Rico were heightened by the passage of the Jones Act in 1917, which granted Puerto Ricans U.S. citizenship without making Puerto Rico into a state. With the entry of the United States into World War I appearing increasingly inevitable, this was seen by some as a way of subjecting Puerto Ricans to the draft without giving them a voice in the United States government.[48]

The limits that Wilson's government placed on the activities of its citizens during World War I and the United States' relations with Latin America under Wilson are not as well remembered today as Wilson's advocacy for peace and a League of Nations, but this cartoon documents a time when Young and many others viewed Wilson as little more than a dictator.

**ABOVE:** Untitled: Two-faced Woodrow Wilson
*Good Morning* (New York City), c. 1919
Ink drawing
8.5″ x 8.75″
Collection of Anthony J. Mourek

**OPPOSITE:** Untitled: Taft as Abandoned Woman
c. 1912, possibly published in *Puck*
Ink and crayon drawing
13.5″x17″
Collection of Anthony J. Mourek

LEFT: Untitled: Arab Pogroms
*Der Groyser Kundes* (New York City),
1920
Ink drawing dated March 19, 1920
16" x 12"
Collection of Anthony J. Mourek

OPPOSITE: Untitled: Abraham Lincoln
and Woodrow Wilson
*Der Groyser Kundes* (New York City),
February 11, 1921
Ink drawing
17" x 11"
Collection of Anthony J. Mourek

## 9. [UNTITLED: ARAB POGROMS]

YOUNG DREW THIS cartoon for *Der Groyser Kundes* ("The Big Stick"), a Jewish humorous weekly edited by Jacob Marinoff. Young supported himself with his work for this publication while he was on trial for sedition, since the editors of most other magazines were reluctant to publish his work during that time.[49]

This cartoon may refer to the Conference of London and the discussions that started there. The conference began on February 12, 1920 and involved British prime minister David Lloyd George, French president Alexandre Millerand, Italian prime minister Francesco Nitti, and, occasionally, the Japanese ambassador. At this conference, the participants discussed the terms of the peace with Turkey and how to divide the territory of the old Ottoman Empire.[50]

Young has depicted the three participating leaders and a somewhat stereotypical Japanese figure seated at a table with a "kosher" stamp on it. The standing figure — labeled "Arabia" and holding a blood-soaked sword — wears a medal that reads "Pogrom medal." He also holds a scroll reading "Arab pogroms — The colony of Matulla completely destroyed, six Jews murdered, 10 wounded, the rest driven out," referring to violence in the Jewish settlement of Metula in the region of Palestine.

Baron Edmond de Rothschild established Metula in 1896, purchasing the land from a Lebanese Christian. In its earliest days the community experienced conflicts with the Druze tenant farmers who originally occupied the land, but had been paid a small compensation and driven off it.[51] Metula was part of French-controlled territory following World War I, but there were conflicts between the French and the local Arab and Druze communities. In February 1920, Metula's residents had to flee to escape violence related to this conflict.[52] Metula passed to British control in December 1920.[53]

This cartoon probably refers to the Arab movement of this time, which sought to create an independent Syrian state with authority over the area of Palestine. An article in *The New York Times* from March 17, 1920, indicates that the Christian and Jewish populations of the impacted areas supported the movement, preferring it to Turkish rule.[54] This cartoon, however, suggests that Young and Marinoff were skeptical that Jewish people would not be persecuted under Arab rule. Additionally, the paper pinned on the side of the desk says that the Poles have earned or deserve a large Poland, referring to the Allies' support for the reconstitution of an independent Polish state. Polish territory had been ruled by Russia, Austria, and Germany for more than one hundred years, but the Allied victory in World War I opened the door for the re-creation of a Polish state in 1918.[55] Reports of pogroms against Jews in Poland began emerging in 1919 and 1920.[56][57] Young and Marinoff clearly feared that the creation of an Arab state would result in similar or worse violence against the Jewish people in its territory.

The stereotypical Arab figure and the subtle reference to Polish anti-Semitism, elements which do not usually appear in Young's cartoons for other publications, suggest that *Der Groyser Kundes*'s editor Jacob Marinoff may have had a great deal of control over the content of the cartoon. Editorial control can easily be seen in most of Young's works for Marinoff, while the influence of other editors on his work is less overt. Political cartoonists are rarely the independent players they say they are.

## 10. [UNTITLED: ABRAHAM LINCOLN AND WOODROW WILSON]

YOUNG'S CRITICISM OF Woodrow Wilson is even harsher in this cartoon for *Der Groyser Kundes* than in his *Good Morning* cartoon. Just after the United States entered World War I, Congress passed the Espionage Act of 1917 at the urging of the Wilson administration. This act criminalized, among other things, anyone who "when the United States is at war ... shall willfully obstruct the recruiting or enlistment service of the United States, to the injury of the service or of the United States."[58]

Eugene V. Debs, who was the Socialist Party of America's candidate for president in 1900, 1904, 1908, and 1912, gave a speech in Canton, Ohio, on June 16, 1918, titled "Socialism is the Answer," which caused him to run afoul of this law. In the speech, Debs stated that "the working class who fight all the battles, the working class who make the supreme sacrifices, the working class who freely shed their blood and furnish the corpses, have never yet had a voice in either declaring war or making peace. It is the ruling class that invariably do both." Thirteen days later, a federal grand jury indicted Debs for violating the Espionage Act.[59] The charges stated that he attempted to cause "insubordination, disloyalty, mutiny, and refusal of duty in the military" and "obstructed and attempted to obstruct the recruiting and enlistment service."[60]

Debs was convicted and sentenced to ten years in prison. He appealed his case to the Supreme Court, but his conviction was unanimously upheld and the 64-year-old Debs went to prison on April 12, 1919.[61]

Debs remained popular during his imprisonment, even running for president in 1920 and receiving over a million votes.[62] Despite appeals from Attorney General A. Mitchell Palmer, labor leader Samuel Gompers, and others,[63] Wilson refused to pardon Debs, saying, "I know there will be a great deal of denunciation of me for refusing this pardon. They will say I am cold-blooded and indifferent, but it will make no impression on me. This man was a traitor to his country and he will never be pardoned during my administration."[64] Debs would not be released until December 25, 1921, by order of President Warren G. Harding.[65]

In this cartoon, published near Abraham Lincoln's birthday, Young shows an elderly Wilson holding to key to Debs's prison cell while the ghost of Lincoln looks on with disappointment. The caption reads "One freed the Blacks, the other Debs." Young compares Wilson's compassion with Lincoln's and finds Wilson wanting. Interestingly, Young has covered the original Yiddish text with paper patches so he could add English text, though he never added the new text in this case. There are other cartoons by Young where he replaced the original Yiddish text with English so the cartoons could be published in *Good Morning*.

## 11. THE SACRED BENCH

WHILE WILLIAM HOWARD Taft is primarily remembered as the 27th president of the United States (1909–1913), he actually served longer as Chief Justice of the United States Supreme Court (1921–1930).[66] Young's cartoon refers to this later period of Taft's career and shows that Young continued to criticize Taft the Chief Justice just as he had Taft the President ("Untitled: Taft as Abandoned Woman" p. 48).

Specifically, this cartoon is a reference to the $10,000 in interest Taft received annually from bonds he held in the United States Steel Corporation. This was a sizable sum at the time, considering Taft's salary as Chief Justice was $15,000 a year.[67] This led some people to worry that this powerful corporation was influencing the United States Supreme Court through Taft.[68] [69]

Young clearly was critical of Taft's acceptance of the money, and he shows the Carnegie "steel trust" padding Taft's seat on the Supreme Court bench. Interestingly, Taft had come under fire from Theodore Roosevelt in 1911 for trying to break up U.S. Steel under the Sherman Antitrust Act of 1890 for anticompetitive behavior in its acquisitions of other companies. The Roosevelt administration and U.S. Steel had shared an understanding that the company would not be subject to antitrust lawsuits for its acquisitions, and Roosevelt felt that Taft had betrayed him by taking action against them. This, along with many other factors, led Roosevelt to try to gain the Republican nomination for president over Taft in 1911.[70]

## 12. FORD FOR PRESIDENT

WHILE HENRY FORD is best known for founding the Ford Motor Company, introducing the Model T automobile, and developing the assembly line,[71] this cartoon refers to the industrialist's less well-known role in politics. Young shows a large hen with Ford's head sitting on a clutch of eggs from which Model T automobiles are hatching, their horns tooting the slogan "Ford for President." This whimsical image depicts the grassroots enthusiasm for Ford as a candidate for president which sprang up between 1916 and 1924.

At the time, many people had a positive impression of Ford, who appeared to have socially progressive views. In 1914, he offered his workers a salary of five dollars a day, more than twice what most other companies offered.[72] Ford also characterized himself as a pacifist, even sponsoring the European Peace Expedition, or "peace ship," in 1915, a private diplomatic mission to Europe which Ford hoped might help bring World War I to an end.[73] All these things made many Americans see Ford as an appealing candidate for president.

In 1916, Henry Ford, without campaigning,[74] won the Michigan Republican presidential primary election with 83,038 votes.[75] Ford did not progress beyond that point that year. In 1918, he ran for the U.S. Senate as a Democrat, but was narrowly defeated.[76] After that lackluster performance, Ford made no further attempts to seek political office. While Ford did not actively seek the presidential nomination, this didn't stop "Ford-for-President" clubs from forming in Michigan and elsewhere in the United States to promote him as a candidate for the 1924 election.[77] Only when Ford endorsed President Coolidge for re-election[78] did this enthusiasm wane.

Today, it is hard to imagine Ford as a popular candidate for president, since he is often associated with anti-Semitism[79] and resistance to unionization.[80] Any reference to Ford's anti-Semitism is conspicuously absent from this cartoon; it raises the question of how the cartoon might have been different had Young drawn it for *Der Groyser Kundes*.

ABOVE: **Ford for President**
*Life*, c. 1916–1923
Ink and colored pencil drawing
11.5″ x 7.5″
Collection of Anthony J. Mourek

OPPOSITE: **The Sacred Bench**
c. 1923, publication status unknown
Ink drawing
12″ x 10″
Collection of Anthony J. Mourek

The Cabinet of Doctor Cali-Coolidge
Investigated and approved by the level headed business-man as sane and sensible.

**The Cabinet of Doctor Cali-Coolidge**
Ink drawing dated December 1927
11.25" x 14.5"
Collection of Anthony J. Mourek

## 13. THE CABINET OF DOCTOR CALI-COOLIDGE

HERE YOUNG MAKES very effective use of a popular culture reference that modern viewers are likely to be less acquainted with than audiences at the time. The cartoon's title refers to the 1920 German film *Das Cabinet des Dr. Caligari*, which is translated into English as *The Cabinet of Dr. Caligari*. In this film, the character Dr. Caligari runs a sideshow that features a fortune-telling somnambulist, Cesare, whom Caligari keeps in a cabinet. During the course of the film, the protagonist discovers that Caligari has been controlling Cesare and using him to commit murders by proxy.[81] The film created a strong reaction among American audiences when it was released.[82]

Young has dressed President Coolidge as the sinister Dr. Caligari, echoed the cubist aesthetics of the film, and covered the cabinet behind him with references to aspects of Coolidge and his presidency that Young found problematic. These include Coolidge's dealings with organized labor, which were not always sympathetic;[83] the Sacco and Vanzetti case, a controversial trial in Massachusetts while Coolidge was governor of that state, in which two Italian immigrants were convicted of murder and sentenced to death on largely circumstantial evidence;[84] and his foreign policy toward Latin America, which included support of strong U.S. business ties and maintenance of U.S. peacekeeping forces in some Latin American countries.[85] Young, who by this time was firmly socialist and drew this cartoon for a socialist publication, clearly viewed the conservative, business-friendly Coolidge[86] as a villainous figure.

Go Gettem!
c. 1928, publication status unknown
Ink and crayon
17″ x 10.75″
Collection of Anthony J. Mourek

## 14. GO GETTEM!

YOUNG COMMENTS ON the 1928 presidential election in this cartoon. Herbert Hoover was the Republican candidate, while Al Smith was the Democratic nominee.[87] Hoover had the benefit of campaigning at a time when the U.S. economy had been thriving under a Republican administration. Smith was handicapped by the fact that he was the first Roman Catholic nominated for president by a major U.S. party, and the campaign prompted an outbreak of anti-Catholic sentiment.[88]

However, despite the significant differences between the candidates, Young points out their similarities. As a socialist, Young viewed them as two sides of the same coin. He depicts both Hoover and Smith as dogs groveling before a figure that represents big business in America. The figure is dressed as a shepherdess while the voters are a flock of sheep in the background. Young has drawn himself in the lower left corner of the drawing saying, "By golly, they like to be sheep." Young seems to see American voters as weak-willed or complacent, their lives completely controlled by powerful businessmen. In his view, political leaders are like sheepdogs — it may seem to the sheep that the dogs are the ones with the power, but the dogs simply do the bidding of the shepherdess. This cartoon is a particularly good illustration of how Young's politics and the context of his work had shifted by this time; rather than supporting either candidate or attacking specific aspects of their policies, he is criticizing the entire system in which they operate.

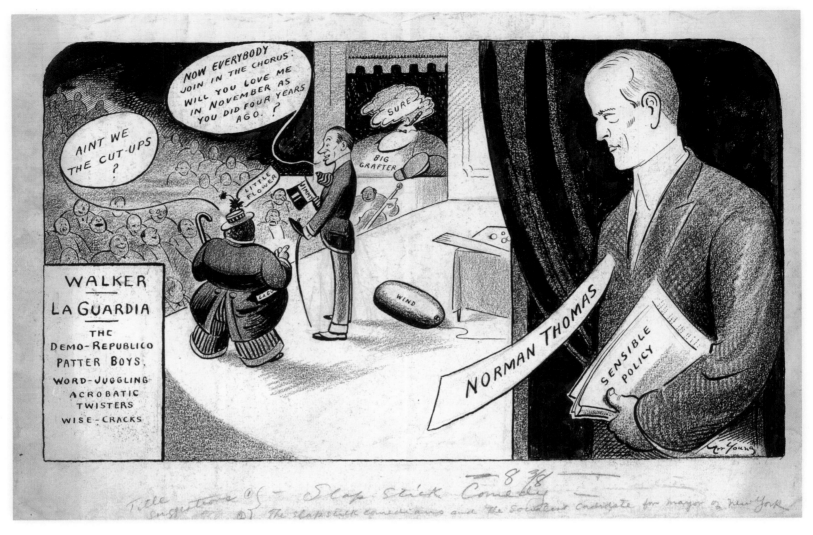

**Slap Stick Comedy**
Date and publication status unknown
Ink drawing
17" x 11"
Collection of Anthony J. Mourek

## 15. SLAP STICK COMEDY

YOUNG AGAIN SHOWS his socialist perspective in this cartoon about the 1929 New York mayoral election. Incumbent Democratic mayor James J. Walker and his Republican challenger, Fiorello H. La Guardia,[89] are shown as "slap stick comedians," performing "word-juggling" and "wise-cracks" for the amusement of their audience, especially the "Big Grafter" with a box seat. Their costumes are those of the vaudeville comics of the day, who frequently caricatured immigrant groups and other minorities, including the Irish, like Walker, and Italians, like La Guardia.[90] Their socialist challenger, Norman Thomas, carries papers labeled "sensible policy" and is dressed as a respectable, middle-class American, but he is relegated

to watching from the wings. Walker won the election by a landslide, receiving 865,549 votes to La Guardia's 368,384, but both far surpassed Norman Thomas, who received only 174,931 votes.[91]

Walker and the powerful Tammany Hall political machine would ultimately come under pressure from governor Franklin D. Roosevelt, who began procedures to have Walker removed from his position as mayor in 1932.[92] Rather than continuing to fight the process, Walker resigned on September 1 of that year.[93] La Guardia would go on to win the 1933 election and serve as mayor for three consecutive terms.[94] Thomas was a perennial socialist candidate for various offices, including the presidency, but never obtained the offices he sought.[95]

## 16. "I WILL NEVER DESERT YOU MR. MICAWBER"

YOUNG DEPICTS PRESIDENT Franklin D. Roosevelt in a way that is unusual to modern viewers. He compares Roosevelt to Wilkins Micawber from Charles Dickens's novel *David Copperfield*, a perpetually destitute character who is convinced that his fortunes will one day turn around and frequently gives others advice. He equates the members of the American public who still faithfully follow Roosevelt to Mrs. Micawber, Wilkins Micawber's loyal wife who continues to support him through all his misfortunes and never doubts that his luck will change. She repeatedly says she "will never desert Mr. Micawber."[96]

In the cartoon, Roosevelt gestures to a document that lists acronyms of some of the organizations and projects that supported the New Deal, such as the National Recovery Administration, the Agricultural Adjustment Administration, and the Tennessee Valley Authority. Young implies that, just as Micawber's attempts to change his fortune always come to naught, Roosevelt's projects have not brought prosperity to the United States. Nonetheless, Roosevelt and his supporters, like Micawber and his wife, remain perhaps foolishly optimistic that continuing on the same path they have followed in the past will lead them to a different outcome.

Young had reason to be skeptical of Roosevelt's ability to turn things around in the United States; in 1929, just before the Depression began, unemployment in the United States was about three percent. In 1933, when the Depression was at its height and Roosevelt entered office, it was just under 25 percent. In 1939, around the time Young drew this cartoon, it was still over 17 percent.[97] Additionally, this high rate of unemployment was at a time when the percentage of the population in the labor force was lower than it is today, since only about 25 percent of women worked outside their homes in the 1930s,[98] while today about 58 percent of women participate in the labor force.[99]

This cartoon is interesting not only because it depicts a usually highly regarded president in a negative light, but also because it relies on a literary reference that is obscure by today's standards. Young, however, clearly expected the reference to be a familiar one to his audience; otherwise, the cartoon could not convey its message effectively.

"I will never desert you Mr. Micawber"
*The Nation* (Washington, D.C.), c. 1939
Ink drawing
10" x 13"
Collection of Anthony J. Mourek

History Repeats

"We are back of you F.D.R. — we know what you are going through"

## 17. HISTORY REPEATS

IN THE LAST year of his life, just a few years after drawing "I will never desert you Mr. Micawber," Young actually defended Franklin D. Roosevelt and compared him to two of America's most respected former presidents. In this image, Roosevelt sits at a desk covered with papers listing the threats he faced, such as New Deal and race haters, enemy agents, quislings, political and industrial fascists, treason, organized obstruction, and organizers of disunity.

There are a number of incidents and situations to which the cartoon might be referring. For example, six Nazi spies were caught in the United States and executed in 1942.[100] Additionally, the American Federation of Labor (AFL) and the Congress of Industrial Organizations (CIO), two large and influential unions, made a "no-strike pledge" when the United States entered World War II, but by 1943 there were increasing numbers of disputes within these labor organizations and growing unrest.[101] This was exemplified by incidents like the 1943 United Mine Workers' strike, which was ultimately unsuccessful and led to the government taking over the mines.[102]

1943 also saw a number of race riots around the country, particularly in Detroit. The Detroit riots lasted three days and stemmed from resistance among white workers to the influx of African American laborers to the city. In one Detroit plant that produced engines for bombers and ships, over 20,000 white workers went on strike to protest the hiring of a few black workers.[103]

It is interesting that Young — who roundly criticized the Espionage Act of 1917 and the Sedition Act of 1918 during World War I, had been a staunch advocate for labor for most of his life, and frequently criticized the status quo — would here support the president against "organized obstruction" and "organizers of disunity." However, attitudes in the majority of the American left-wing milieu of which Young was a part were pro-war and anti-strike at this time, and had been since Germany invaded the Soviet Union in 1941.

The Communist Party USA (CPUSA) was supportive of Stalin and supported the United States against the Axis Powers, which threatened the Soviet Union, while groups like the Socialist Workers Party, a Trotskyist organization, opposed Stalin and opposed the war efforts of the United States and Britain on the grounds that they were engaged in an imperialist war.[104] James P. Cannon, national secretary of the Socialist Workers Party, was indicted and jailed in 1941 under the Alien Registration Act of 1940 for plotting to overthrow the United States government.[105] This bore some resemblance to the imprisonment of Eugene V. Debs during World War I, but in this case CPUSA — and, this cartoon seems to indicate, Young — supported the action. Young's implied support for the New Deal in this cartoon is also a noteworthy contrast to his criticism of Theodore Roosevelt's watered-down socialism in his "Stealing Thunder" cartoon decades earlier and his "I will never desert you Mr. Micawber" cartoon just a few years before.

OPPOSITE: History Repeats
1943, publication status unknown
Ink drawing
11" x 15"
Collection of Anthony J. Mourek

## ENDNOTES

1. Young, Art. *The Best of Art Young*, with an Introduction by Heywood Broun. New York: The Vanguard Press, 1936: xv.

2. Young, Art. *The Best of Art Young*, with an Introduction by Heywood Broun. New York: The Vanguard Press, 1936: xv.

3. Young, Art. *The Best of Art Young*, with an Introduction by Heywood Broun. New York: The Vanguard Press, 1936: xvi.

4. "Cholera's seven pandemics." CBC News: Technology and Science. Canadian Broadcasting Corporation: 09 May 2008. (http://www.cbc.ca/news/technology/cholera-s-seven-pandemics-1.758504)

5. "The Only Safe Course." *The New York Times*, 1892 September 1: 4.

6. "Immigration Suspended." *The New York Times*, 1892 September 2: 4.

7. "Two More Cholera Ships." *The New York Times*, 1892 September 4: 1.

8. "December 6, 1892." Public Papers and Addresses of Benjamin Harrison, Twenty-third President of the United States, March 4, 1889, to March 4, 1893. U.S. Government Printing Office, 1893: 153-154. (https://play.google.com/store/books/details?id=cX74MiF8Pm0C&rdid=book-cX74MiF8Pm0C&rdot=1)

9. Young, Art. *Art Young: His Life and Times*. John Nicholas Beffel, ed. New York: Sheridan House, 1939: p. 149.

10. "Nast, Thomas." *Authors and Artists for Young Adults*. Ed. Dwayne D. Hayes. Vol. 56. Detroit: Gale, 2004. p119-125.

11. "Title: Financial Statements from World's Columbian Exposition, Chicago, 1893, and Atlanta Exposition, 1895." Trans-Mississippi and International Exposition. (http://trans-mississippi.unl.edu/memorabilia/view/TMI04418.html)

12. Rydell, Robert W. "World's Columbian Exposition (May 1, 1893–October 30, 1893.)" *Encyclopedia of Chicago*. Chicago Historical Society: 2005. (http://www.encyclopedia.chicagohistory.org/pages/1386.html)

13. "WELCOMED TO THE CITY: Mayor Hempstead Washburne Addresses the Assemblage." *Chicago Daily Tribune* (1872-1922) [Chicago, Ill] 22 Oct 1892: 9.

14. Rydell, Robert W. "World's Columbian Exposition (May 1, 1893–October 30, 1893.)" *Encyclopedia of Chicago*. Chicago Historical Society: 2005. (http://www.encyclopedia.chicagohistory.org/pages/1386.html)

15. "Mayor Washburne's Administration." *Chicago Daily Tribune* (1872-1922) [Chicago, Ill] 18 Apr 1893: 4.

16. "Pleased with the Nomination: The "Freie Presse" Thinks Mr. Allerton a Desirable Mayoralty Candidate. *Chicago Daily Tribune* (1872-1922) [Chicago, Ill] 17 Mar 1893: 9.

17. "Is a True Chicagoan: Sketch of Washington Hesing's Life and Local Work." He Has Ever Been Devoted to the Welfare of the City and Is Deemed a Promising Candidate for the Mayoralty on the Democratic Ticket — His Education Here and Abroad — Becomes Identified with the "Staats-Zeitung" — Has Been Appointed to Many Important Offices. Has Held Important Offices.

18. *Chicago Daily Tribune* (1872-1922) [Chicago, Ill] 22 Jan 1893: 6.

19. "Harrison's Easy Victory." *Chicago Daily Tribune* (1872-1922); Apr 5, 1893; ProQuest Historical Newspapers: Chicago Tribune, pg. 4.

20. "Viewed from Above: The Gathering and Massing of that Great Audience." *Chicago Daily Tribune* (1872-1922) [Chicago, Ill] 02 May 1893: 5.

21. "Harrison and Hesing." *Chicago Daily Tribune* (1872-1922) [Chicago, Ill] 03 Oct 1893: 4.

22. "Harrison, Carter Henry, (1825-1893)." *Biographical Directory of the United States Congress*. (http://bioguide.congress.gov/scripts/biodisplay.pl?index=H000267)

23. "People & Events: Carter Harrison (1825-1893)" *Chicago: City of the Century*. PBS: 2003. (http://www.pbs.org/wgbh/amex/chicago/peopleevents/p_harrison.html)

24. "Story of His Life." *Chicago Daily Tribune* (1872-1922); Oct 29, 1893; ProQuest Historical Newspapers: Chicago Tribune pg. 3.

25. "The Kangaroo Ballot: A Most Exciting Municipal Election in Chicago." *Los Angeles Herald*, April 5, 1893. (http://cdnc.ucr.edu/cgi-bin/cdnc?a=d&d=LAH18930405.2.18#)

26. "Germans in Line for Allerton." *Chicago Daily Tribune* (1872-1922); Mar 21, 1893; ProQuest Historical Newspapers: Chicago Tribune, pg. 1

27. "People & Events: Carter Harrison (1825-1893)" *Chicago: City of the Century*. PBS: 2003. (http://www.pbs.org/wgbh/amex/chicago/peopleevents/p_harrison.html)

28. "Haymarket Riot." *St. James Encyclopedia of Labor History Worldwide*. Ed. Neil Schlager. Vol. 1. Detroit: St. James Press, 2004. p423-428. Copyright 2003 St. James Press, copyright 2006 Gale, copyright 2007 Gale, Cengage Learning

29. Young, Art. *Art Young: His Life and Times*. John Nicholas Beffel, ed. New York: Sheridan House, 1939: p. 108.

30. Ditmore, Melissa Hope. *Encyclopedia of Prostitution and Sex Work*. Vol. 1. Santa Barbara, CA: Greenwood Publishing Group, 2006, p. 96.

31. Heap, Chad. *Slumming: Sexual and Racial Encounters in American Nightlife*, 1885-1940. Chicago, IL: University of Chicago Press, 2009, p. 39.

32. "The Progressive Era (1890–1930)." *Gale Encyclopedia of U.S. History: Government and Politics*. Vol. 2. Detroit: Gale, 2008. *Gale Virtual Reference Library*. Web. 15 July 2013.

33. "Blacks and Watermelons." Jim Crow Museum of Racist Memorabilia. Ferris State University, May 2008. Web. 24 July 2013. (http://www.ferris.edu/jimcrow/question/may08/)

34. "Theodore Roosevelt." *Encyclopedia of World Biography*. 2nd ed. Vol. 13. Detroit: Gale, 2004. 280–283. *Gale Virtual Reference Library*. Web. 24 July 2013, pp. 282–283

35. "Standard Oil Check Used for Roosevelt." *The New York Times* 5 October 1912: 1. ProQuest Historical Newspapers: *The New York Times* (1851–2009). Web. 24 July 2013, p. 1.

36. "Roosevelt Says Big Gifts Didn't Purchase Favor." *The New York Times* 19 August 1912: 2. ProQuest Historical Newspapers: *The New York Times* (1851–2009). Web. 24 July 2013, p. 2.

37. "Blacks and Watermelons." Jim Crow Museum of Racist Memorabilia. Ferris State University, May 2008. Web. 24 July 2013. (http://www.ferris.edu/jimcrow/question/may08/)

38. Young, Arthur. *Art Young, His Life and Times*. New York: Sheridan House, 1939, pp. 260–261.

39. Young, Arthur. *Art Young, His Life and Times*. New York: Sheridan House, 1939, p. 200.

40. "Roosevelt, Theodore." *Gilded Age and Progressive Era Reference Library*. Ed. Lawrence W. Baker and Rebecca Valentine. Vol. 2: Biographies. Detroit: UXL, 2007. 151–171. Gale Virtual Reference Library. Web. 22 July 2013, pp. 168–170.

41. "Taft, William Howard." *UXL Encyclopedia of U.S. History*. Sonia Benson, Daniel E. Brannen Jr., and Rebecca Valentine. Vol. 8. Detroit: UXL, 2009. pp. 1507-1510. Copyright 2009 Gale, Cengage Learning: 1510.

42. "Campaigns and Elections." *American Presidents: A Reference Resource*. http://millercenter.org/president/taft/essays/biography/3

43. "Roosevelt, Theodore." *Gilded Age and Progressive Era Reference Library*. Ed. Lawrence W. Baker and Rebecca Valentine. Vol. 2: Biographies. Detroit: UXL, 2007. 151–171. Gale Virtual Reference Library. Web. 22 July 2013, pp. 168–170.

44. "Roosevelt, Theodore." *Gilded Age and Progressive Era Reference Library*. Ed. Lawrence W. Baker and Rebecca Valentine. Vol. 2: Biographies. Detroit: UXL, 2007. 151–171. Gale Virtual Reference Library. Web. 22 July 2013, pp. 168–170.

45. "Wilson, Woodrow." *UXL Encyclopedia of U.S. History*. Sonia Benson, Daniel E. Brannen Jr., and Rebecca Valentine. Vol. 8. Detroit: UXL, 2009. 1696–1699. Gale Virtual Reference Library. Web. 15 July 2013, p. 1699.

46. Young, Arthur. *Art Young: His Life and Times*. New York: Sheridan House, 1939, p. 311.

47. "Sedition Act, 1918." *American Decades Primary Sources*. Ed. Cynthia Rose. Vol. 2: 1910–1919. Detroit: Gale, 2004. 410–413. Gale Virtual Reference Library. Web. 15 July 2013, p. 410.

48. Krenn, Michael L. "Dominican Republic, Relations with." *Dictionary of American History*. Ed. Stanley I. Kutler. 3rd ed. Vol. 3. New York: Charles Scribner's Sons, 2003. 75–77. Gale Virtual Reference Library. Web. 15 July 2013, p. 76.

49. Santiago-Irizarry, Vilma. "Puerto Rico." *Dictionary of American History*. Ed. Stanley I. Kutler. 3rd ed. Vol. 6. New York: Charles Scribner's Sons, 2003. 543–547. Gale Virtual Reference Library. Web. 15 July 2013, p. 544–545.

50. Young, Arthur. *Art Young, His Life and Times*. New York: Sheridan House, 1939, p. 340.

51. Wagner, Heather Lehr. *The Division of the Middle East: The Treaty of Sèvres*. New York: Chelsea House Publishers, 2004. p 2-6.

52. Morris, Benny. *Righteous Victims: A History of the Zionist-Arab Conflict, 1881-1998*. New York: Vintage, 1999, p 55.

53. Rubinstein, Danny. "Once, long before Nasrallah was born." Haaretz. 9 August 2006.

54. (http://www.haaretz.com/print-edition/features/once-long-before-nasrallah-was-born-1.194735)

55. Biger, Gideon. *The Boundaries of Modern Palestine, 1840-1947*. (Routledge Studies in Middle Eastern History). New York: Routledge, 2004, p. 133-134.

56. "Allies ask out views on Turkey." *The New York Times* 19 August 1912: 2. ProQuest Historical Newspapers: *The New York Times* (1851–2009). Web. 3 July 2015, p. 3.

57. "Poland Confident of Great Future." *The New York Times* (1857-1922) [New York, N.Y] 17 Nov 1918: 50.

58. "The Facts About Pogroms in Poland." A Review by Herman Bernstein. *The New York Times* (1857-1922) [New York, N.Y] 12 Dec 1920: BR4.

59. "Poland." *Encyclopaedia Judaica*. Ed. Michael Berenbaum and Fred Skolnik. Vol. 16. 2nd ed. Detroit: Macmillan Reference USA, 2007. p287-326.

60. "Espionage Act of 1917." *Gale Encyclopedia of American Law*. Ed. Donna Batten. Vol. 4. 3rd ed. Detroit: Gale, 2010. p234-235.

61. "Debs, Eugene Victor." *Development of the Industrial U.S. Reference Library*. Ed. Sonia G. Benson, Jennifer York Stock, and Carol Brennan. Vol. 2: Biographies. Detroit: UXL, 2006. p 49-59.

62. "Debs, Eugene 1855–1926." *Encyclopedia of the Supreme Court of the United States*. Ed. David S. Tanenhaus. Vol. 2. Detroit: Macmillan Reference USA, 2008. p 11-13.

63. "Debs, Eugene Victor." *Development of the Industrial U.S. Reference Library*. Ed. Sonia G. Benson, Jennifer York Stock, and Carol Brennan. Vol. 2: Biographies. Detroit: UXL, 2006. p 49-59.

64. "Debs, Eugene Victor." *Development of the Industrial U.S. Reference Library*. Ed. Sonia G. Benson, Jennifer York Stock, and Carol Brennan. Vol. 2: Biographies. Detroit: UXL, 2006. p 49-59.

65. Cooper, John Milton. *Woodrow Wilson: A Biography*. New York: Vintage Books, 2011. p. 573.

66. Pietrusza, David. *1920: The Year of the Six Presidents*. New York: Basic Books, 2008. p 277.

67. "Debs, Eugene 1855–1926." *Encyclopedia of the Supreme Court of the United States*. Ed. David S. Tanenhaus. Vol. 2. Detroit: Macmillan Reference USA, 2008, p 11-13. p 12.

68. "William Howard Taft." *Encyclopedia of World Biography*. 2nd ed. Vol. 15. Detroit: Gale, 2004. 78–81. Gale Virtual Reference Library. Web. 16 July 2013, pp. 79–81.

69. "Say Taft Gets Pension from Carnegie Fund." *The Evening News* 17 April 1923: 3. Web. 15 July 2013, p. 3.

70. "Debs Attacks Taft." *The New York Times* 14 May 1923: 17. ProQuest Historical Newspapers: *The New York Times* (1851–2009). Web. 15 July 2013, p. 17.

71. "Socialists Assail Taft." *The New York Times* 30 April 1923: 44. ProQuest Historical Newspapers: *The New York Times* (1851–2009). Web. 15 July 2013, p. 44.

72. "TR & Taft Split." eHistory. Ohio State University, 2013. Web. 3 August 2013.

73. (http://ehistory.osu.edu/osu/mmh/1912/trusts/trtaft.cfm)

74. "Ford, Henry." Business Leader Profiles for Students. Ed. Sheila Dow and Jaime E. Noce. Vol. 1. Detroit: Gale, 2002. 284–288. Gale Virtual Reference Library. Web. 31 May 2013, p. 284.

75. "Ford, Henry," pp. 284–288.

76. Peace Ark Starts; Ford is Buoyant." *The New York Times* 5 December 1915: 1. ProQuest Historical Newspapers: *The New York Times* (1851–2009). Web. 9 July 2013, p. 1.

77. Kosek, Joseph Kip. "Henry Ford for President!" George Mason University's History News Network. George Mason University, 27 Apr. 2011. Web. 31 May 2013.

78. (http://www.hnn.us/articles/138750.html)

79. "The Palladium." *The New York Times* 5 May 1916: 10. ProQuest Historical Newspapers: *The New York Times* (1851–2009). Web. 31 May 2013.

80. "Ford, Henry." *UXL Encyclopedia of World Biography*. Ed. Laura B. Tyle. Vol. 4. Detroit: UXL, 2003. 725–729. Gale Virtual Reference Library. Web. 31 May 2013, p. 728.

81. "Organize for Ford, Ignoring his Wish: Backers at Detroit Conference Decide to Start a National Movement." *The New York Times* 13 December 1923: 4. ProQuest Historical Newspapers: *The New York Times* (1851–2009). Web. 31 May 2013, p. 4.

82. "Ford for Coolidge; President Sends Him Thanks for Support." *The New York Times* 20 December 1923: 1. ProQuest Historical Newspapers: *The New York Times* (1851–2009). Web. 31 May 2013, p. 1.

83. "Henry Ford Invents a Jewish Conspiracy." *Jewish Virtual Library*. The American-Israeli Cooperative Enterprise, 2013. Web. 18 July 2013.

84. (http://www.jewishvirtuallibrary.org/jsource/anti-semitism/ford1.html)

85. Boehmke, Phil. "Organizing Ford; the 1941 River Rouge strike." *American Thinker* 6 September 2010. Web. 9 July 2013.

86. White, M. B. "Das Kabinett des Dr. Caligari." *International Dictionary of Films and Filmmakers*. Ed. Sara Pendergast and Tom Pendergast. 4th ed. Vol. 1: Films. Detroit: St. James Press, 2000. 620–622. Gale Virtual Reference Library. Web. 1 June 2013, p. 622.

87. "A Cubistic Shocker." *The New York Times* 20 March 1921: X2. ProQuest Historical Newspapers: *The New York Times* (1851–2009). Web. 1 June 2013, p. X2.

88. McCoy, Donald R. "Coolidge, Calvin." *Presidents: A Reference History*. Ed. Henry F. Graff. 3rd ed. Detroit: Charles Scribner's Sons, 2002. 401–413. Gale Virtual Reference Library. Web. 1 June 2013, p. 403.

89. "The Sacco and Vanzetti Case." *American Decades*. Ed. Judith S. Baughman, et al. Vol. 3: 1920–1929. Detroit: Gale, 2001. Gale Virtual Reference Library. Web. 1 June 2013.

90. "Calvin Coolidge and Nicaragua." *American Decades Primary Sources*. Ed. Cynthia Rose. Vol. 3: 1920–1929. Detroit: Gale, 2004. 104–108. Gale Virtual Reference Library. Web. 1 June 2013, pp. 104–108.

91. "John Calvin Coolidge." *Encyclopedia of World Biography*. 2nd ed. Vol. 4. Detroit: Gale, 2004. 217–219. Gale Virtual Reference Library. Web. 1 June 2013, p. 218.

92. "Hoover, Herbert." *Great Depression and the New Deal Reference Library*. Ed. Allison McNeill, Richard C. Hanes, and Sharon M. Hanes. Vol. 2: Biographies. Detroit: UXL, 2003. 104–112. Gale Virtual Reference Library. Web. 2 Aug. 2013, p. 106.

93. Lichtman, Allan J. "Smith, Alfred E." *Encyclopedia of the Great Depression*. Ed. Robert S. McElvaine. Vol. 2. New York: Macmillan Reference USA, 2004. 890–892. Gale Virtual Reference Library. Web. 2 Aug. 2013, p. 891.

94. "Official Plurality for Mayor 499,847." *The New York Times* (1923-Current file) [New York, N.Y] 23 Nov 1929: 3.

95. Springhall, John. *The Genesis of Mass Culture: Show Business Live in America, 1840 to 1940*. New York: Palgrave Macmillan, 2008. p. 140.

96. "Final Results of the Election on Tuesday." *The New York Times* (1923-Current file) [New York, N.Y] 07 Nov 1929: 20.

97. Duffus, R. L. "The Facts Revealed in the Seabury Inquiry." *The New York Times* (1923-Current file) [New York, N.Y] 14 Aug 1932: XX1.

98. "Walker's Statement Explaining His Decision to Resign as Mayor." *The New York Times* (1923-Current file) [New York, N.Y] 02 Sep 1932: 1.

99. "Fiorello, Henry La Guardia." *Encyclopedia of World Biography*. Vol. 9. 2nd ed. Detroit: Gale, 2004. p166-167.

100. "Thomas, Norman." *Encyclopedia of the Great Depression*. Ed. Robert S. McElvaine. Vol. 2. New York: Macmillan Reference USA, 2004. P 979-980.

101. "David Copperfield." *Novels for Students*. Ed. Ira Mark Milne. Vol. 25. Detroit: Gale, 2007. 83–109. Gale Virtual Reference Library. Web. 16 July 2013, p. 92.

102. "Unemployment Statistics during the Great Depression." *United States History*. Web. 26 July 2013. (http://www.u-s-history.com/pages/h1528.html)

103. "Working Women in the 1930s." *American Decades*. Ed. Vincent Tompkins. Vol. 4. Detroit: Gale, 2001. CRSN. 17 November 2010. Web. 30 July 2013.

104. "Women in the Labor Force in 2010." United States Department of Labor. U.S. Department of Labor, 2010. Web. 30 July 2013.

105. (http://www.dol.gov/wb/factsheets/Qf-laborforce-10.htm)

106. "1942: German saboteurs executed in Washington." *This Day in History*. A&E Television Networks: 2015.

107. "No-strike Pledge, World War II." *St. James Encyclopedia of Labor History Worldwide*. Ed. Neil Schlager. Vol. 2. Detroit: St. James Press, 2004. p51-57.

108. "United Mine Workers of America." *Ohio History Central*. Ohio History Connection.

109. (http://www.ohiohistorycentral.org/w/United_Mine_Workers_of_America?rec=995)

110. Cosgrove, Ben. "Hatred on the Home Front: The Detroit Race Riots During WWII." *Life*. Time.com: 18 June 2014.

111. (http://time.com/3880177/detroit-race-riots-1943-photos-from-a-city-in-turmoil-during-wwii/)

112. "The Smith Act." *American Decades*. Ed. Judith S. Baughman, Victor Bondi, Richard Layman, Tandy McConnell, and Vincent Tompkins. Vol. 5: 1940-1949. Detroit: Gale, 2001.

113. 29 Reds Indicted in 'Overthrowplot.' Special to *The New York Times*. *The New York Times* (1923-Current file) [New York, N.Y] 16 July 1941: 7.

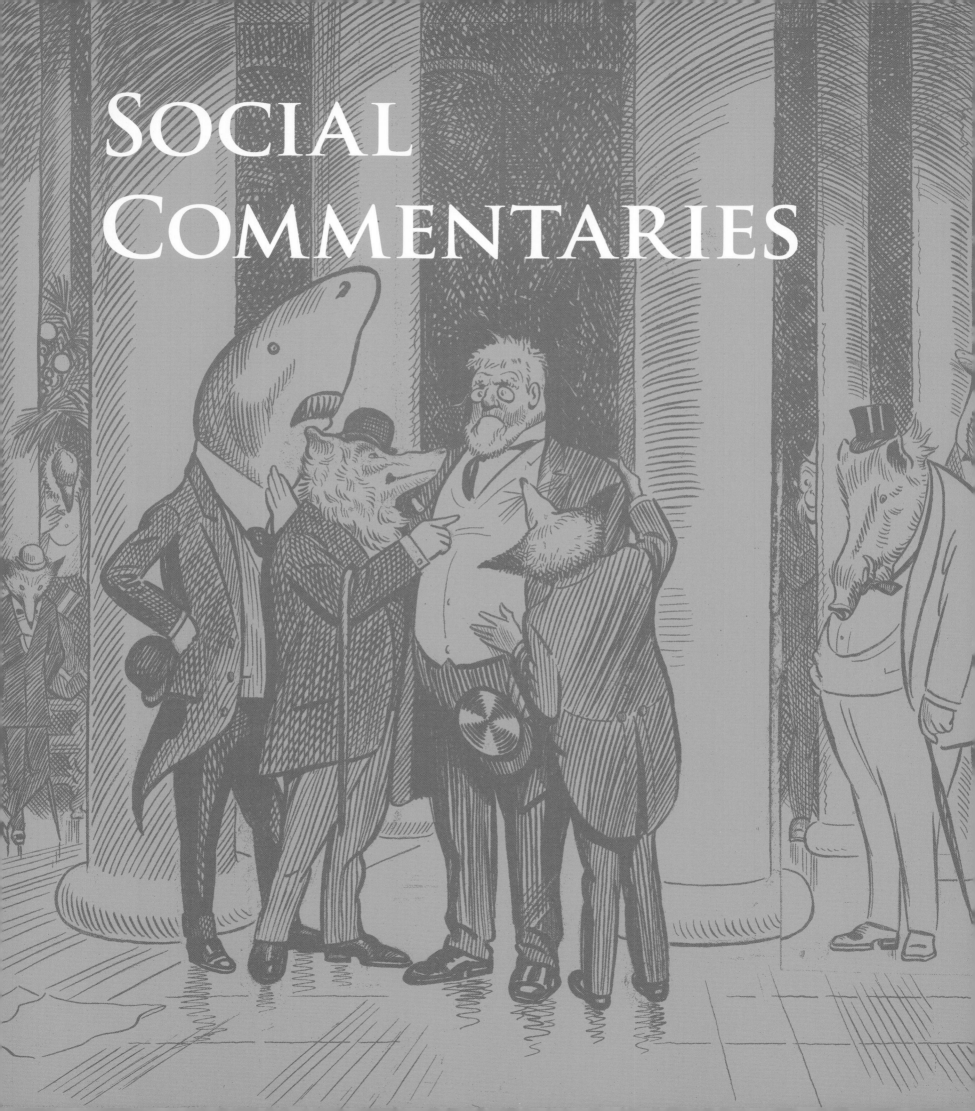

# SOCIAL COMMENTARIES

## 04

RIGHT: Original art for the cover of *The Socialist Primer* by Art Young, 1930
(Printed version, p. 251)
9.5" x 12.5"

**ABOVE:** Protest
*The Liberator,* January 1923
14.25" x 9.25"

**BELOW:** Progress
*Labor:* "Where are we going Mamma?"
*Capital:* "Never you mind where we are going."
*The Liberator,* October 1922
7.25" x 9.5"

**OPPOSITE:** Getting Rich
11.75" x 13.5"

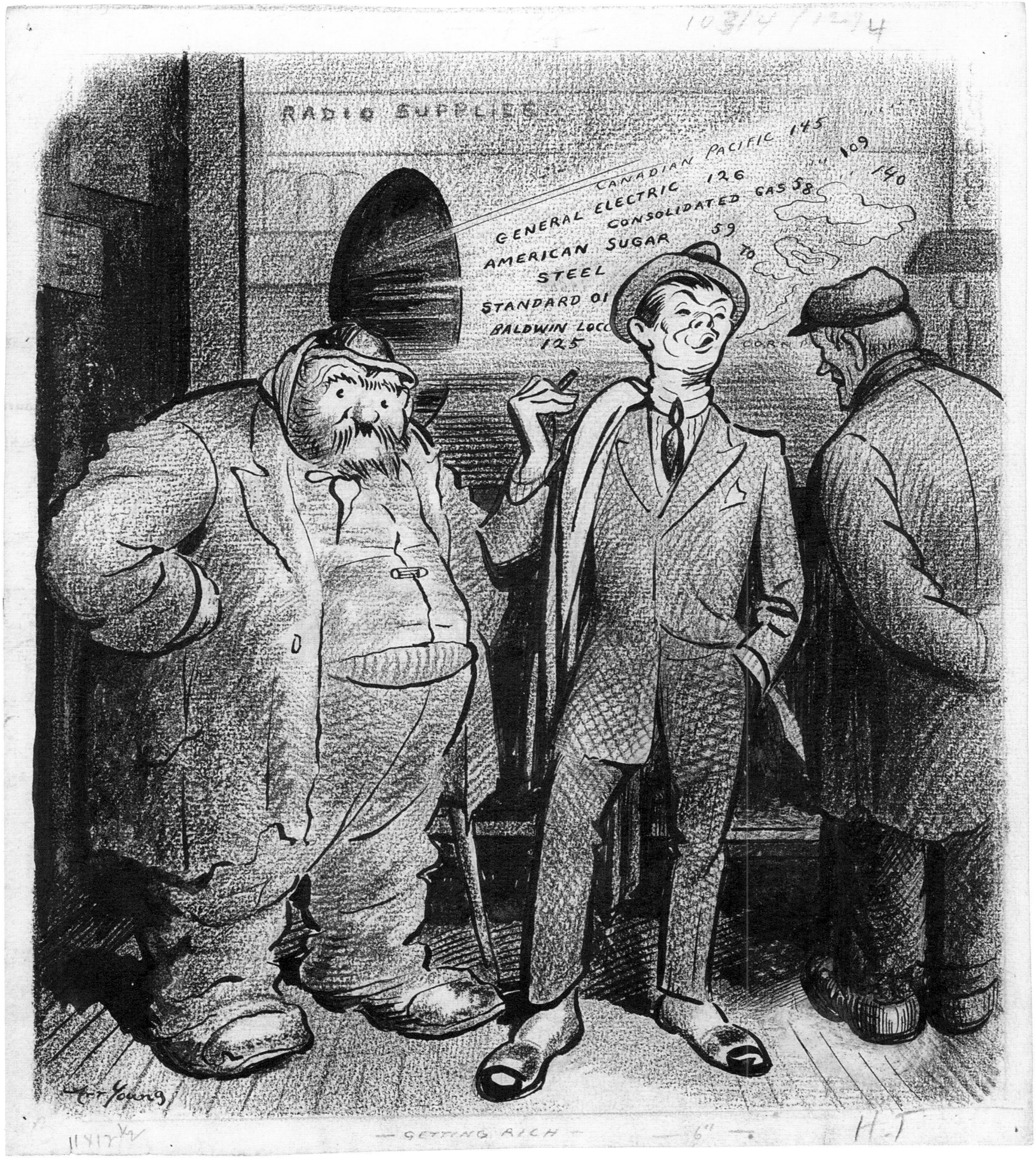
RADIO SUPPLIES
CANADIAN PACIFIC 145
GENERAL ELECTRIC 126
CONSOLIDATED GAS 58
AMERICAN SUGAR 59
STEEL
STANDARD OI
BALDWIN LOCO
125
109
140
TO
Art Young
— GETTING RICH —

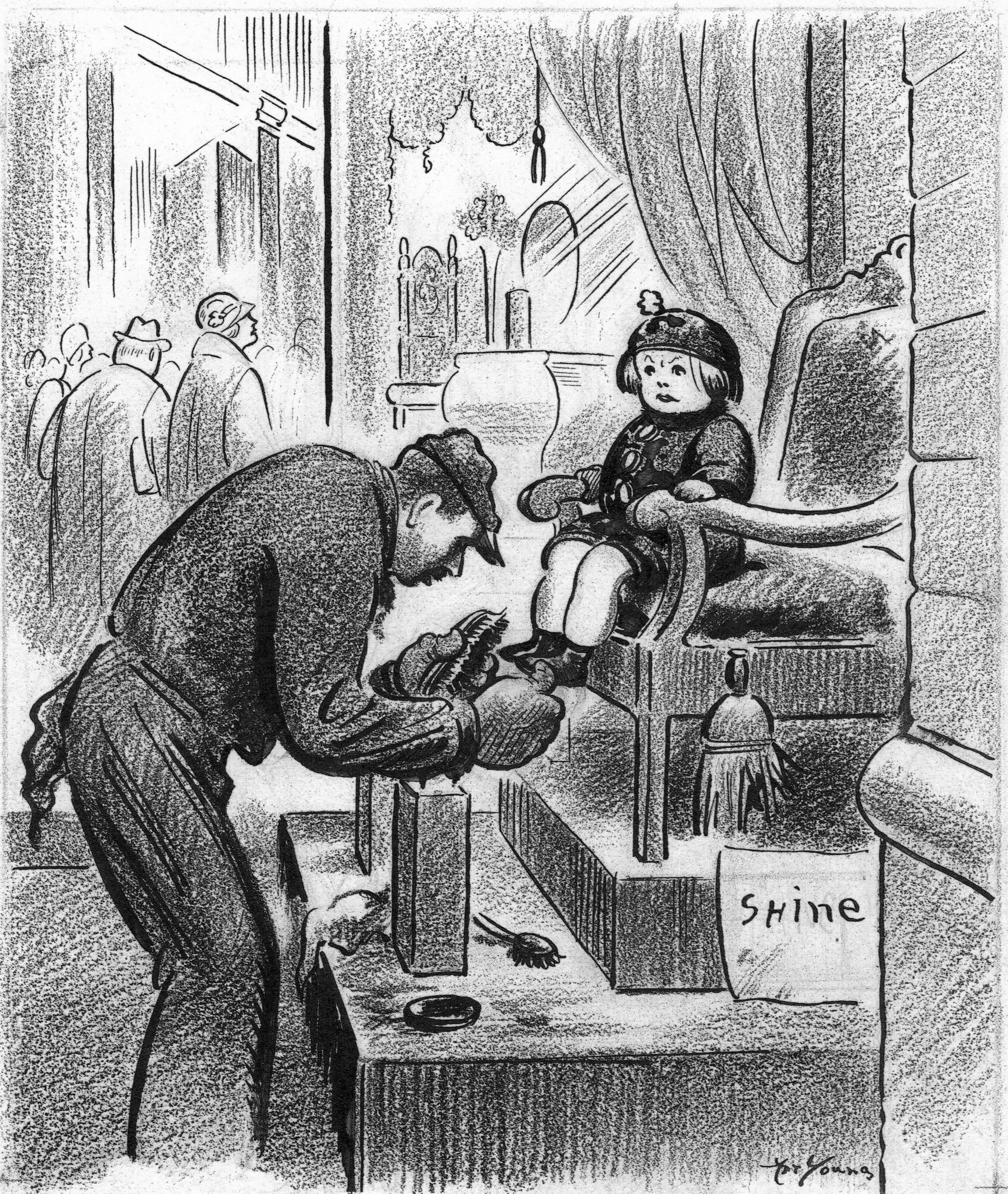
SHINE

**ABOVE: Progress**
*Art Young's Inferno*, 1934
8.75" x 13"

**OPPOSITE: Capital and Labor**
13" x 22"

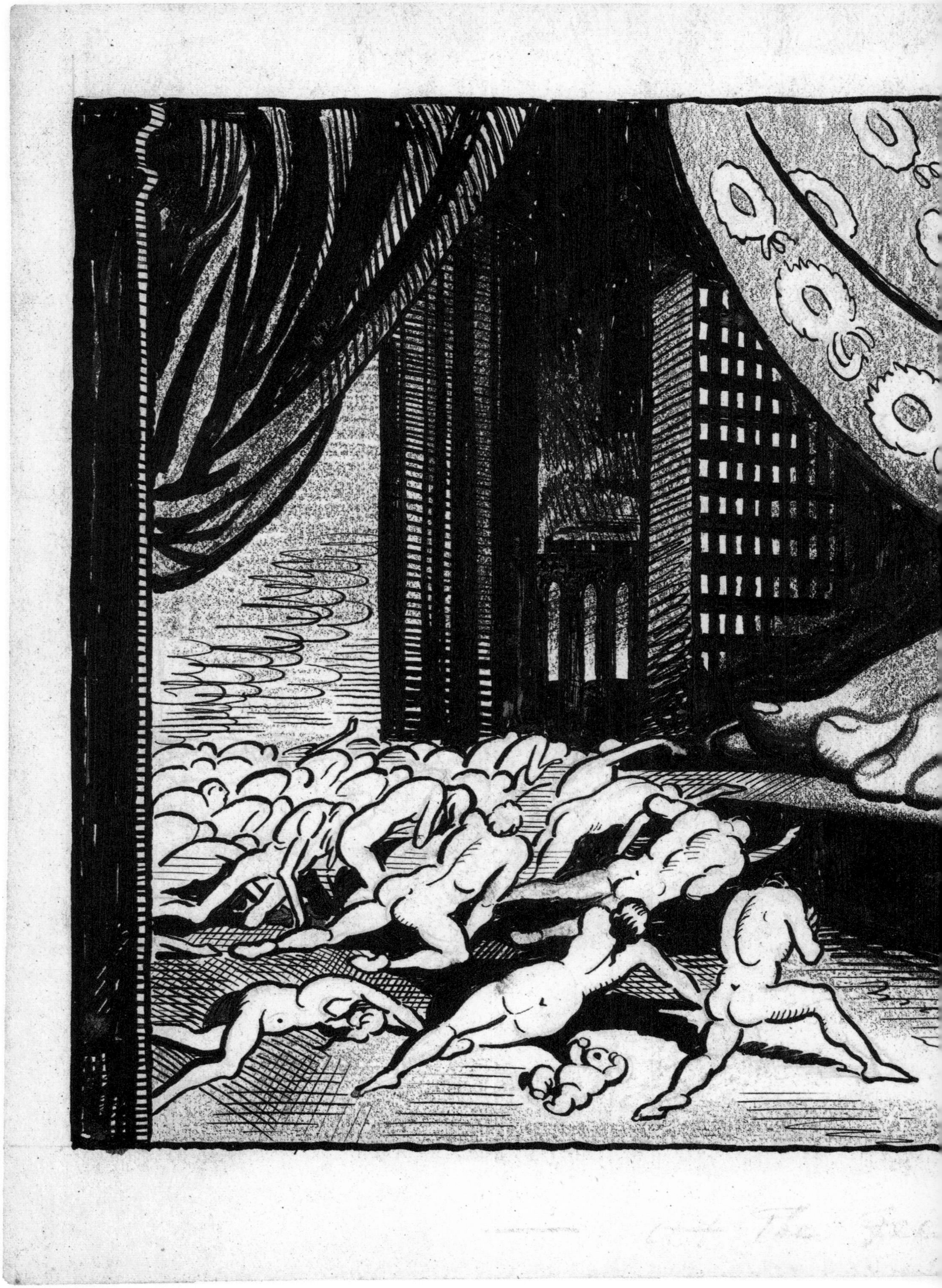

**Feet of Power**
12.25" x 8.25"

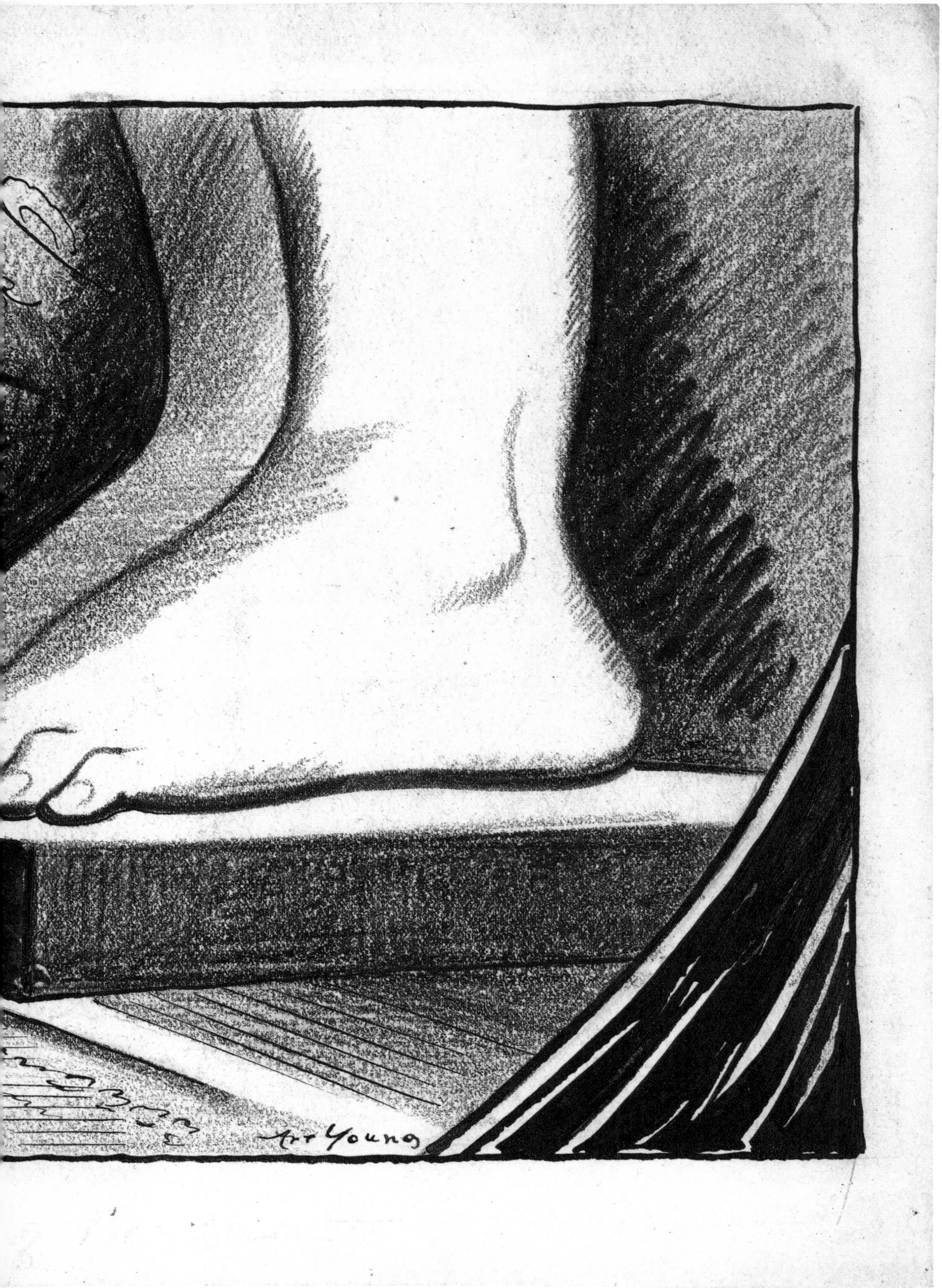
Art Young

**Guardian of the Dividends**
*Life*, March 18, 1913
7.5" x 9.5"

This world of creepers

**This World of Creepers; Afraid of Themselves and of Others,
Afraid of the Almighty, of Life and of Death**
*Life*, November 14, 1907
From Art Young's personal tear sheet file,
with handwritten notation
19.5" x 12.5"

**ABOVE: Pit and Dome**
*Metropolitan Magazine*, June 1914
7" x 9.5"

Here is a view of the dome that is not seen on postcards or guide-books. I made the sketch from an inhabited alley a few blocks southeast of the Capitol, not because the view is typical of all that surrounds the House of Congress ~ that would be untrue ~ but because it is characteristic of our country as a whole. Dedicated to democracy, we have become a nation with a pit and dome.

**RIGHT: Hunting a Job**
"It develops character"
12.75" x 16.5"

**Heaven Help the Law-Abiding Citizen**
Our law-making bodies are like a kind of gatling-cannon — and
Mr. Citizen is the target.
*Metropolitan Magazine,* February 1914
22.5" x 11.5"

**The Streets for Democracy**
*Driver (to pedestrian who happens to be the eminent publicist Prof. Highbrow PhD
and profound thinker and author of several scientific books):* "Say, are yous tryin'
to take a nap on de street? Shake yer pegs, no brains!"
13.75" x 15.75"

**The Public Impulse**
13.75" x 18.625"

It is often argued against the recall of judges that the public mind is swayed by "gusts of violent passion" that suddenly, on the strength of a rumor that a judge is corrupt, the public will storm the court and drag his Honor to the nearest lamp post.

I have drawn the cartoon above to illustrate the fact that the public does not sin on the side of impulse so much as it does on the side of apathy. When you think of all the abuses the people submit to — the corruption, the tyranny, the degradation, and the toleration of the system that breeds them — it becomes plain that the public mind moves with the "violence" of a snail with rheumatism.

No, there is no need to worry over the possibility of a public revolt now and then. Rather let us deplore the fact the people shamefully submit like patient cattle to countless acts of injustice inflicted by a master class.

**The Prisoner Who Came Clean**
*Life*, May 6, 1926
From Art Young's personal tear sheet file

**The Age of Advertising**
*Puck*, date unknown
From Art Young's personal tear sheet file

CERTIFICATE OF MARRIAGE

THIS IS TO CERTIFY

That on the _____ une

Nineteen _____ eight

at no 231 _____ City of

New York _____ New York

or any other city

I JOINED TOGE _____ HOLY MATRIMONY

J. Hamilton _____ Brute

and Lucile _____ Meek

according to the Rite _____ he Average Church in

the United States of _____ onformity with the Laws

of the State of Ne _____

IN WITNESS WHEREOF I h _____ y name this fourth

day of June _____ undred and eight

Bertha Anybody }

George Orwell } WI _____ J. Dontcare D.D.

RIGHT: **The Animals He Meets When He Has Money to Invest**
14.25″ x 16.5″

BELOW: **Train Crowds**
"A young lady writes to the Good Form department of a newspaper to know if she should "precede or follow her escort into the subway car."
May 5, 1910
9″ x 15″

OPPOSITE: **Not to Be Taken From Her Cross — by Order of the Bishops of the Episcopal Church**
*Life*, date unknown
13.75″ x 17.25″

*From "Rugged" to Ragged Individualism.*

*The story of the middle-class American.*

WHAT IS A REASONABLE PROFIT?
10, 20, 40 or 90 PERCENT,
OR IS IT ALL YOU CAN GET?

ABOVE: **The Crime Wave**
*The Liberator*, February 1921
11" x 8.5"

OPPOSITE ABOVE: **From Rugged to Ragged Individualism —
The Story of the Middle-Class American**
13.5" x 10"

OPPOSITE BELOW: **What Is a Reasonable Profit?**
What is a "Reasonable Profit?"
Is it ten — twenty — eighty or ninety percent?
A committee of thinking people will report as soon as possible
*Metropolitan Magazine*, November 1917
11" x 8.5"

**The Speculative Pit**
*Today Magazine,* May 1935
10" x 13.5"

**ABOVE:** Extinct
*Metropolitan Magazine,* August 1914
10.75″ x 8.5″

**RIGHT:** Authority
9.5″ x 8.25″

**Successful Selfishness**
*The Society of Illustrators Album 1911*
7.75" x 7.75"

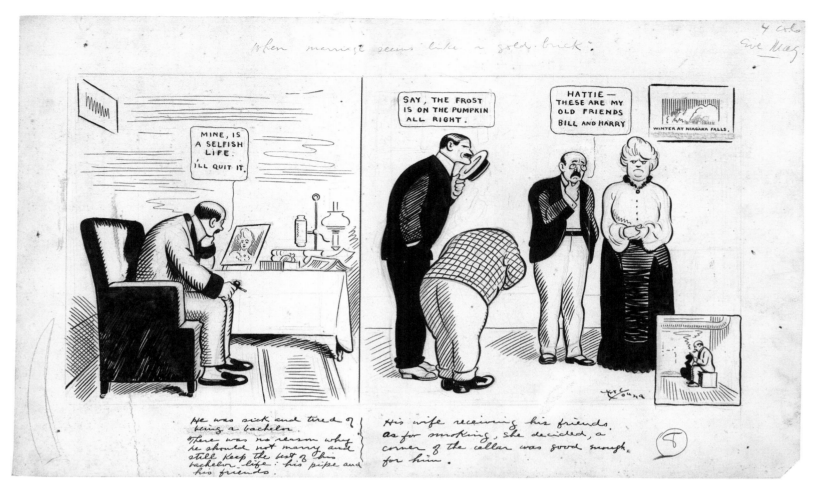

**His Wife Receiving His Friends**
"He was sick and tired of being a bachelor. There was no reason why he should not marry and still keep the best of his bachelor life: his pipe and his friends. His wife receiving his friends. As for smoking, she decided, a corner of the cellar was good enough for him."
23.75" x 14.5"

**ABOVE:** Next!
From the Cradle to the Mill
Originally published in *Puck*, April 10, 1912, centerfold
*What Fools These Mortals Be!: The Story of Puck Magazine*
Courtesy The Library of American Comics/IDW Publishing

**OPPOSITE:** Fool's Paradise
15" x 18.75"

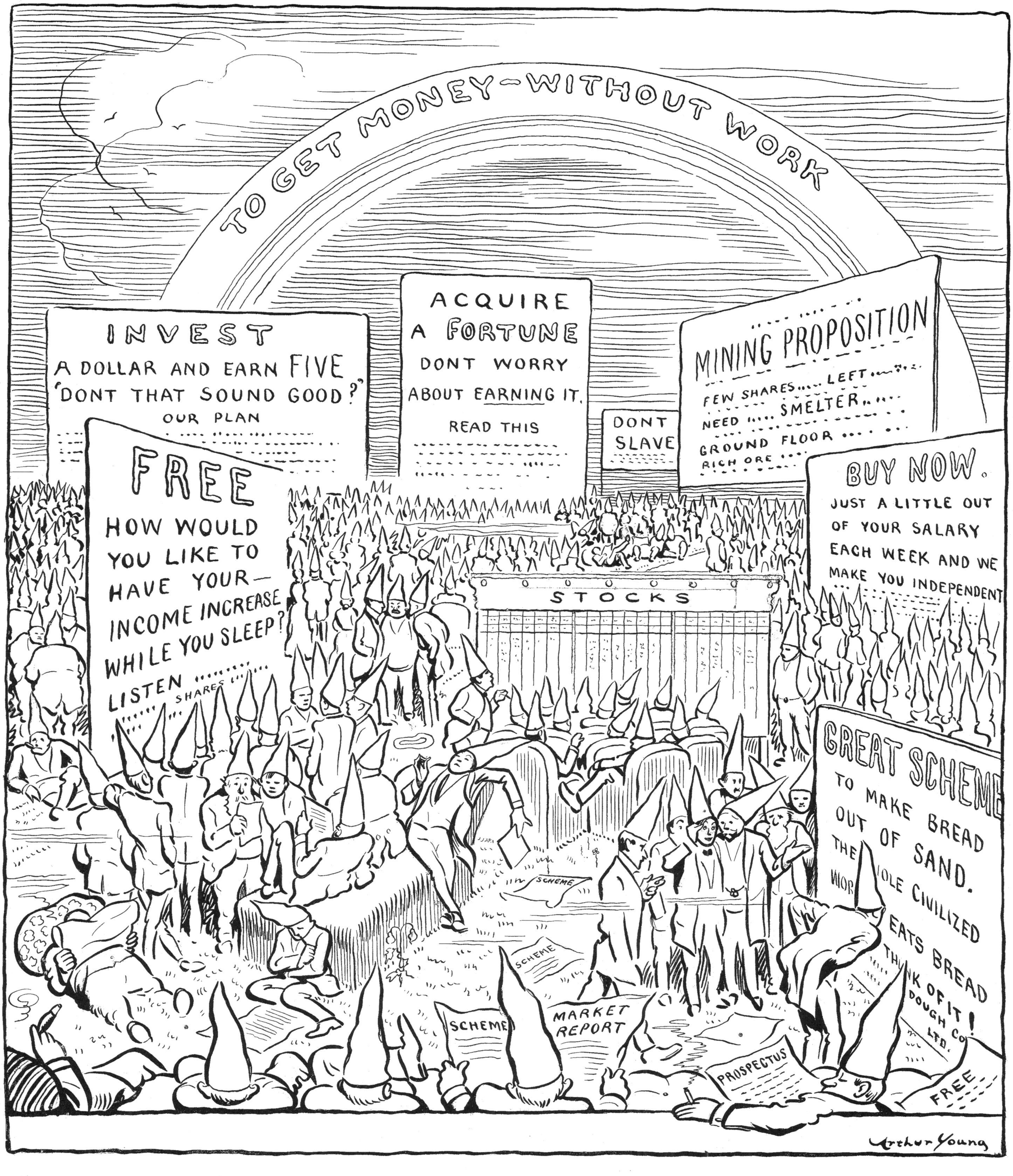
TO GET MONEY — WITHOUT WORK
INVEST
A DOLLAR AND EARN FIVE
"DONT THAT SOUND GOOD?"
OUR PLAN
ACQUIRE
A FORTUNE
DONT WORRY
ABOUT EARNING IT.
READ THIS
DONT
SLAVE
MINING PROPOSITION
FEW SHARES LEFT
NEED SMELTER
GROUND FLOOR
RICH ORE
FREE
HOW WOULD
YOU LIKE TO
HAVE YOUR —
INCOME INCREASE
WHILE YOU SLEEP?
LISTEN
SHARES
BUY NOW.
JUST A LITTLE OUT
OF YOUR SALARY
EACH WEEK AND WE
MAKE YOU INDEPENDENT
STOCKS
GREAT SCHEME
TO MAKE BREAD
OUT OF SAND.
THE
WOR
OLE CIVILIZED
EATS BREAD
DOUGH CO
LTD.
SCHEME
SCHEME
SCHEME
MARKET
REPORT
PROSPECTUS
FREE
Arthur Young

More Comments and Advice for People Who
Are Compelled to Ride in Street Cars
21" x 23"

**Three Cheers for The Supreme Court**
*The Liberator*, 1918
20" x 19"

On June 3rd [1918], the Supreme Court, by a vote of five to four, declared unconstitutional the Federal Child Labor Law of 1916. This law forbade the shipment across state lines of the products of all "mills, factories, canneries, workshops, mines and quarries" employing children under 14, or children between the ages of 14 and 16 at night, or more than 8 hours a day. It went into effect Sept. 1, 1917, and when in full operation would have released 150,000 children.

— *The Liberator,* August 1918

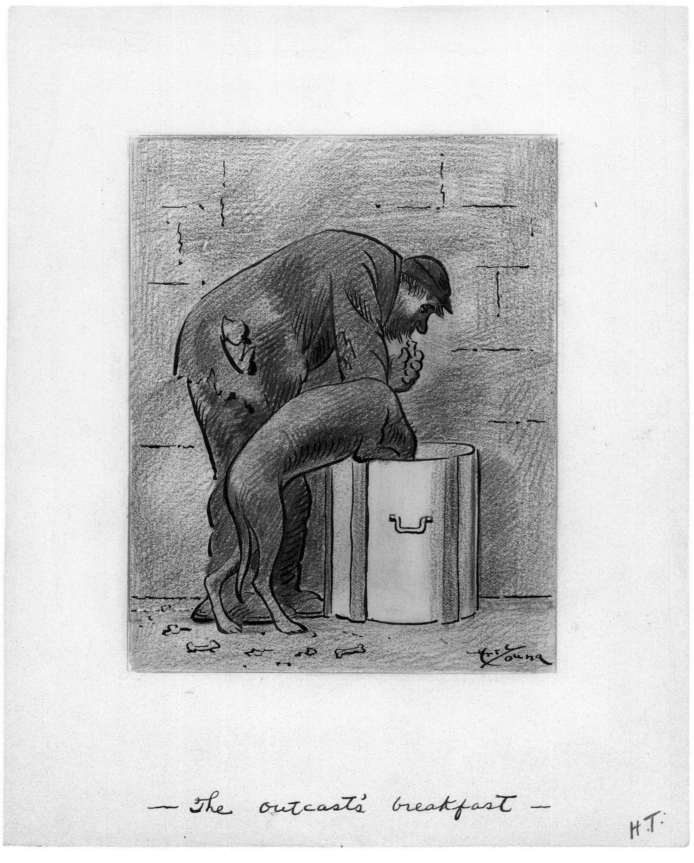

The Outcast's Breakfast

**The Outcast's Breakfast**
8″ x 10″

**The Goose-Step**

ABOVE: Art for the dust jacket of *The Goose-Step: A Study of American Education* by Upton Sinclair, 1923
15.5" x 14.5"
RIGHT: Spine, front cover, and front flap of the printed dust jacket

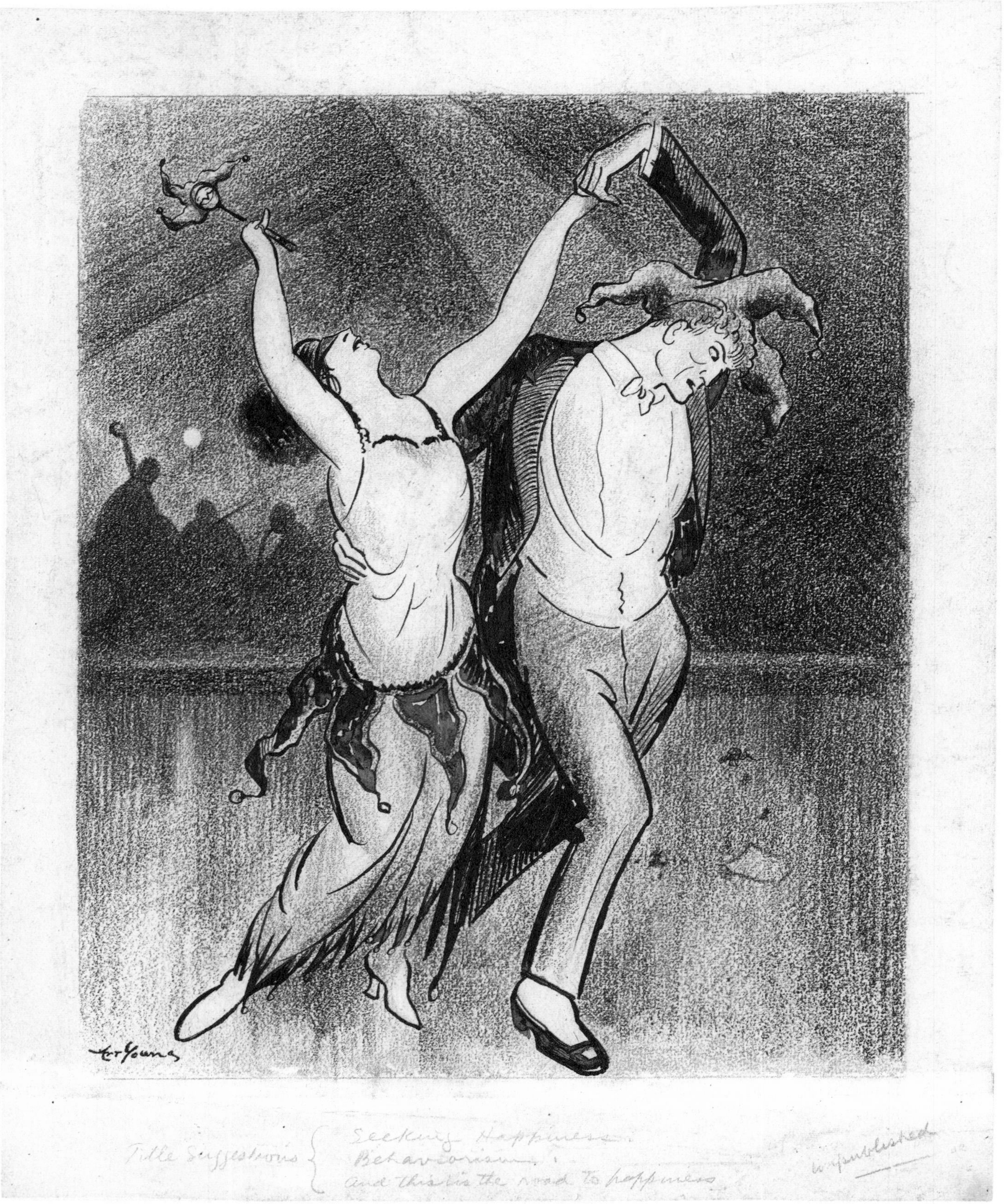
Art Young
Title Suggestions
Seeking Happiness.
Behaviorism.
and this is the road to happiness
unpublished

Seeking Happiness
13"x 16"

To Defenders of Tipping
16" x 21"

**The Counterfeiters of Coin and the
Counterfeiters of Securities**
As published in color in *Puck*, September 28, 1910, centerfold

What is the difference morally between making and circulating valueless paper in the guise of money, and making and circulating valueless paper in the form of securities? Both kinds of counterfeits get real money in exchange for fake; only, one kind gets a few hundreds of dollars, perhaps, and then goes to jail, while the other gets millions, maybe, and says: "Don't! You'll destroy confidence," to anybody who ventures to criticize.

TOP: Pride of Ownership — But No Appreciation of Those Who Made the Thing Owned
26″ x 14.75″

ABOVE: Poor Old Civilization
10.5″ x 6″

**The Man Who Agitates**
*Puck*, 1909 and *Good Morning*, 1919
22" x 16.75"

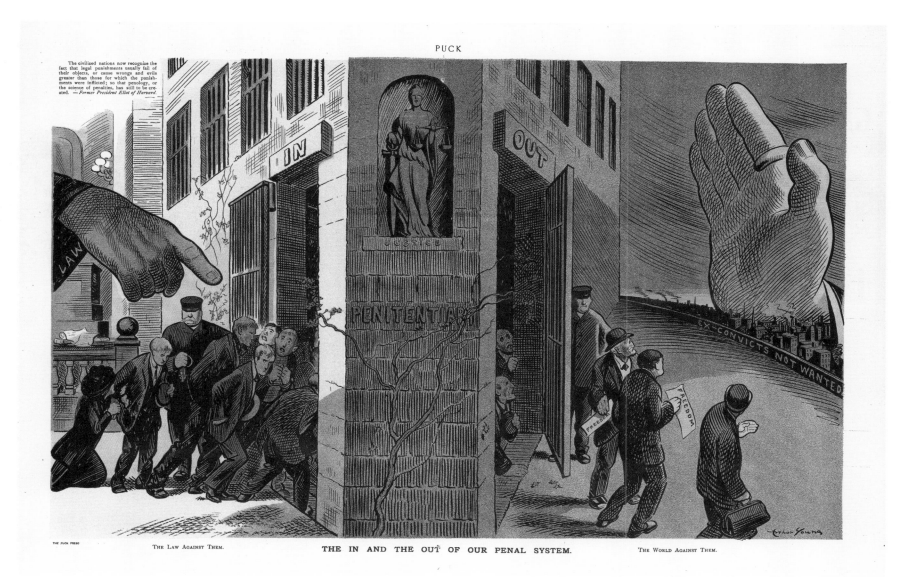

THE IN AND THE OUT OF OUR PENAL SYSTEM.

THE LAW AGAINST THEM.

THE WORLD AGAINST THEM.

**The In and the Out of Our Penal System**
*Puck*, May 20, 1909
22» x 17»

The civilized nations now recognize the fact that legal punishments
usually fail of their objects, or cause wrongs and evils greater than
those for which the punishments were inflicted; so that penology,
or the science of penalties, has still to be created.

— Former President Eliot of Harvard

**That Disturbing Light**
27" x 17"

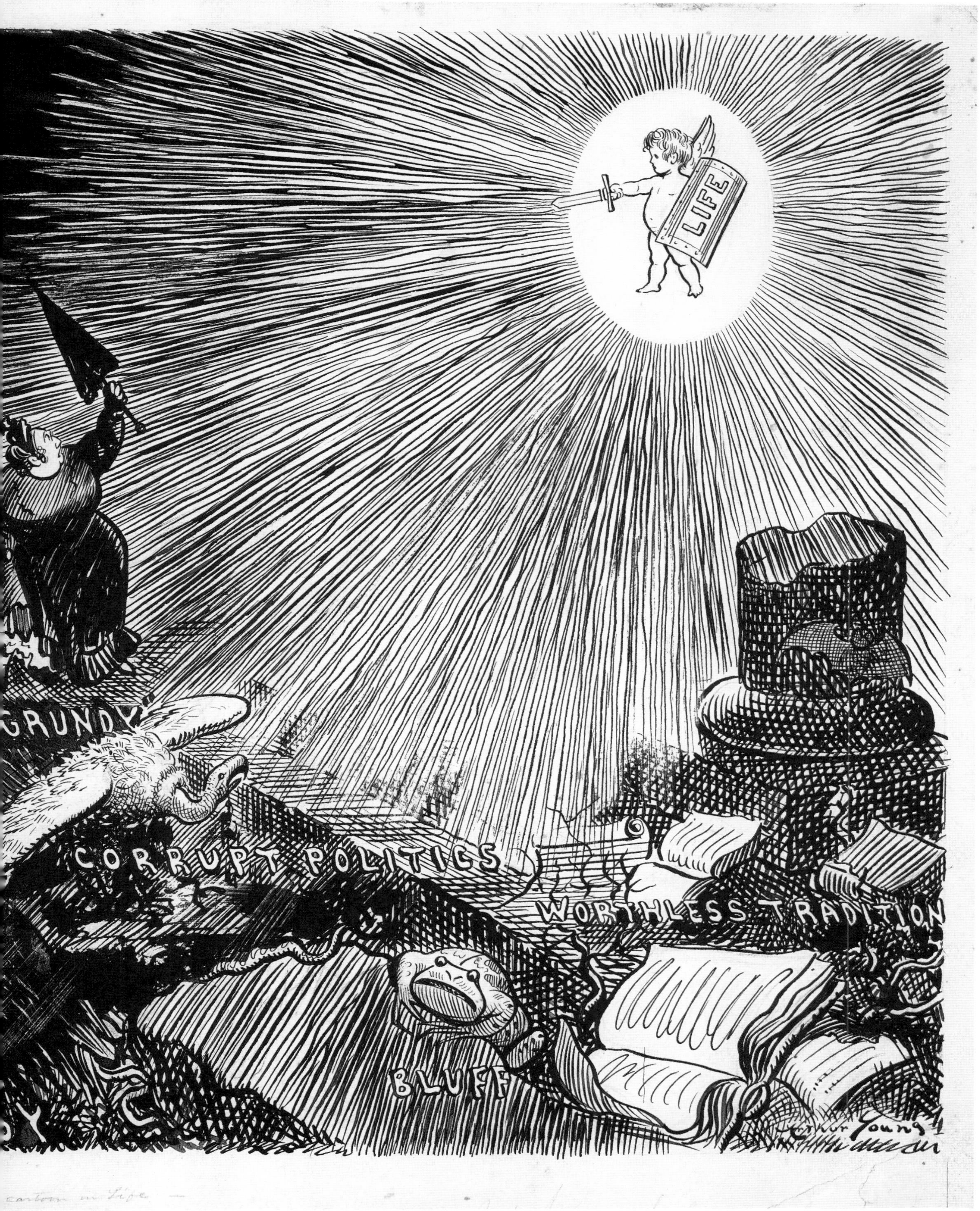
LIFE
GRUNDY
CORRUPT POLITICS
WORTHLESS TRADITION
BLUFF

**ABOVE: April Fool**
*Laborer:* "Say! I've got to have work! My family is starving!"
*Capitalist:* "Ah, but I've got overproduction. The joke is on you, why don't you laugh?"
Dated March 3, 1911 on reverse
27.5" x 21"

**OPPOSITE: The Interest of the Nation in the Campaign Has Reached Fever-heat**
17.5" x 24"

The interest of the nation in the campaign has reached fever-heat

**The Old Game ~ It Ruins Many**
16.75» x 22.5»

The effort to GET SOMETHING FOR NOTHING, to make the vice of gambling replace honest work. It is played in Wall Street, at the race track, and wherever men gamble. It ruins all of its foolish followers in the end and makes criminals of many.

It fills poorhouses and lunatic asylums, digs graves in Potter's field, breaks up countless homes. It has gone on for centuries and still nothing but experience teaches. No man will feel that this cartoon applies TO HIM.

When Married Life Seems Like a Gold Brick (To the Man)
23.125" x 16.75"

An Anarchist in the Making
*Puck*, July 26, 1909, centerfold

**Gas vs. Guns**
To make New York safe, 75,000 pistol permits have
been granted.
*The Nation,* May 3, 1922
8.5" x 7"

**ABOVE: War Dog**
A political cartoon, date and publication status unknown
10.25" x 5.75"

**RIGHT: Can't See It — The Blind Pig**
8.5" x 10.5"

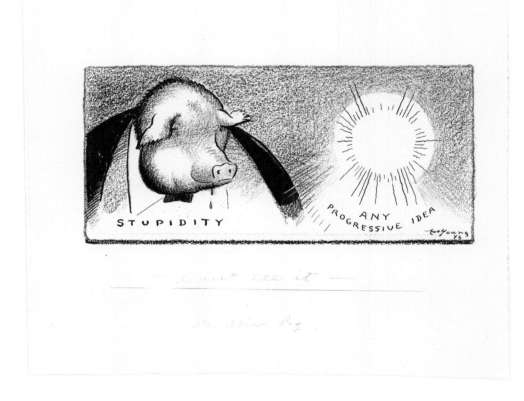

**I Christen Thee**
*Life*, November 18, 1915
25.25» x 15.75»

**World Progress**
*Teacher:* "Jimmie Proletariat, take the head of the class. You can certainly do better than this doddering imbecile."
*The Liberator* #31, October 1920
13.75" x 10.75"

**The Thinker**
"Would I have been worse off if Germany had won?"
*Good Morning*, Jan. 1, 1921
9.25" x 7.25"

**Signs**

*Judge (to man arrested for violating the no-smoking law):* "What's the matter, can't you read?"
*Culprit:* "Sure I can read. I see many signs: Drink Moxie. Use Lye Tooth Powder. Eat Heiny's Pickles. Do I do it?"
*Good Morning* #7, June 1919

"My Secret, Brother, is Brains"
14" x 17"

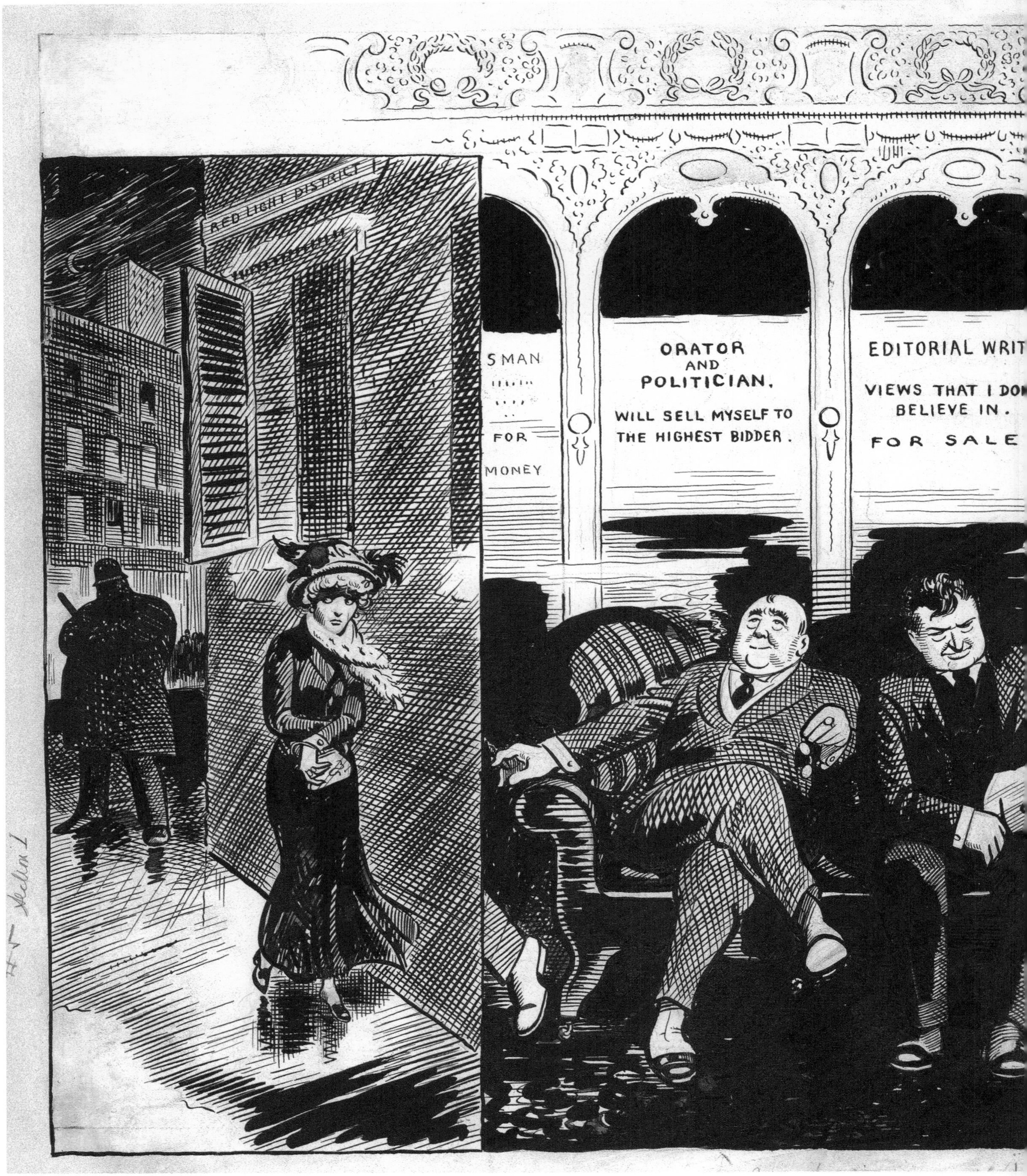
RED LIGHT DISTRICT
SMAN
FOR
MONEY
ORATOR
AND
POLITICIAN.
WILL SELL MYSELF TO
THE HIGHEST BIDDER.
EDITORIAL WRIT
VIEWS THAT I DON
BELIEVE IN.
FOR SALE

**Prostitution — Illegal and Legal**
(Art Young's original title)
Which is the greater evil — the
woman of the streets or these mental
prostitutes?
Published as "For Sale," *Puck*,
December 20, 1911, centerfold
27.75" x 17.25"

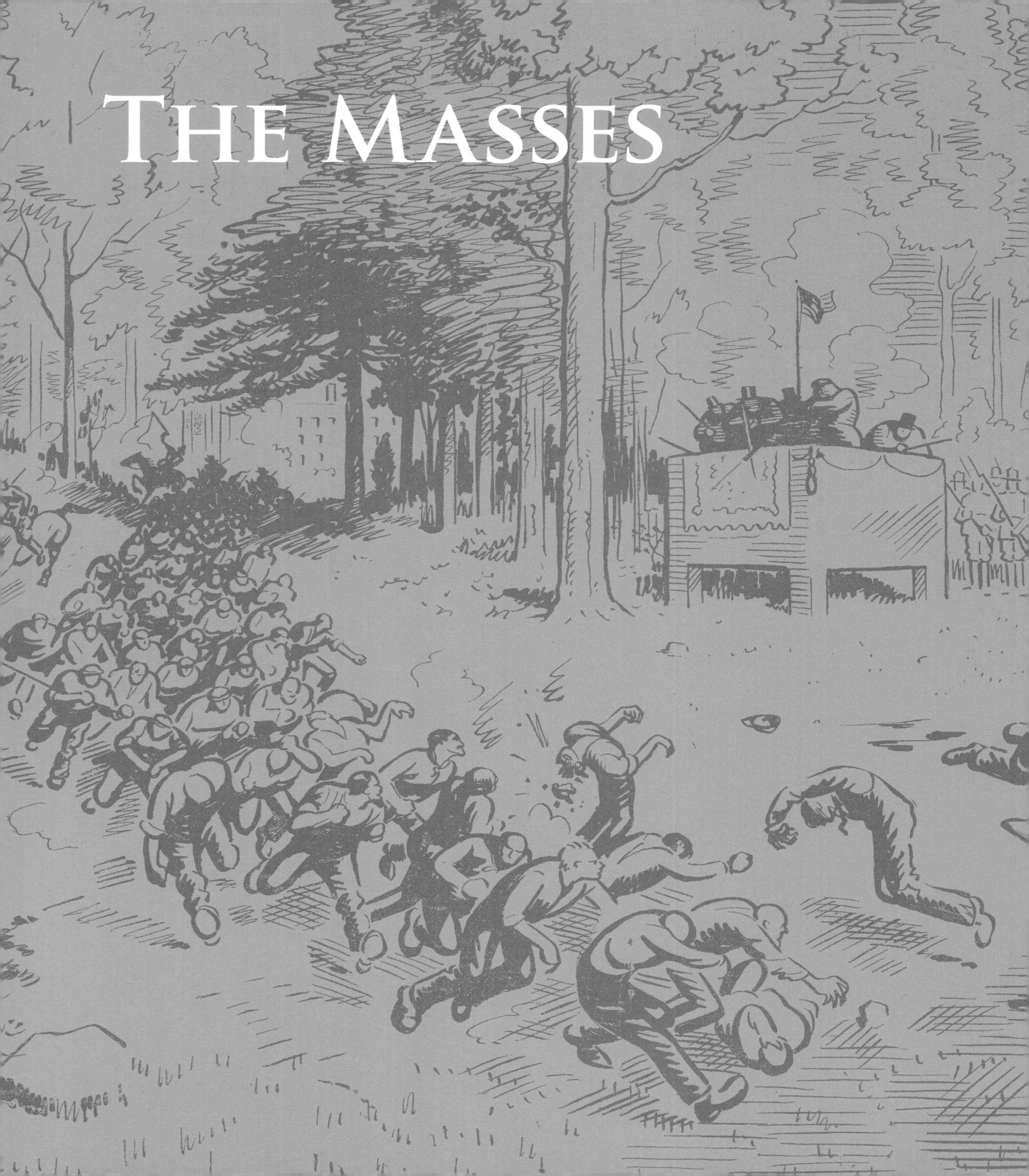
THE MASSES

## 05

**MARC MOORASH**

Very Unfortunate Situation
*The Masses*, February 1913, back cover print
From Art Young's personal tear sheet file
10.5" x 13.5"

This magazine is owned and published cooperatively by its editors. It has no dividends to pay, and nobody is trying to make money out of it. A revolutionary and not a reform magazine; a magazine with a sense of humour and no respect for the respectable; frank; arrogant; impertinent; searching for true causes; a magazine directed against rigidity and dogma wherever it is found; printing what is too naked or true for a money-making press; a magazine whose final policy is to do as it pleases and conciliate nobody, not even its readers ...

— from the masthead of *The Masses*

It is in the pages of *The Masses* (1911–1917) that Art Young truly began to find his voice. He had occasionally been able to place some of his increasingly socialist political cartoons in other magazines (whose regular checks allowed Young to work for *The Masses*, which didn't pay its contributors), but when Max Eastman became editor, Young, for the first time, found himself in a position to mold a publication in which he had the freedom to fully ink his mind.

Young (who also functioned as one of the magazine's contributing editors) published more than 150 illustrations and writings. His poignant pen avoided no major issue of the times, touching on an astoundingly wide range of subjects including: women's suffrage ("Breed," December 1915); child labor ("Mill Owner: 'Mrs. Crumb, I Have Called to Assist You...'," April 1914); family struggles ("Hell on Earth," March 1915); workers' rights ("A Strike-Breaking Agency," August 1915); attacks against anti-immigration sentiment ("If They Should Come Back Via Ellis Island," March 1913); the struggle of labor ("April Fool," April 1913); corruption in the legal system ("The Majesty of the Law," March 1914); war ("Millions for 'Defence'," January 1916); and capitalism ("A Compulsory Religion," December 1912 and "Business As Usual," January 1916).

It was also through the pages of *The Masses* that Young would find himself under legal duress.

**Reward**
Jesus Wanted Poster
Original lettering; pasted-up Jesus image
13.75″ x 16″

In July 1913, Young's cartoon, "Poisoned at the Source," accused the Associated Press of purposely covering up the news of the 1912 Paint Creek/Cabin Creek coal miners' strike in West Virginia. The AP's complaint led to Young and Eastman being indicted on two counts of criminal libel — for which they were arrested and jailed, then released after posting bail — and which were later quietly dropped.

Just a few years later, as the Great War progressed, *The Masses* took an increasingly staunch and loud stance, stating that it was big business and propaganda that were driving the United States to enter the fray. *The Masses* was barred from being delivered through the U.S. Mail and banned from newsstands and libraries, which resulted in ever-greater difficulty in filling subscriptions and paying for printing.

In 1917, Young, Eastman, John Reed, Floyd Dell, and Merrill Rogers were indicted for "conspiracy to obstruct recruitment and enlistment" under the newly passed Espionage Act for their work in *The Masses*. In Young's case, it was his cartoon, "Having Their Fling"

Why is the capitalist burning with indignation?
Why is he cursing the delegate of a labor union?
Why does he always curse a labor delegate?
Why? Because the labor delegate faces him and says: "The men demand their rights."

He isn't used to being ordered. He wants to do all the ordering himself.
He does'nt know as Abraham Lincoln knew that "Labor is prior to capital."—But he will know it some day.—*Arthur Young.*

**Vulture Capitalism**
*The Masses,* January 1911
Young's first published cartoon for *The Masses*

(*The Masses*, September 1917; see p. 30) that provoked the government's wrath.

The two trials that followed, which were little more than an attack on the freedom of the press in wartime, might be best known for Young's sketch of his sleeping self during the first trial, cheekily titled "Art Young On Trial for His Life" (p. 126). The first trial ended in a hung jury. The government initiated a retrial in September 1918 — with the same inconclusive result.

However, *The Masses* had folded by then (though it was quickly reborn as *The Liberator* — with the same contributors but less-collective ideals), and the great experiment in combining socialism, art, literature, and an ideologically free press had ended.

Also ended, at least for a few years, was Young's inclusion in the mainstream magazines that had been his lifeline. But the trade-off for all of the struggles was that Young's legacy and legend were emblazoned in the hearts of the radical movements of the first half of the 20th century. And that led him to turn his attention to what would become his pride and joy — his next magazine endeavor, *Good Morning*.

**The God of War**
*The Masses*, September 1915
From Art Young's personal tear sheet file, with handwritten notations
10" x 11"

**Respectability**
*The Masses*, August 1915
12" x 15.5"

**A Compulsory Religion**
*The Masses*, December 1912
print
(Handwritten manuscript,
p. 279)
10.5" x 13.5"

"The trouble with the world is the insane worship of money."

How often we hear this thundered from the pulpit, emphasized in the press and in ordinary conversation. Yes that's the trouble. But what drives people to this insanity?

In the first place, life is a fight for food, shelter and clothing. No matter how high the price of food soars, we must struggle to pay the cost. No matter how high the cost of apparel goes, we must keep a degree of comfort and a decent appearance. No matter how far the landlord advances his rent, we must struggle to pay for shelter.

We must fight to get these things or die, and the average man does die fighting for them between 45 and 50 years of age. You might truthfully write over the tombstones of four-fifths of the human race: "Died fighting for food, shelter, and clothing — in a world of plenty."

The fear that they will not get the necessities of life, and that their children will suffer for them, drives the restless spirits on.

It is this kind of civilization that breeds an insane worship of money. That some men want more, after they have been assured a life of comfort, merely emphasizes the tragic baseness of this mad movement. In a world that is running amuck, individuals cannot stop, even if they would, for back of it all is the original cause — FEAR.

A stampede of cattle carries all with it, even if one of the herd is ready to stop.

So, bend your back to the lash, cringe, crawl, prostitute yourselves mentally and physically, bribe, graft, do anything to get money. "Get it," says father to son; "marry for money," says mother to daughter.

Under the circumstances, how can the average individual worship any God — but Mammon?

**Ancient Bill of Rights — The Right to Worry!**
Raising a family in an atmosphere of fear and trouble
*The Masses*, March 1915
15.75" x 19"

**Breed!**
*The Masses*, December 1915
From Art Young's personal tear sheet file
20" x 12.75"

# DANGER!

## To the Free Press of America

The Associated Press is now trying to send to prison two men who have dared to criticise it.

Do you know about the case of Max Eastman and Art Young, and the proceedings against The Masses?

### COME AND HEAR

**Inez Milholland Boissevain**

**John Haynes Holmes**     **Morris Hillquit**

**Lincoln Steffens**     **Amos Pinchot**

**Charlotte Perkins Gilman**

## FREE MASS MEETING
### Thursday, March 5, 8 P.M.

# COOPER UNION

Danger!
Original handbill from Art Young's files, c. 1913
6″ x 9.5″

**ABOVE: It's a Great Country**
The munition maker made us hate Europe, and now we must buy munitions from him to defend ourselves against that hatred.
*The Masses*, February 1916
10.75" x 8.5"

**OPPOSITE: The Sport of Kings**
*The Masses*, December 1914
From Art Young's personal tear sheet file, with handwritten notations
18" x 13.5"

*Drawn by Arthur Young.*

THE MASSES, December, 1914.

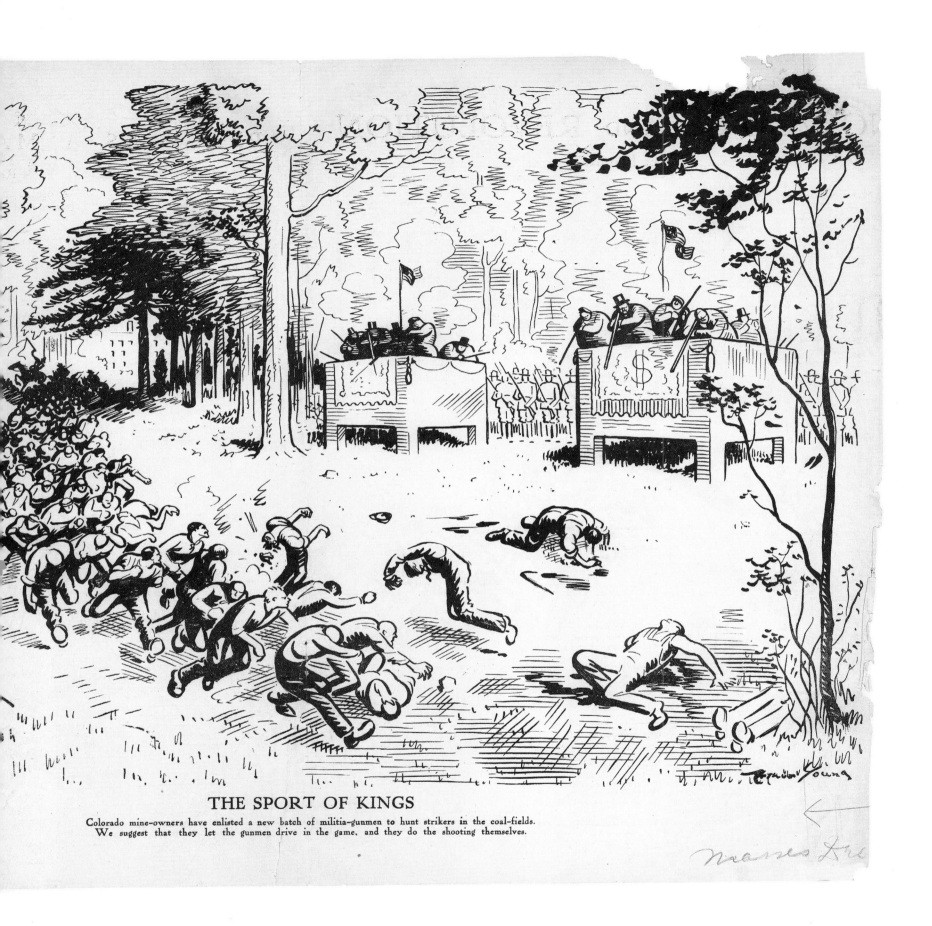

## THE SPORT OF KINGS

Colorado mine-owners have enlisted a new batch of militia-gunmen to hunt strikers in the coal-fields.
We suggest that they let the gunmen drive in the game, and they do the shooting themselves.

**ABOVE: Art Young Sleeping in Court**
*Art Young: His Life and Times*, 1939

**RIGHT:** *Attorney for Defendant:* "Your honor, the defendant was out of work. He has a sick wife and three small children." *Prosecuting Attorney:* "Your honor, I object on the ground that the evidence is irrelevant, incompetent and immaterial." *— and the Judge yawned.*
*The Masses*, September 1916
14.5" x 11.25"

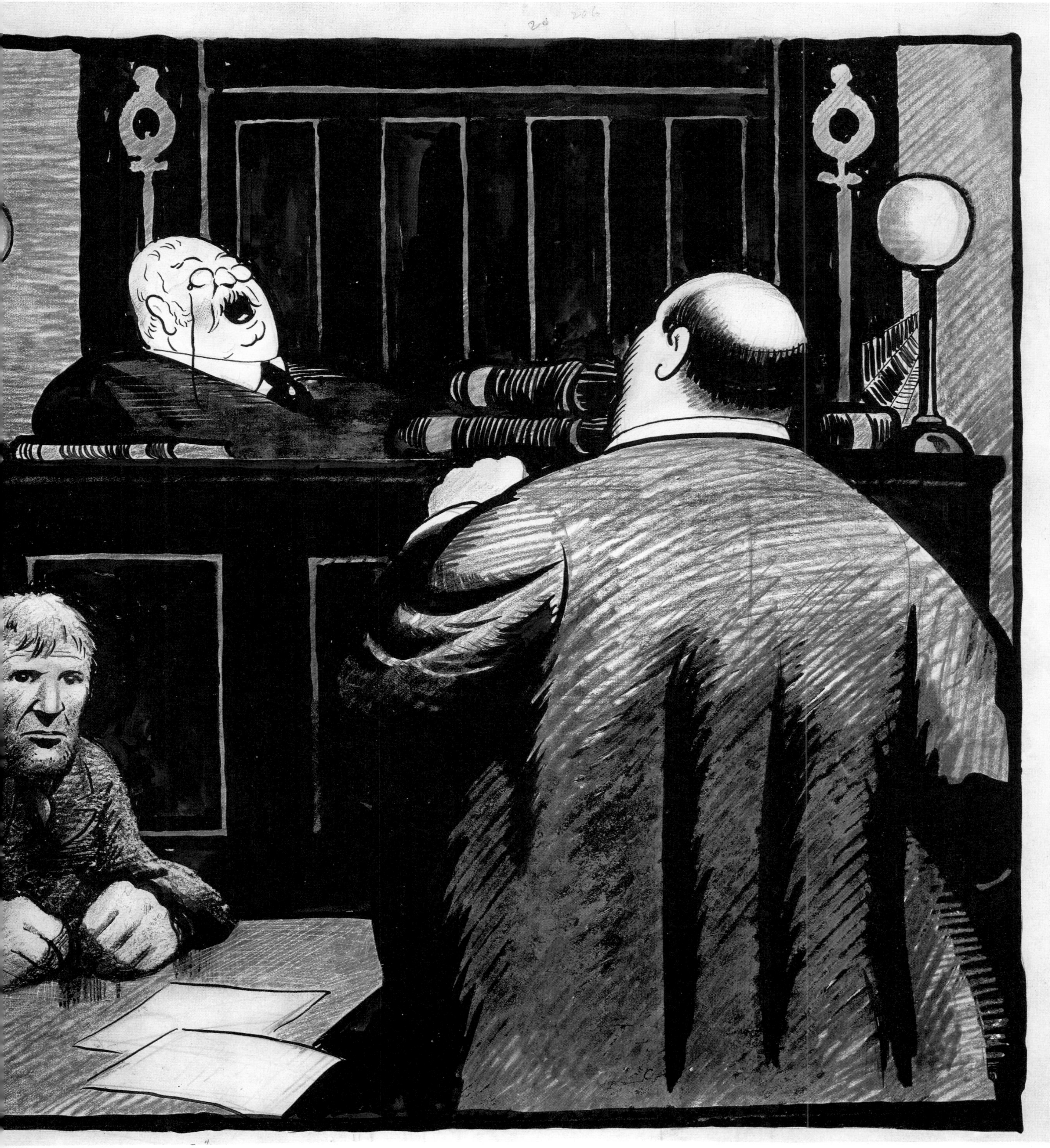

*The New York Call,* November 29, 1913, front
page, top half

**The A.P. and The Masses Editors**
*The Masses*, April 1914
18.5″ x 22″

**Man Not Improved**
*The Masses,* April 1917
21.25" x 24.5"

TO LAUGH THAT WE MAY NOT WEEP

**Predatory Wealth**
*The Masses*, July 1913
"They who bend to power and lap its milk"
Dedicated to: educators, editors, lawyers, legislators, ministers
16.25" x 20"

# GAGS

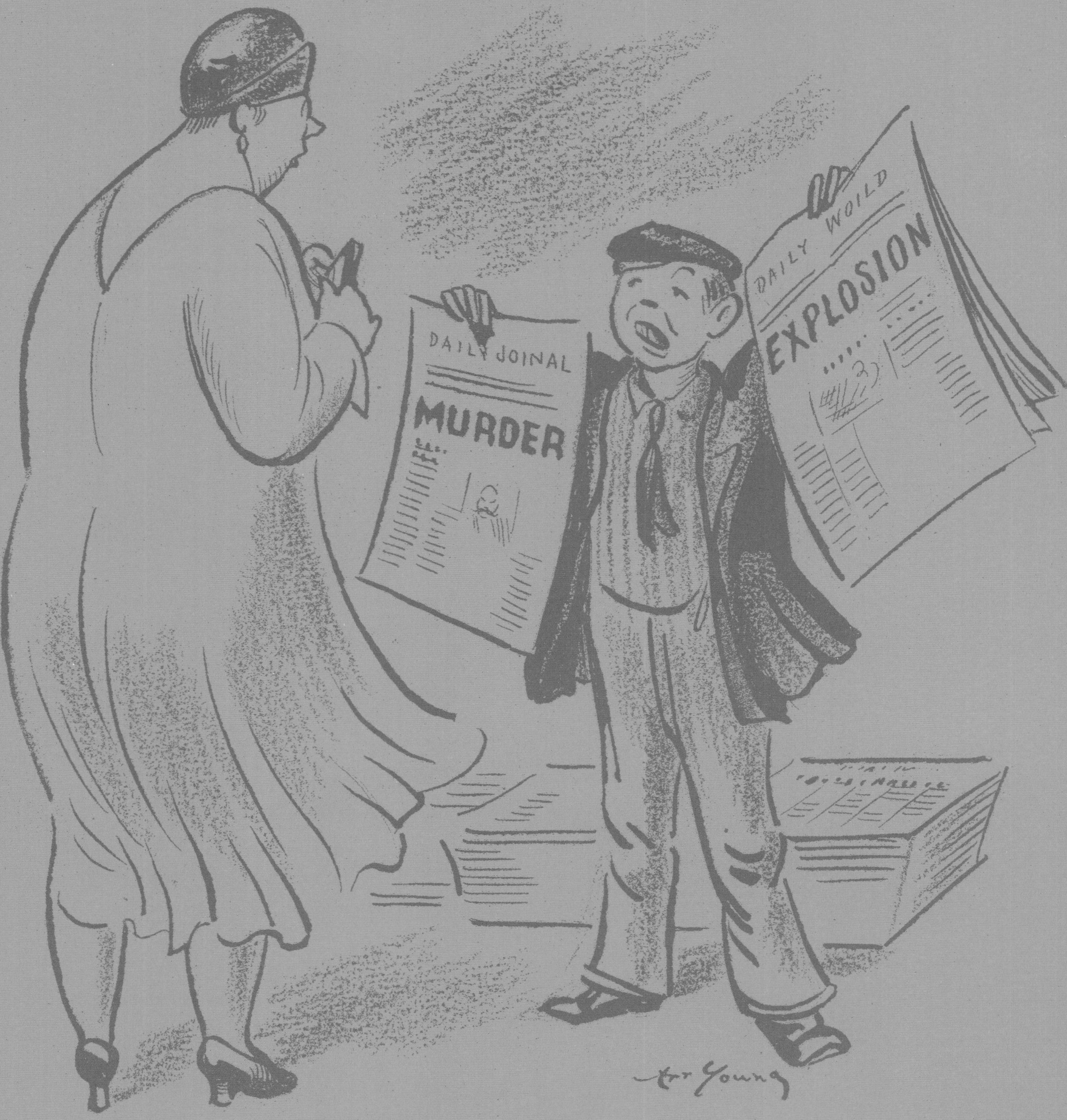
DAILY JOINAL
MURDER
DAILY WOILD
EXPLOSION
Art Young

## 06

**Kindness to Animals Week**
10.75" x 9.25"

"Git up offen there Bill, don't you know yer (hic)
liable to catch pneumonia?"
12.25" x 10"

ABOVE: "Well, go on then, I didn't want to talk to you nohow, I only spoke to you 'cause I seen you."
11.5" x 9"

RIGHT: *Girl:* "Yes, an some day I'm gonna act in the movies."
*Boy:* "Gowan! You aint got no sex appeal."
*New Masses*, June 1926
8.75" x 11"

Inside the illustration sign:

READ RATES.  B. UPPAN DEWING M.D.  HOURS 2 TO 5
$5. FOR ENTERING THE HOUSE.
$10. FOR ONE LOOK AT TONGUE.
$15 FOR TWO LOOKS AT TONGUE.
$4.50 FOR MEDICINE THAT COSTS AT WHOLESALE ABOUT 10 CTS.
IF YOU HAVEN'T A LARGE INCOME, AND ARE NOT AN
INFLUENTIAL CITIZEN AND HAVE A LARGE FAMILY
TO SUPPORT, FIVE DOLLARS EXTRA WILL BE CHARGED
AS WE DON'T CARE TO ENCOURAGE YOUR CUSTOM.

*why not be honest about it. Life*

ABOVE: **Why Not Be Honest About It?**
For *Life*, date and publication status unknown
7.5" x 10"

RIGHT: *Class:* "What is your sister's name?"
"Thelma"
"How Lovely!"
"Yes'm — we got it outen a book"
9" x 13"

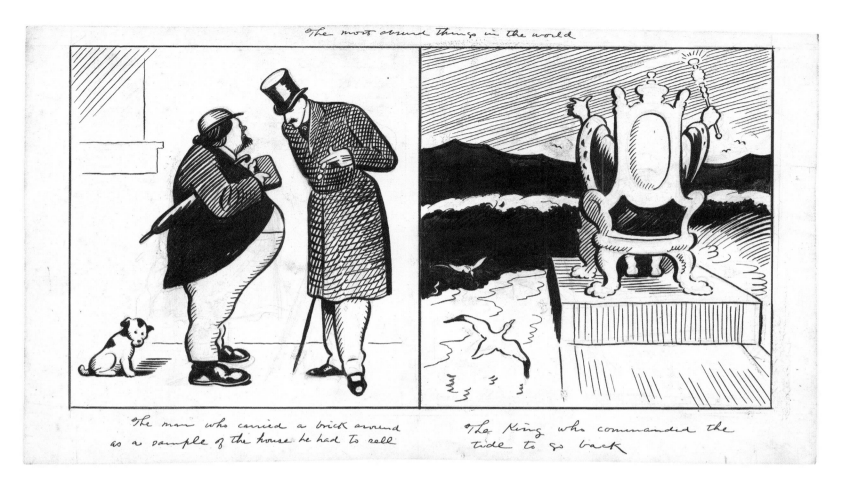

The most absurd things in the world

The man who carried a brick around as a sample of the house he had to sell

The King who commanded the tide to go back

**ABOVE:** The Most Absurd Things in the World
The man who carried a brick around as a sample of the house he had to sell
The King who commanded the tide to go back
14.75″ x 8.25″

**LEFT:** *Kindly woman:* "You should brace up, my man, think of what you owe to society."
*Bum:* "I don't owe society nuthin' lady. Wha' do you think I been doin'? Playin' bridge?"
11″ x 12″

"Is Doc Bartlett a well-informed man?"
"Is he! Say, you just ort to hear Doc give the
  guvmunt hell."
8.5" x 9.75"

**The Man Who Got a Seat on the Opposing Side**
9.25" x 11.5"

**Stageworthy**
If all the people who have been told they deserve to be on stage — did
For *Life*, date and publication status unknown
11.5″ x 9.25″

*Housewrecker:* "Golly! What a fine
building that will be to tear down!"
9" x 12.75"

**ABOVE: Arrested for Hissing**
11.5" x 11"

**RIGHT: Next**
12.25" x 10"

**OPPOSITE: The Comic Artist**
Dated February 17, 1911 on reverse
22" x 18"

THE COMIC ARTIST
DREAMS A FUNNY IDEA

IN HIS DREAM HE TELLS IT TO HIS WIFE

A HORSE LAUGHS SO HARD AT IT
HE BREAKS A BLOOD VESSEL

AN EDITOR ROLLS ALL OVER HIMSELF
WITH MIRTH — AND GIVES HIM FIVE
HUNDRED DOLLARS FOR IT.

SIX HUNDRED AND THIRTY FOUR THOUSAND READERS
LAUGH THEMSELVES SICK

BUT— WHEN HE WAKES
UP, HE CAN'T REMEMBER IT

**ABOVE:** *Lady (after the hero has tied the villain's hands, backed him into a corner, slapped his face and shot him):* "Isn't he darling?"
*Life*, April 19, 1923
10.5" x 8.75"

**OPPOSITE:** **Aftah**
*Aunt Lucy:* "Marrid yet Miss Pearl?"
*Miss Pearl:* "No Aunt Lucy, I think I am destined to be an old maid."
*Aunt Lucy (consolingly):* "Well Honey, ole maids is bettah off — that is — aftah they git done strugglin"
*Puck*, May 25, 1916
11.75" x 17.25"

— After —

Aunt Lucy: "Marrid yet Miss Pearl"

Miss Pearl: "No Aunt Lucy, I think I am destined to be an old maid"

Aunt Lucy: (consolingly) "Well Honey, ole maids is bettah off — that is — aftah they git done strugglin"

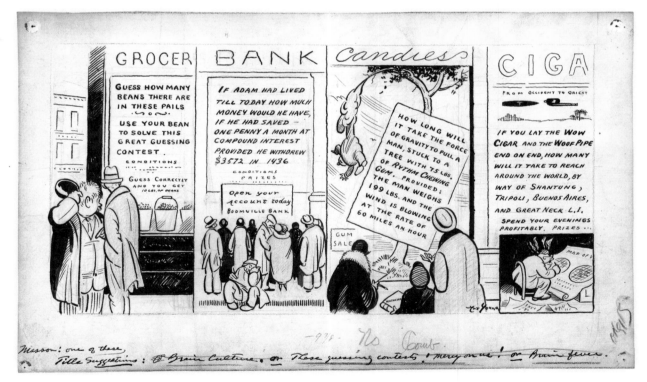

ABOVE: The Husband Show
*Life*, July 15, 1910
21.75» x 14»

RIGHT: Brain Fever
*The Saturday Evening Post*,
February 20, 1926
19» x 11.75»

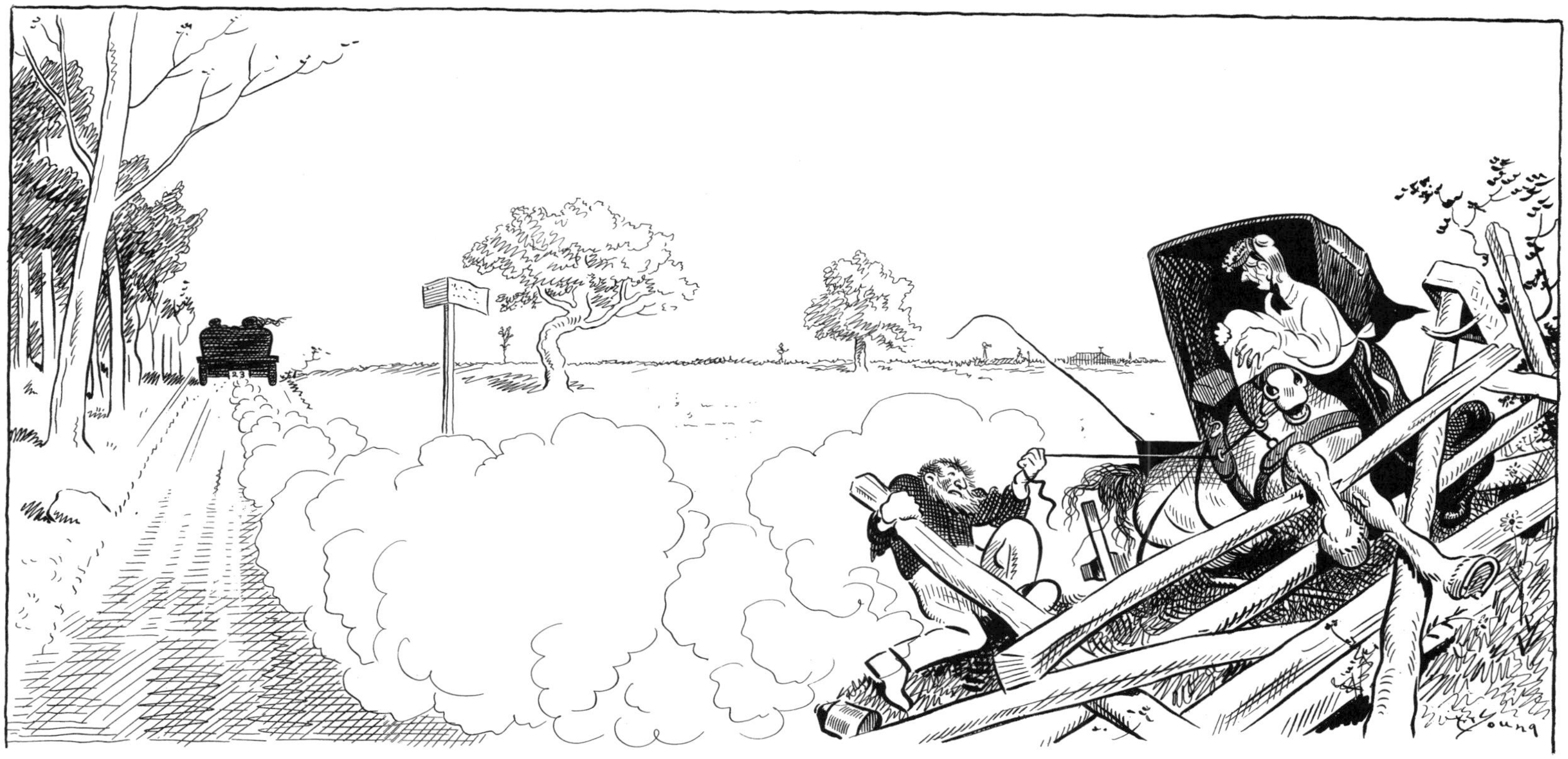
Young

**ABOVE:** Carriage Wreck
*Puck*, July 6, 1906
20.75"x 10.75"

**RIGHT:** "I Think I'll Take the Murder"
*The New Yorker*, June 14, 1930
9.5"x 10"

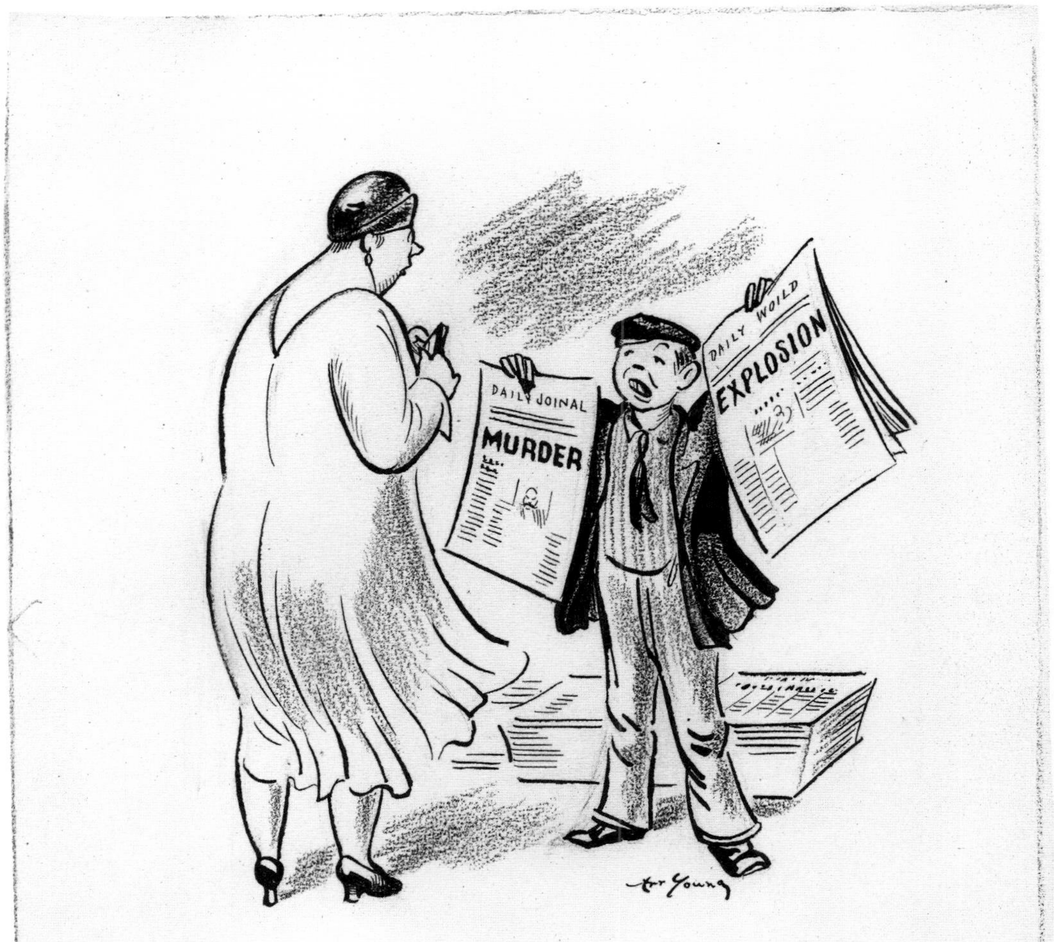
DAILY JOINAL
MURDER
DAILY WOILD
EXPLOSION
Art Young
"I think I'll take the murder"
New Yorker
June 14 1930
H.T.

"Mother, when you were a single girl, didn't you find it a
 bore to be a virgin?"
*New Masses*, July 1926
12.5" x 9.25"

THE "COMMON PEOPLE."—A PICTURE FOR CARTOONISTS.

LINCOLN.—Are these the Common People I said God must have Loved Because He made so Many of Them?

The "Common People" — A Picture for Cartoonists
*Puck* color page print
17" x 13"

WHEN JONES WAS SICK

HE DIDN'T FALL IN LOVE WITH HIS TRAINED NURSE
AS SO OFTEN HAPPENS.

TIME TO TAKE HIS MEDICINE

WHERE THE FRUIT GOES

GROANS AND TOSSES FROM 1 TO 4 A.M.

NURSES RECORD

Passed a comfortable night — a little restless toward morning.

WHEN THE DOCTOR ARRIVES.

When Jones Was Sick
15" x 13.5"

TOP: Advalorum Ad Nauseum
21.5" x 12.75"

ABOVE: Queer Animals We See at Summer Resorts
22.5" x 12.75"

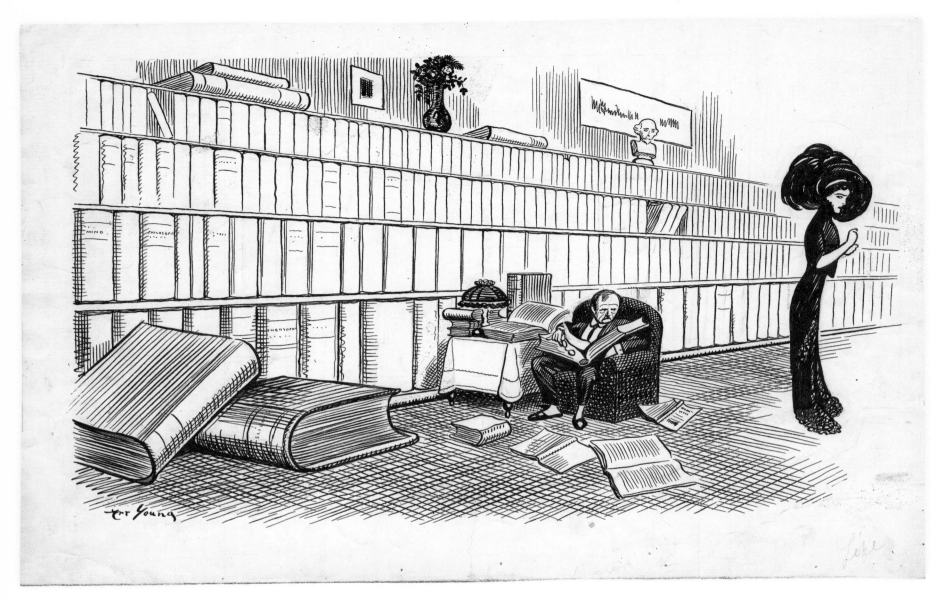

"Howard, I've got to know the truth. Do you love me?"
"Blanche, according to the thesis of soul-harmony as upheld
by esoteric thinkers, we are as near subliminal unity and
cosmic harmony as finite matter can approximate in a world of
limitations and destructive forces."
*Life*
Dated June 16, 1910 on reverse
14.25" x 22.5"

**Reduction Ad Absurdum**
Dated May 18, 1909 on reverse
24.5" x 19.5"

# FANTASY & MUSINGS

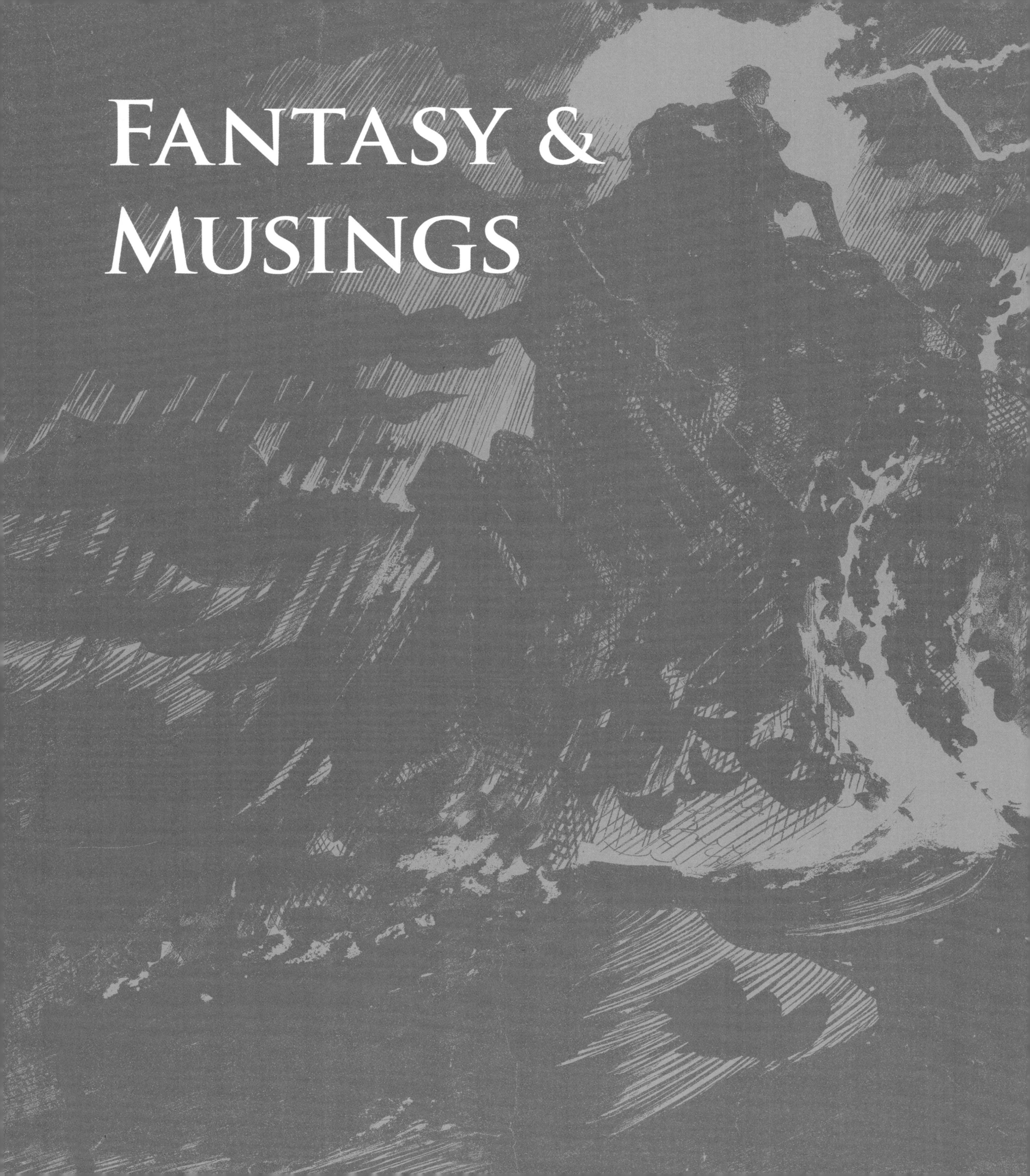

## 07

**Victory of The Will**
Dated 1887
14.5" x 19.25"

The time calls for men who can hold the pathway of life against the attacks of their weaknesses and vices. Not to be turned from, a career of manliness, this is the most honorable triumph in the political, business and private life of the American citizen.

**ABOVE: The Meet**
*Author's Readings,* 1897
16.5" x 10.75"

**OPPOSITE: His Master's Footsteps**
14.5" x 18"

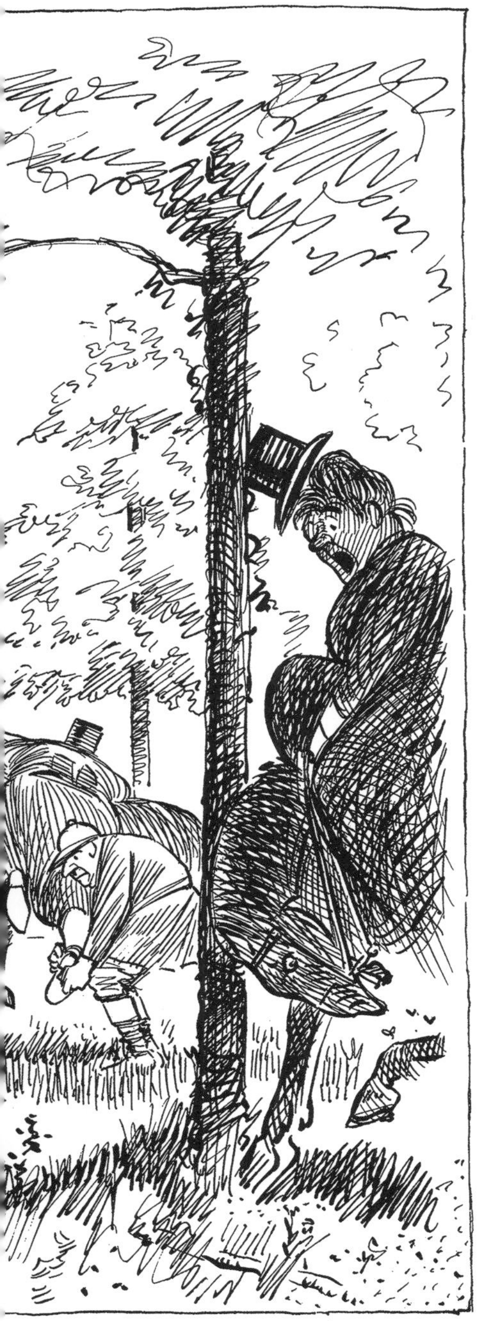

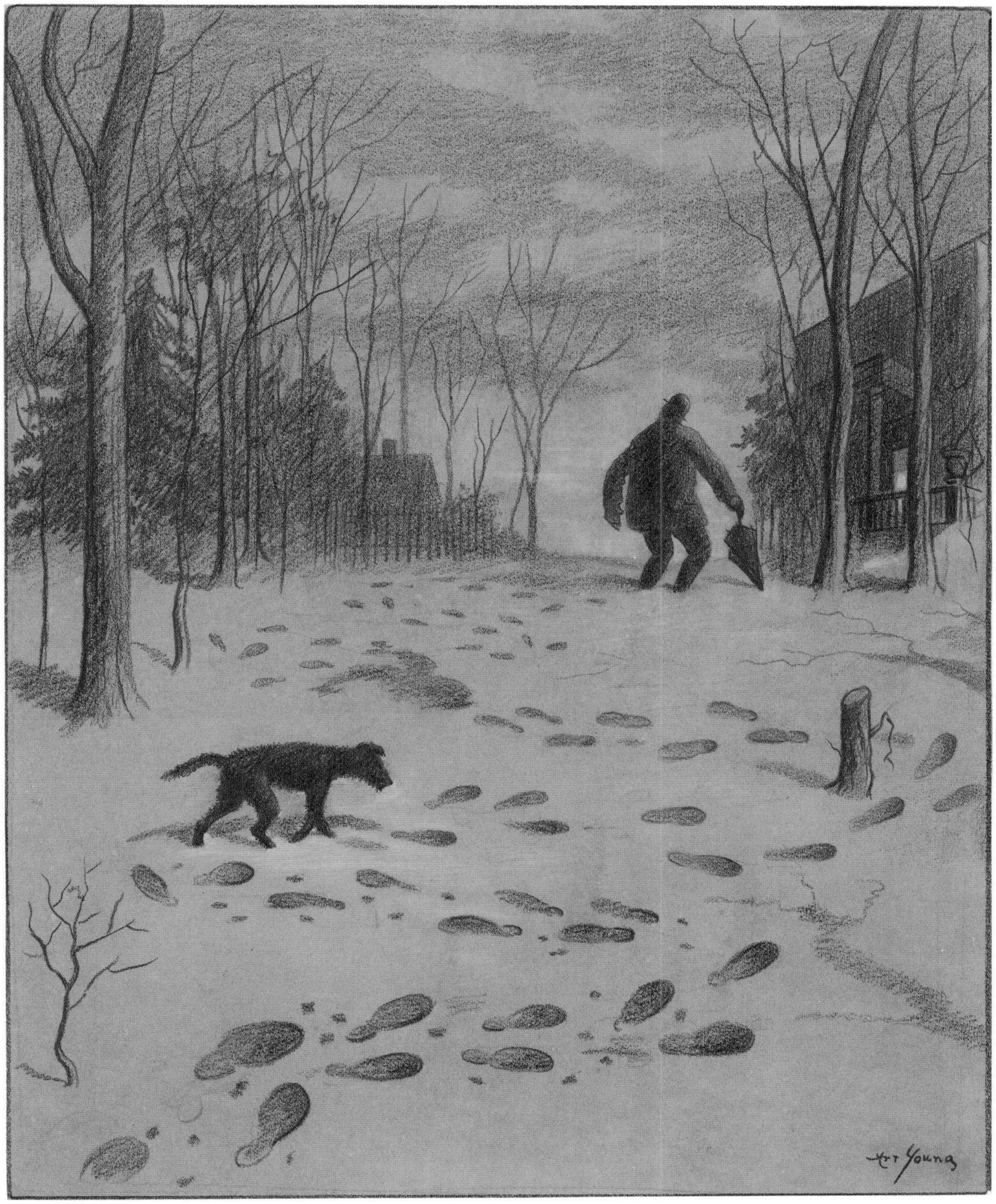
Art Young

**It's A Dog's Life**
*New Masses*, January 1927
14" x 10.25"

The City Beautiful of the Future
16.75" x 21"

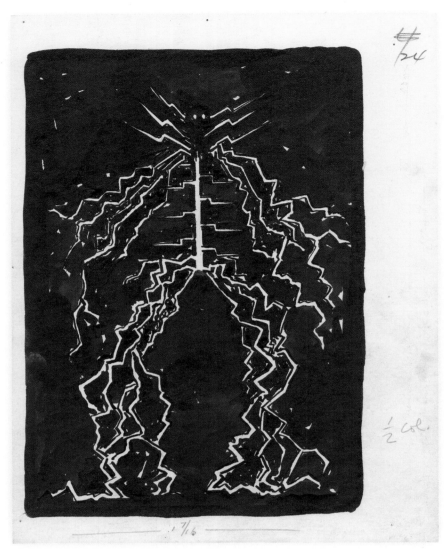

**ABOVE: Nervous System of Congress**
*Metropolitan Magazine*, 1915
8.5" x 11"

**BELOW: Washington Square**
*Life,* February 21, 1924
9.5" x 9.5"

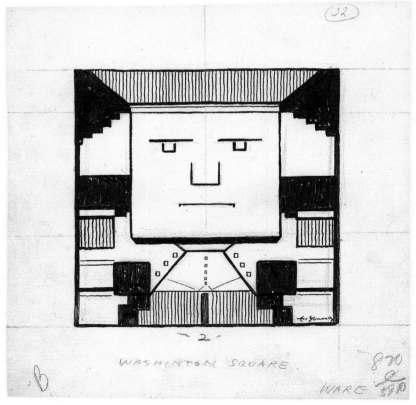

Beach-Strolling Indians
c. 1885
28.5" x 14"

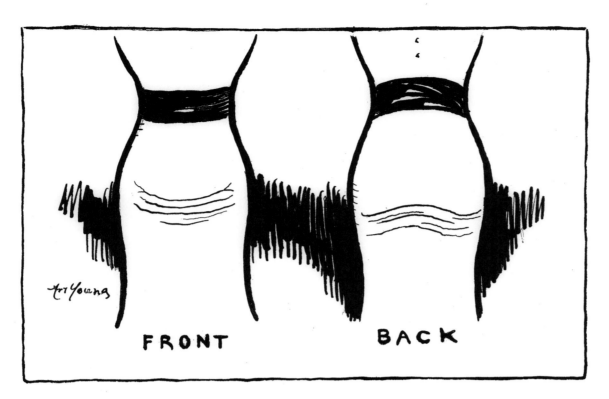

ABOVE: Not That We Care, But This Is the Way a
Woman's Dress Wrinkles
9.5" x 7"

RIGHT : Noise Glutton
7" x 10.5"

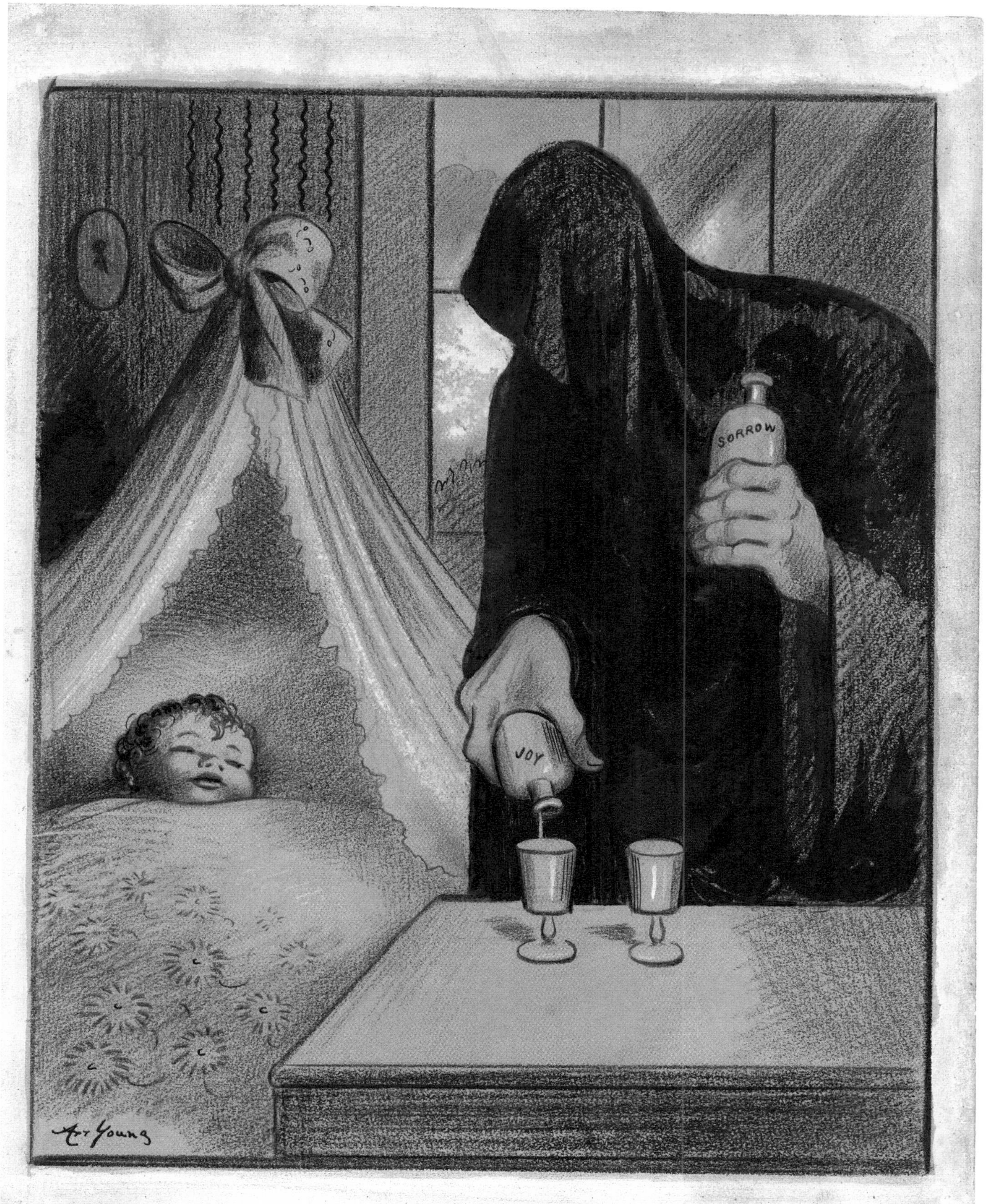
SORROW
JOY
Art Young
Our Portion

Our Portion
12"x 15.5"

**Useful Repurposing**
*Puck*, July 3, 1908
28.5" x 18.25"

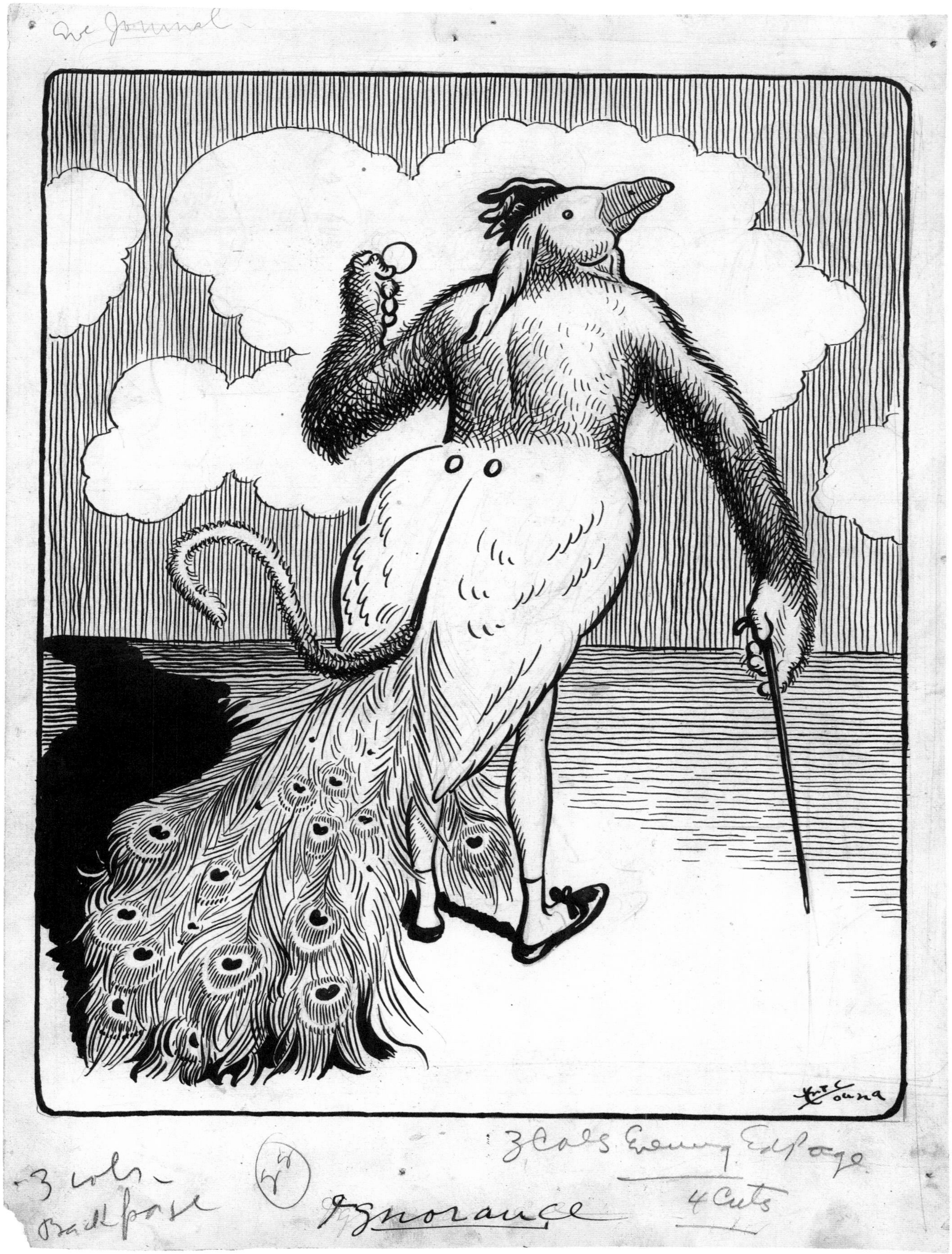
3 Cols Evening Ed Page
4 Cuts
Ignorance

Ignorance
11.75" x 16"

Strength
26" x 16.5"

TO LAUGH THAT WE MAY NOT WEEP

The Perfection of the Machine age — Human Beings Starting on a Pleasure Trip, About 50 Years Hence
*Life,* March 22, 1923
11.75" x 10.75"

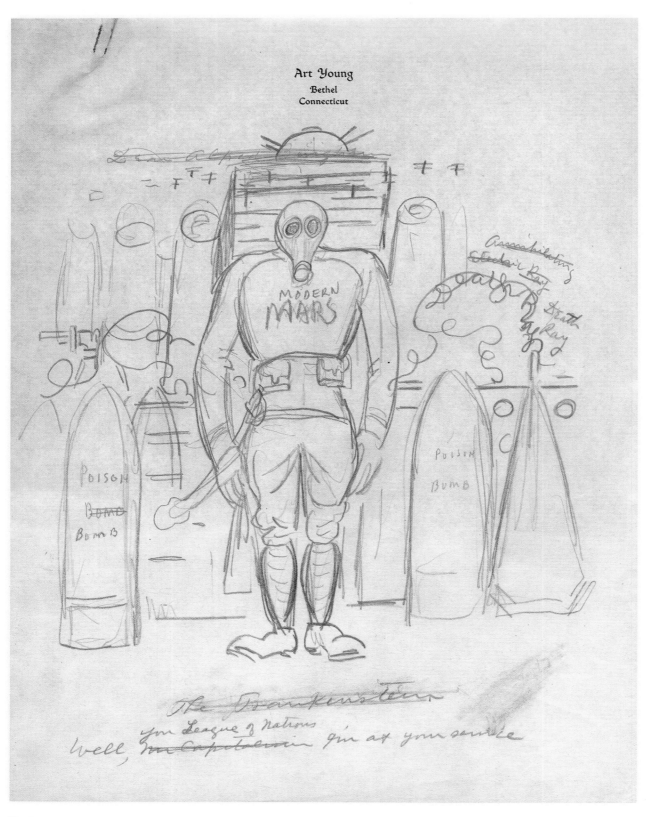

**The Frankenstein of 1933**
"Well, you League of Nations, I'm at your service."
Pencil on paper
Bethel, Connecticut
8.5" x 11"

## More Deadly Gases Made for the Next War Can Wipe Out Cities, Says Lord Halsbury

Special Cable to THE NEW YORK TIMES.

LONDON, Dec. 31.—New details of terribly potent gases which are already available for employment in the next war are revealed by the Earl of Halsbury, writing in The British Legion Journal.

"We cannot judge the nature of future wars from the known effects of chlorine or phosgene used in the World War," he says. "Some modern gases have an arsenical base and can be carried in light containers in liquid form and blown into fine smoke by a comparatively small charge of explosive."

Lord Halsbury goes on:

"Even air containing one part in 200,000,000 of diphenyl-chlorarsine produces nasal irritation. One part in 50,000,000 causes marked symptoms, and with such a mixture five minutes is said to be the limit of human tolerance.

"The symptoms are intense mental distress and utter dejection. If severely gassed, people would be driven mad by the pain and misery and would lose all mental control. If a town were first attacked with arsenical gas bombs, then others containing modern asphyxiant gas, its population would be obliterated."

"One modern asphyxiant bomb would kill everybody within a radius of a half mile, the victims being driven so mad with irritation that they could not stand respirators.

"Inquiries made from three foreign firms of the highest integrity show that any one could easily manufacture these gases in a very short time. Within a week they could be producing 100 tons of diphenyl-chlorarsine daily, which could easily be converted into diphenyl-cyanoarsine. The total amount of poison required to fill the main part of the London area with a lethal mixture of arsenical poison gas to a height of forty feet is only forty tons."

Another gas mentioned is lewisite, which "aircraft could spray through hose pipes in liquid form."

Defense squadrons, Lord Halsbury concludes, cannot protect towns from aerial bombers.

"Air manoeuvres in 1927 were intended to reassure the public that our defenses against hostile aircraft were adequate, but actually proved that London cannot be defended," he declares.

### RATES LUCK ABOVE WALL ST. EXPERTS

because the history of inflation is the history of disaster."

This drew the immediate reply from Dr. Irving Fisher of Yale that he believed Colonel Ayres had

**ABOVE:** More Deadly Gases Made for the Next War
From Art Young's personal tear sheet file
*The New York Times,* January 1, 1933

**RIGHT:** The Latest English Fashions for the Next War
From Art Young's personal tear sheet file

THE LATEST ENGLISH FASHIONS FOR THE NEXT WAR: A GROUP OF FACTORY GIRLS, Red Cross Camp Near Winchester, Try Out Their New Gas Masks During a Life-Saving Drill in a Simulated Gas Attack.
(Times Wide World Photos.)

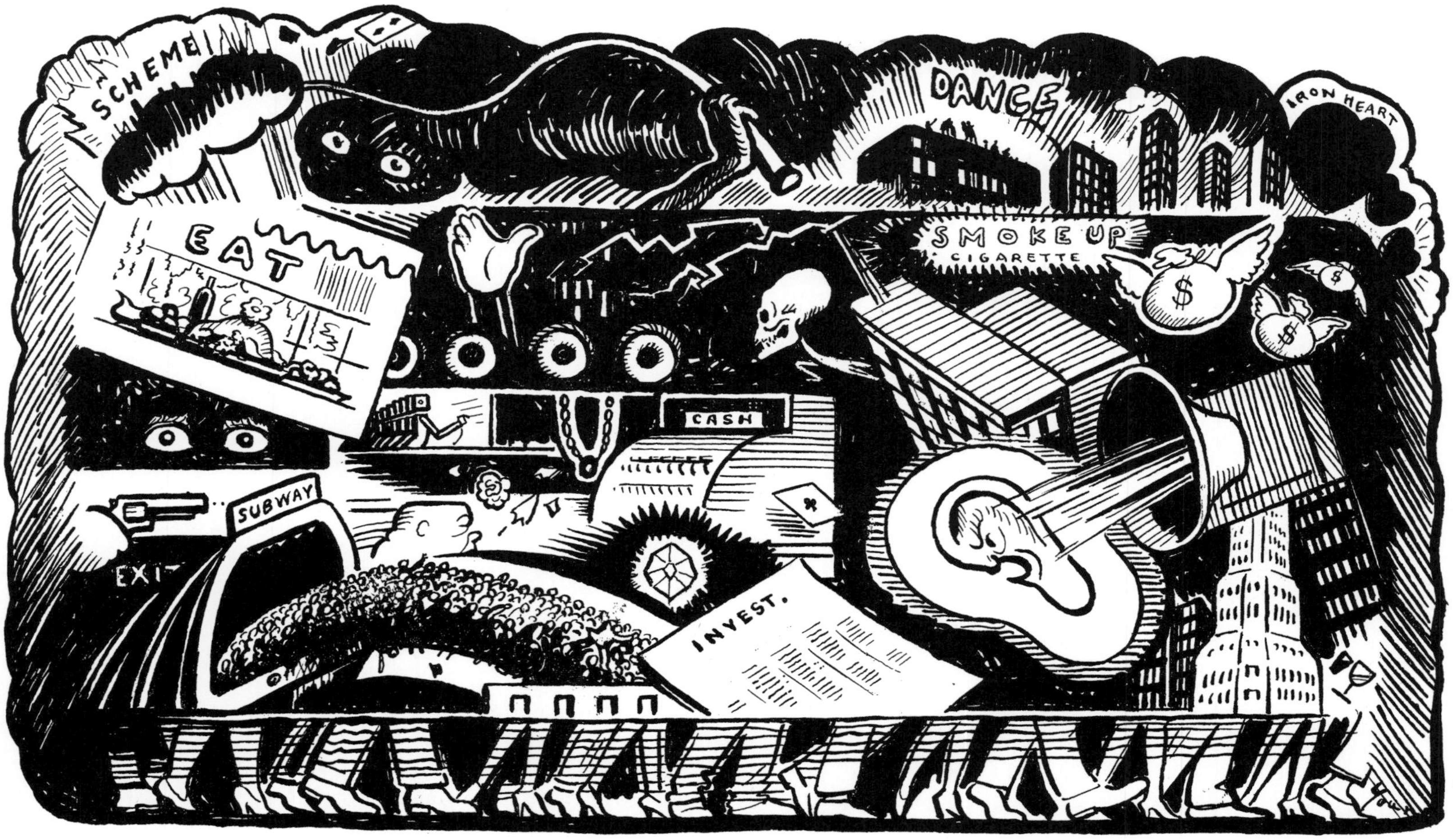
SCHEME
DANCE
IRON HEART
EAT
SMOKE UP
CIGARETTE
CASH
SUBWAY
INVEST.

*a slice of the city*

A Slice of the City
13" x 8.5"

Selected
full page
y.

unpublished

Bird in the rain,

**Bird in the Rain**
11" x 14"

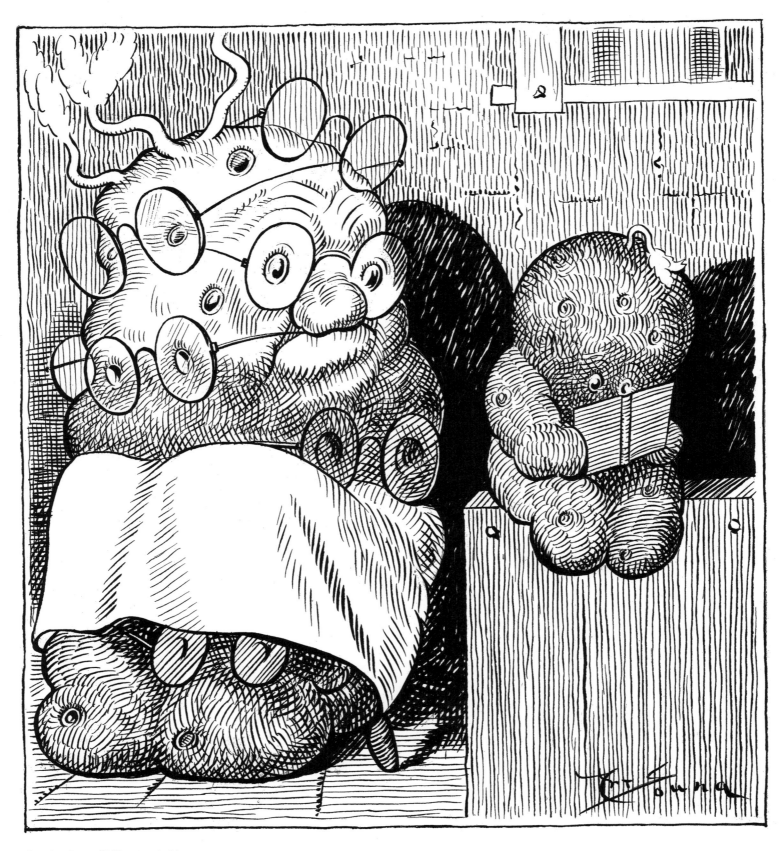

*Grandma Potato:* "Willie, stop straining your
eyes — do you want to get spectacles all over
yourself like grandma?"
9" x 10"

*Cedar Tree:* "Say neighbor, I wish you'd make up your mind which way you want to grow."
10" x 12"

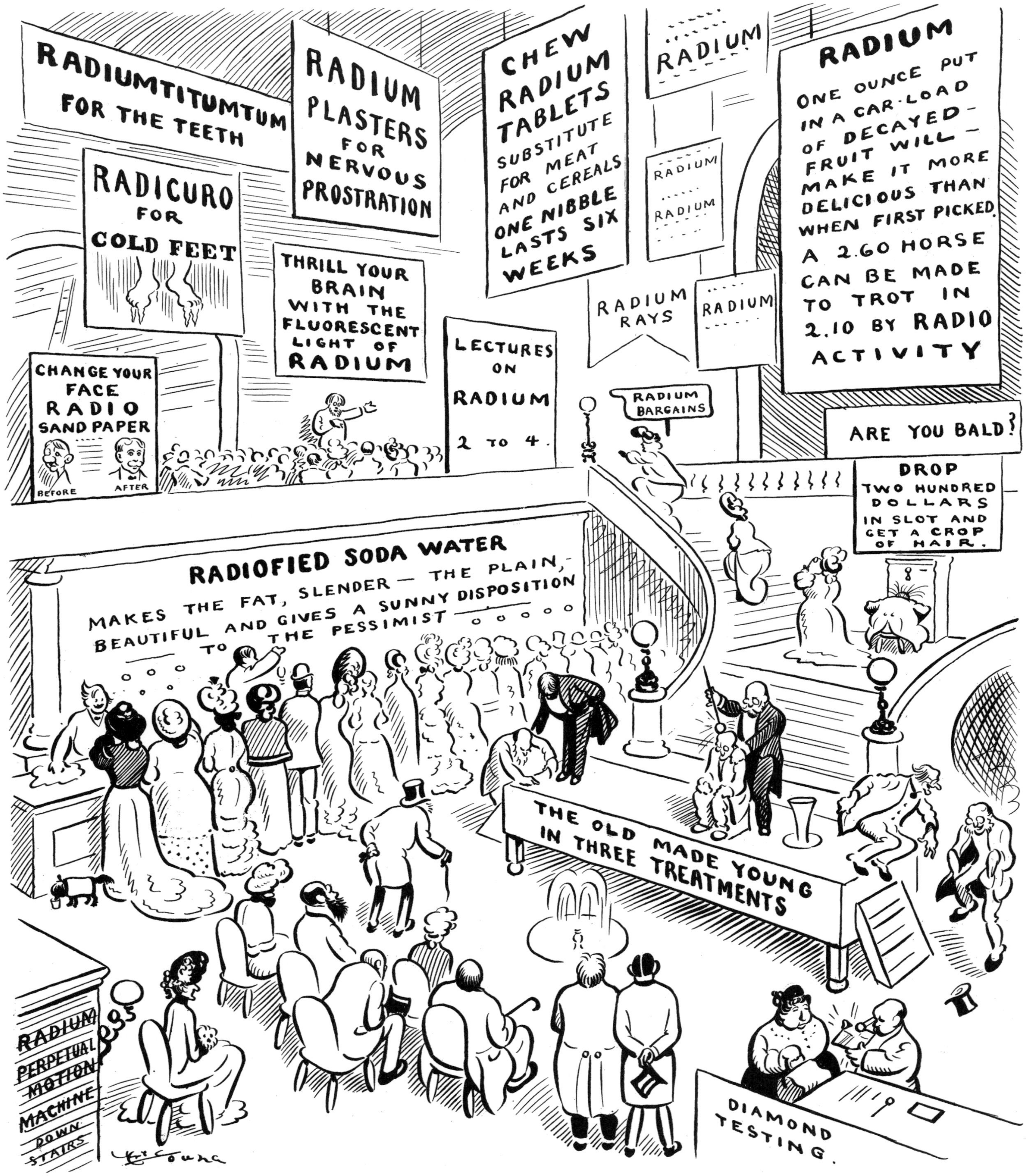
RADIUMTITUMTUM FOR THE TEETH
RADIUM PLASTERS FOR NERVOUS PROSTRATION
CHEW RADIUM TABLETS SUBSTITUTE FOR MEAT AND CEREALS ONE NIBBLE LASTS SIX WEEKS
RADIUM
RADIUM ONE OUNCE PUT IN A CAR-LOAD OF DECAYED-FRUIT WILL-MAKE IT MORE DELICIOUS THAN WHEN FIRST PICKED. A 2.60 HORSE CAN BE MADE TO TROT IN 2.10 BY RADIO ACTIVITY
RADICURO FOR COLD FEET
RADIUM
RADIUM
THRILL YOUR BRAIN WITH THE FLUORESCENT LIGHT OF RADIUM
RADIUM RAYS
RADIUM
CHANGE YOUR FACE RADIO SAND PAPER
BEFORE
AFTER
LECTURES ON RADIUM 2 TO 4.
RADIUM BARGAINS
ARE YOU BALD?
DROP TWO HUNDRED DOLLARS IN SLOT AND GET A CROP OF HAIR.
RADIOFIED SODA WATER
MAKES THE FAT, SLENDER — THE PLAIN, BEAUTIFUL AND GIVES A SUNNY DISPOSITION TO THE PESSIMIST
THE OLD MADE YOUNG IN THREE TREATMENTS
RADIUM PERPETUAL MOTION MACHINE DOWN STAIRS
DIAMOND TESTING.

*Migration of Gnomes*

**ABOVE:** **Migration of Gnomes**
On reverse: "Illustration to Elizabeth North Young's story for children"
17" x 9.25"

**RIGHT:** Gnome In Tree
10" x 14.25"

**OPPOSITE:** Radium Treatments
14.5" x 17.75"

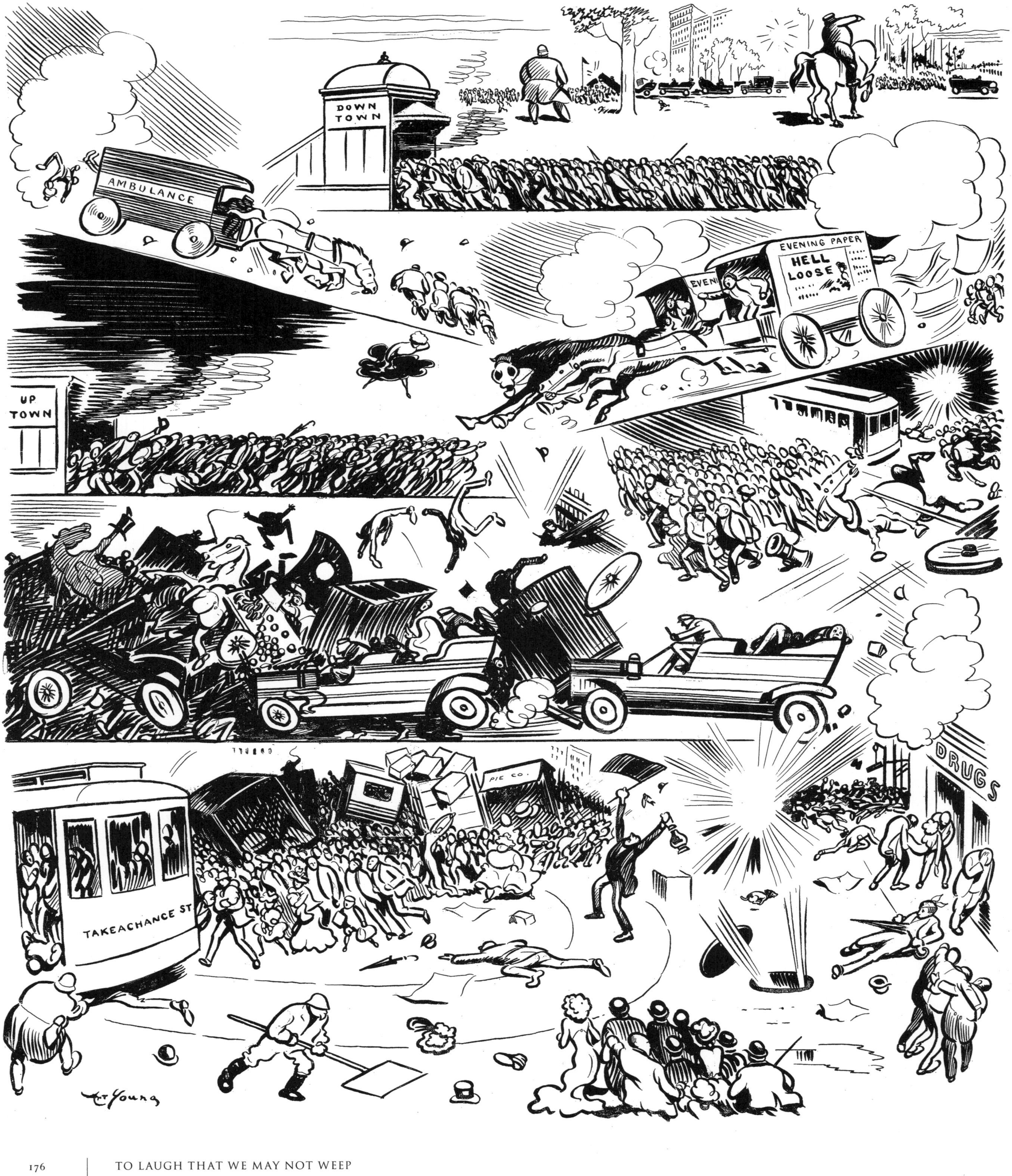
DOWN TOWN
AMBULANCE
EVENING PAPER
HELL LOOSE
EVENI
UP TOWN
PIE CO.
DRUGS
TAKEACHANCE ST
Art Young

—7'/8"—

**ABOVE:** The Machine May Have a Soul
14.375" x 11"

**OPPOSITE:** New York City — Is It Worth It?
*Life*, April 29, 1909
17.5" x 21.25"

Camphor Ball

Phantasy

well, what do you think of it?

The Drug Store word-artist.

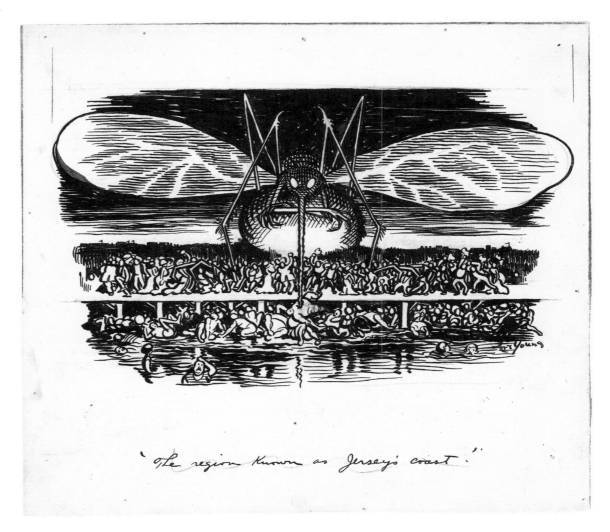

"The region Known as Jersey's coast."

ABOVE: **What Matter Can Do With The Mind**
*Metropolitan Magazine*, c. 1915
11" x 8.5"

After a brief month or week in the country, Mr. Backflat returns to the city and plunges into the frenzy of city life. I have tried to illustrate the effect of environment on the human mind in the above cartoon. Fortunate is he who can keep something of that tranquility and health that he found beside still waters. The supply cannot be too large while he struggles in the city vortex.

LEFT: **Demon Rum**
10" x 7.25"

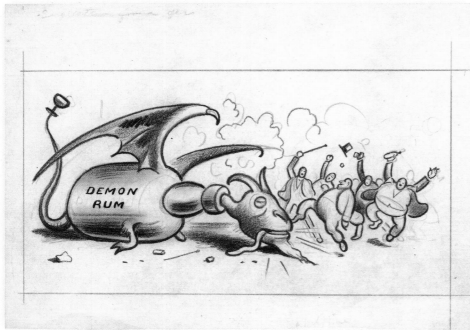

Mrs. Grundy — Why Not? A Statue to the Ruler
12.25" x 14.5"

**The Last Christmas Tree Surrenders**
12" x 9"

**Camel Riding on the Plaisance**
*The Inter Ocean Illustrated Supplement* (Chicago), June 21, 1893
Scene from the World's Columbian Exposition, 1893
(Printed version, p. 23)
19" x 22"

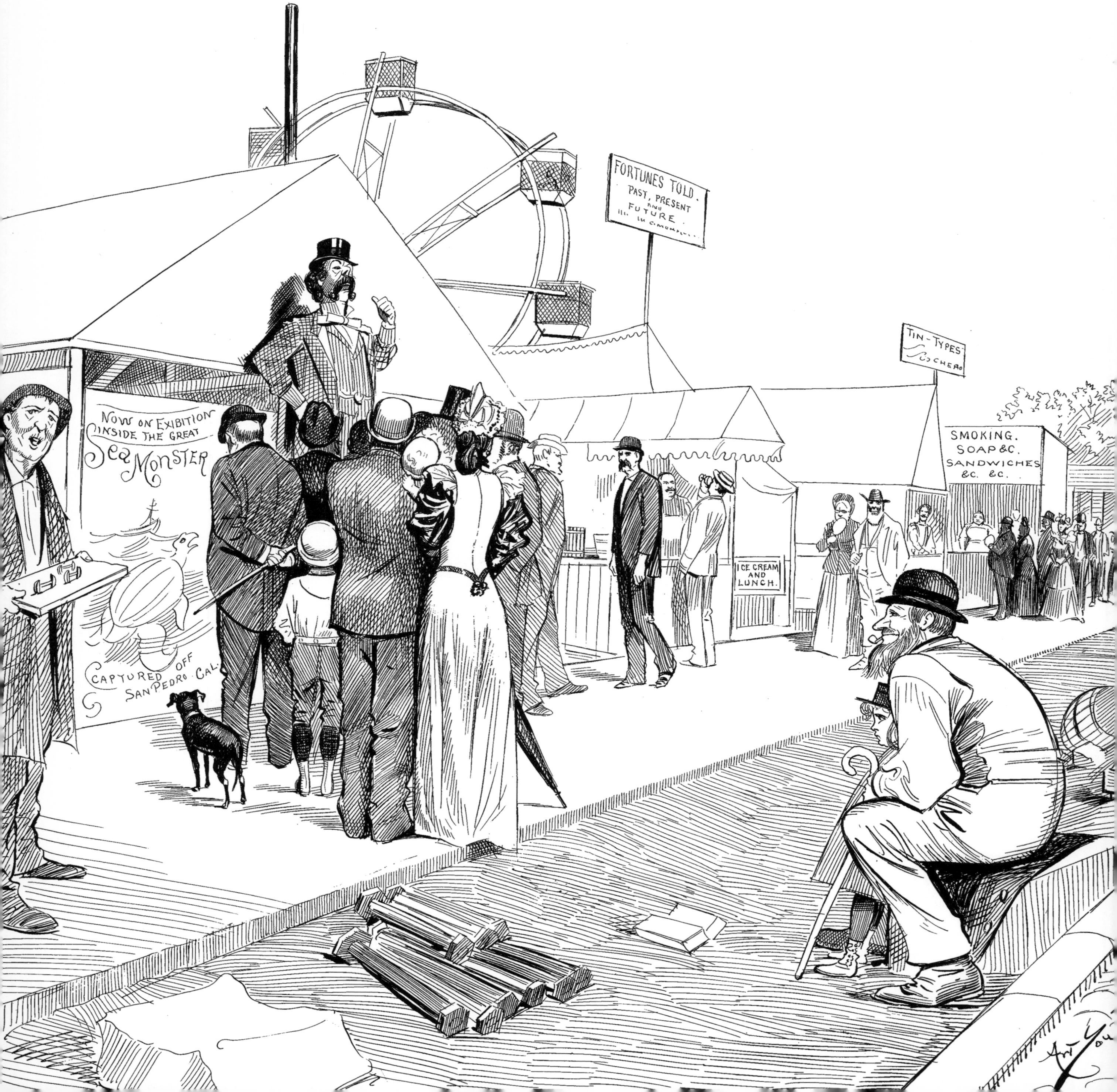
FORTUNES TOLD.
PAST, PRESENT AND FUTURE.
TIN-TYPES
NOW ON EXIBITION INSIDE THE GREAT
Sea Monster
CAPTURED OFF SAN PEDRO CAL.
ICE CREAM AND LUNCH.
SMOKING. SOAP &C. SANDWICHES &C. &C.

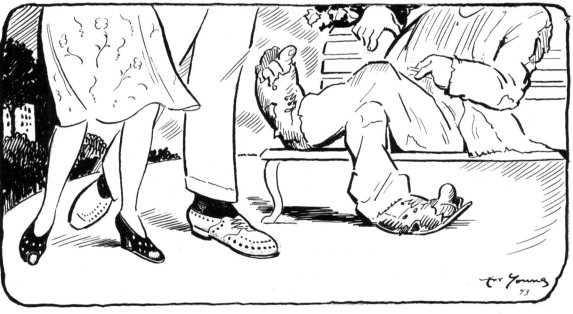

**ABOVE:** How Time Passes — In Youth and in Age
Scene from the World's Columbian Exposition, 1893
23.5″ x 15″

**LEFT:** Air Conditioned Footwear
12.375″ x 8.5″

**OPPOSITE:** Midway
Scene from the World's Columbian Exposition, 1893
19″ x 22″

The Dead Lamb.

**The Dead Lamb**
*20" x 11.75"*

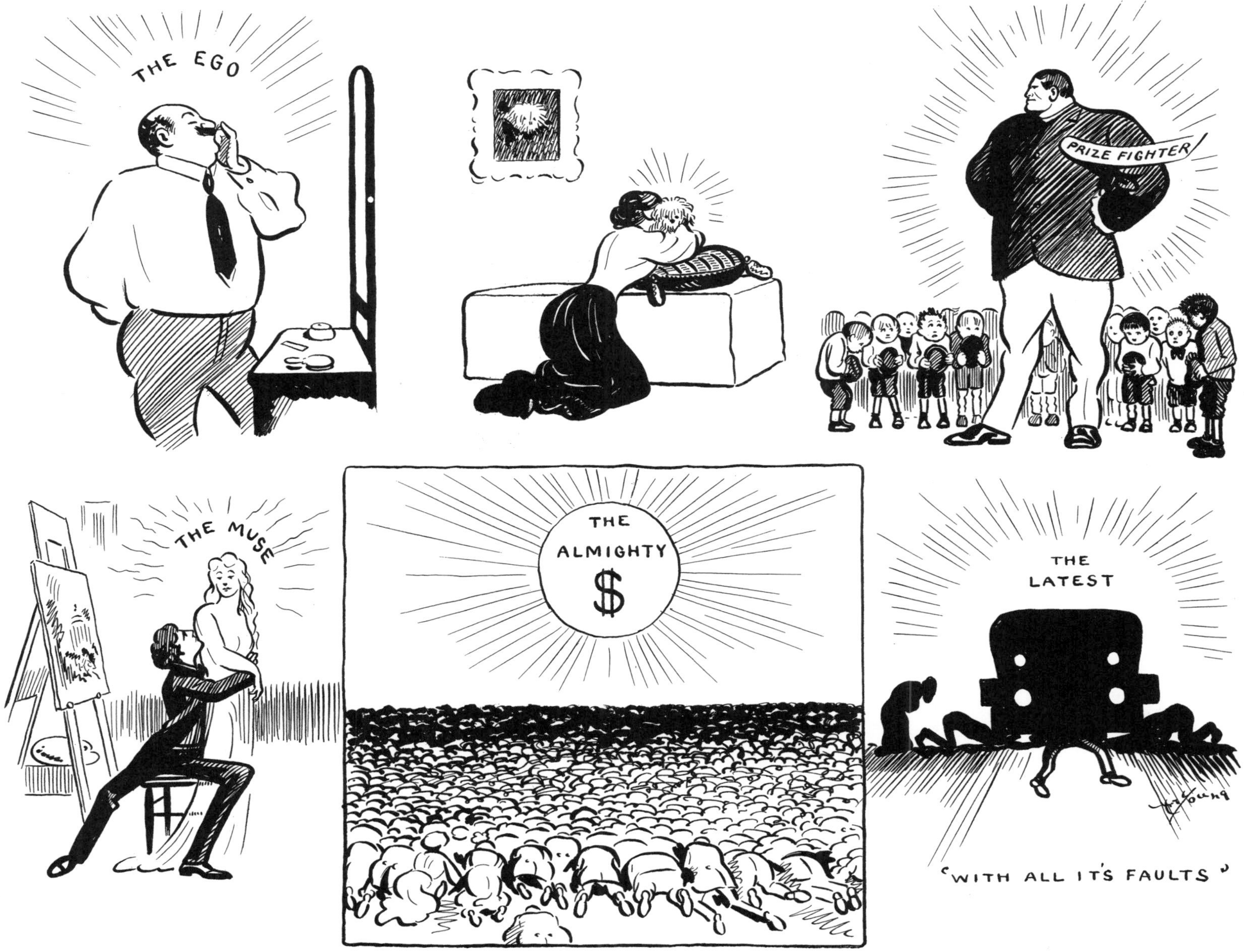
THE EGO
PRIZE FIGHTER
THE MUSE
THE ALMIGHTY $
THE LATEST
"WITH ALL IT'S FAULTS"

Worship
15" x 12.75"

ABOVE: **Anticipation and Reality**
22.5" x 14"

LEFT: **Golden Calf, Mammon, And Baal**
Dated February 1, 1912. Marked for *Life*
12.5" x 8.25"

For those who have the courage to admit that Money is their God ~~ we have a large collection of Gold Idols. (send for booklet)

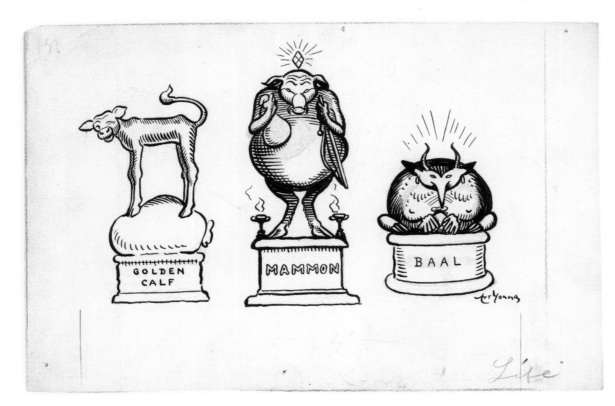

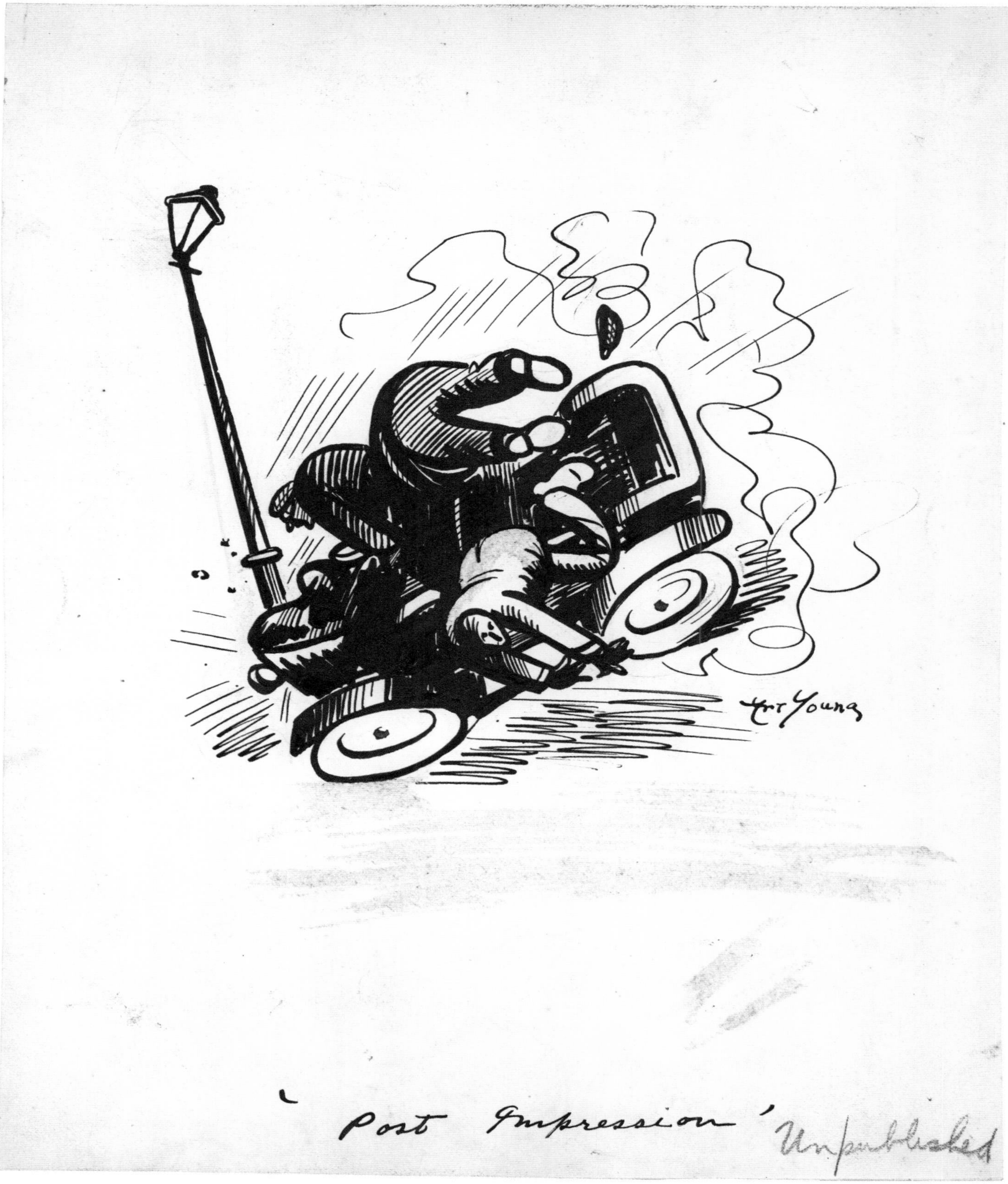
Art Young
'Post Impression'
Unpublished

Post Impression
10.5" x 13"

**Drain the Dismal Swamp of the Mind**
Copyright 1904 Star Publishing Co.
26" x 19.25"

**The Struggle for Popularity**
21.5" x 19.5"

Annual Athletic Festivities on the Dog-Town Reservation
c. 1885
28.5" x 17.5"

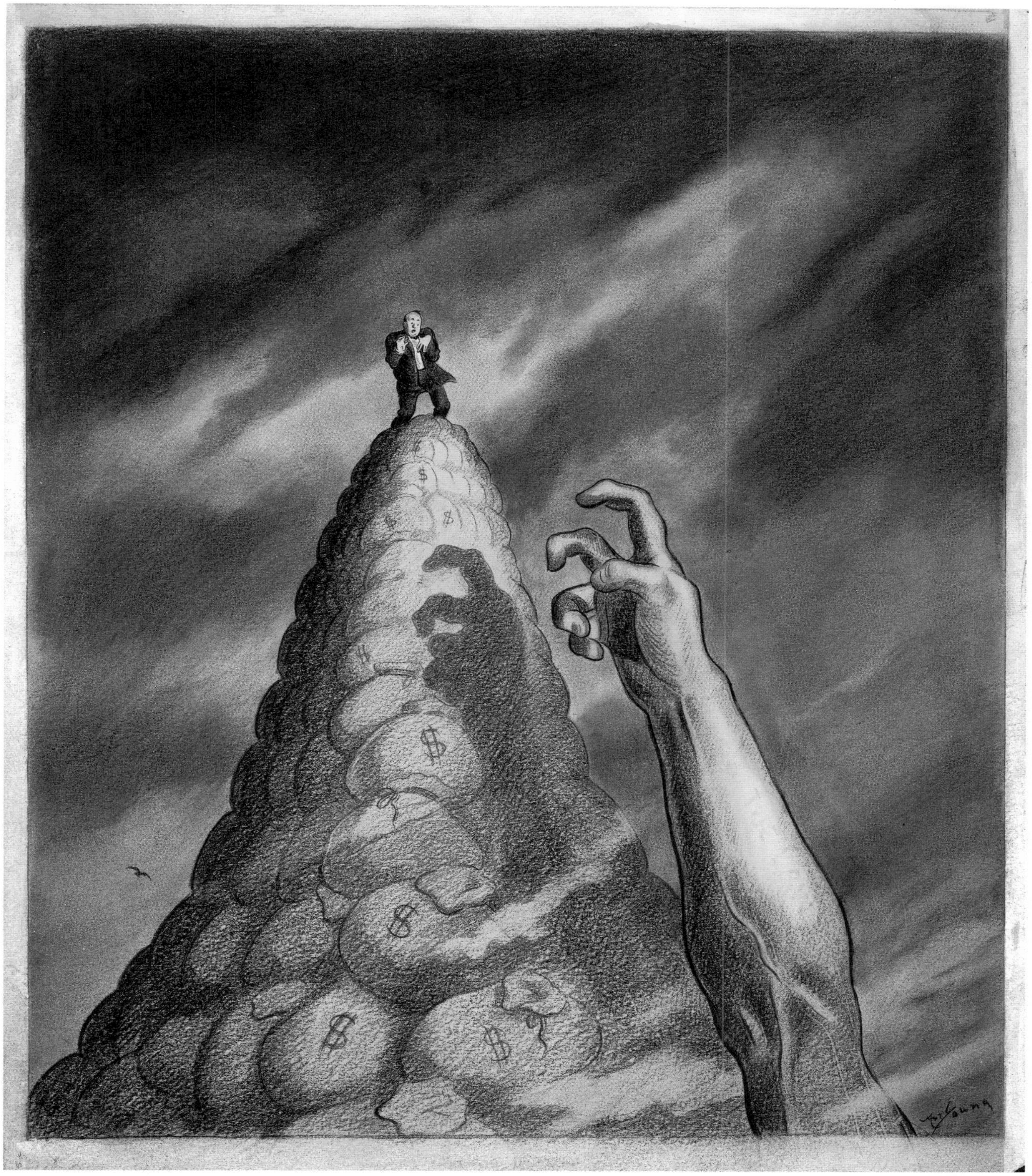

Getting Nearer
20.75" x 24.5"

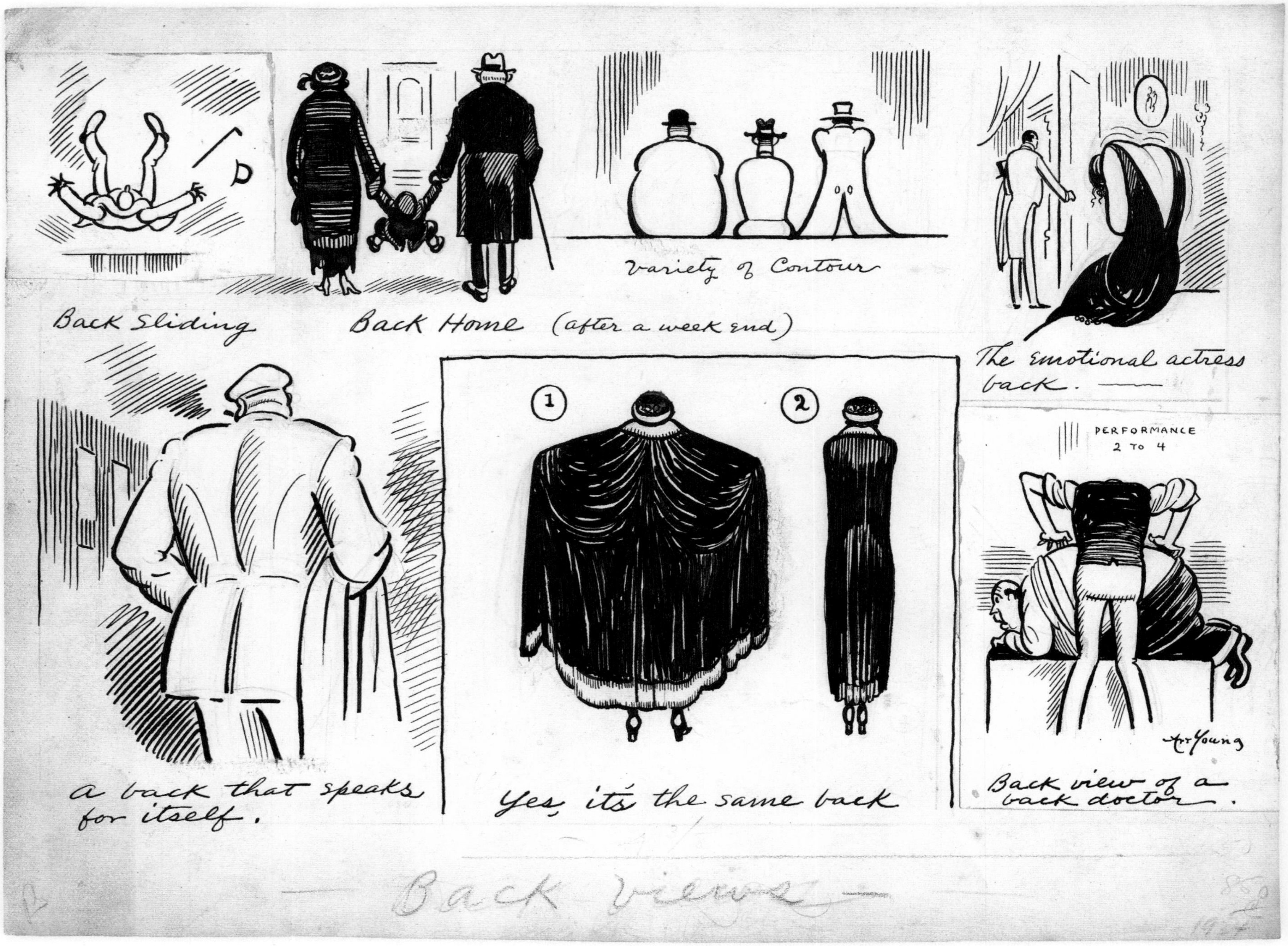
Back Sliding
Back Home (after a week end)
Variety of Contour
The emotional actress back.
1
2
PERFORMANCE 2 TO 4
Art Young
a back that speaks for itself.
Yes, it's the same back
Back view of a back doctor.
Back Views

**Back Views**
*Life,* April 26, 1923
15.5″ x 11.5″

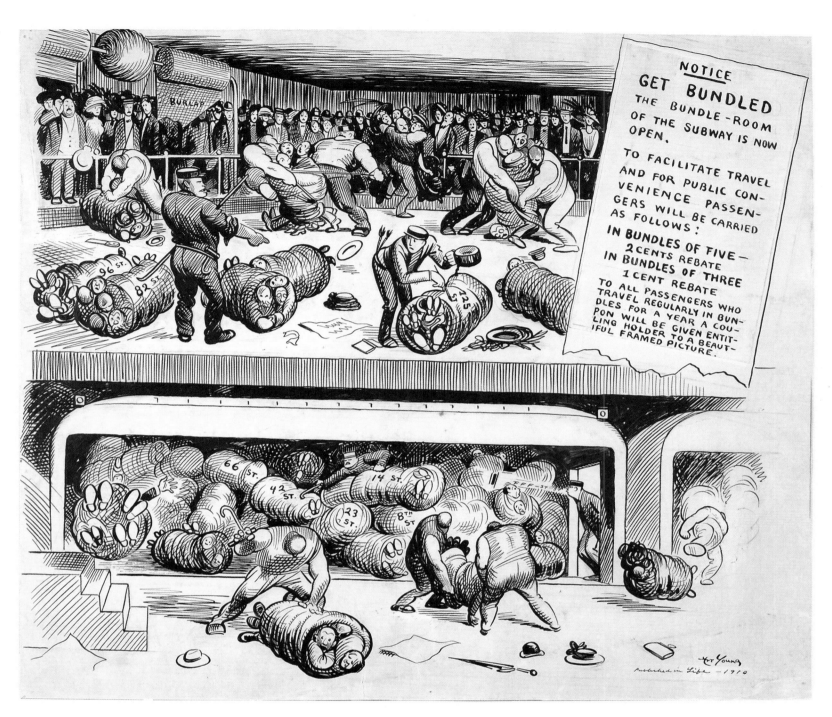

**A Suggestion to Streetcar Companies**
It can't be worse than it is, and the above scheme, besides other
advantages, may insure putting you off at the right station
*Life*, May 6, 1910
21.5" x 18"

**Greenwich Village Party**
*On My Way*, 1928
9.5" x 9"

The newer generation of artists who take up their abode in this famous part of New York City may, or may not, have the artistic and liberty seeking propulsion of the original invaders — here's hoping that they have! — but, however tawdry and commercial the Village has become, it is still the old home where once a band of neophytes from the monastery of custom started something — different.

**The Crown Store**
Dated December 27, 1910
19.5" x 12"

When everything else fails, the Capitalists can try this:

*ORATOR*: "We live under the grandest government in the world's history, — we are a people that knows no monarch of divine pretence, that accepts no ermine of heredity nor bends the calloused knee to mitered might.

But instead we recognize that every citizen is a sovereign in his own right. That each individual is a king and rules the destinies of a glorious commonwealth.

In conclusion, gentlemen, I have a pleasant surprise for you — as you pass out of the hall each of you will be presented with a beautiful crown."

(a week later, they pawn them to pay the butcher.)

# Complexes

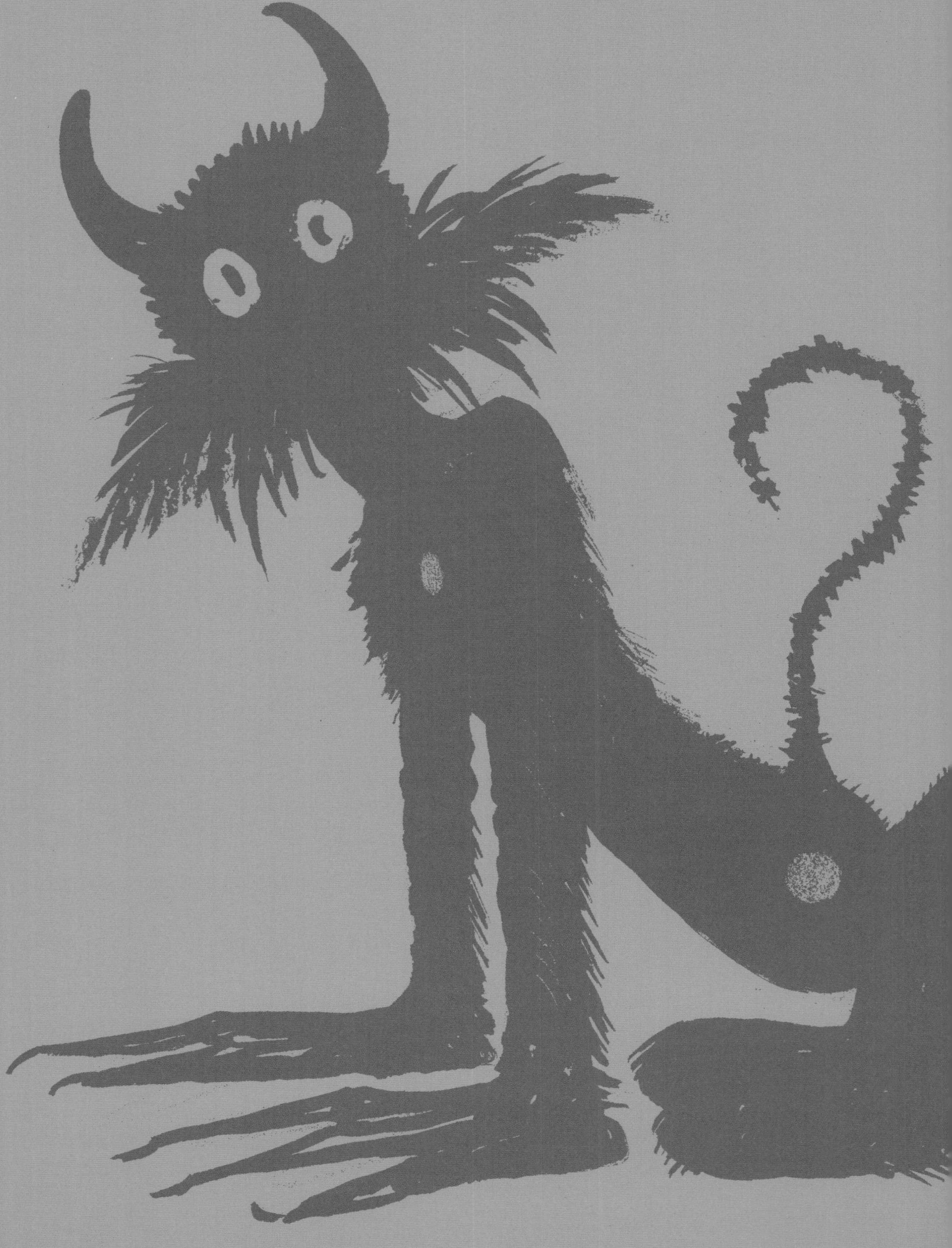

## 08

A complex is modern name for a fault; something good that is carried too far; a virtue devilized. It is an imp that hovers about us but which can be seen only by the Psychoanalyst — so they say — and sent back to normal — whatever normal is — where no complex can exist. In the interests of science we have pictured a few of the most noted complexes believing that it is best to come face to face with them and talk it over.

**Superiority Complex**
*The Saturday Evening Post*, August 30, 1924
10.75" x 12.5"

The Superiority Complex — Roosterius Frogismo — sings a song about itself. It feathers its own nest and is ready at any time to pose for its picture. It never recognizes any other Complex unless it belongs to the superior species. Its favorite habitat is in the minds of college graduates, the new-rich, literary cults, public officials, or wherever a sense of proportion has been lost or neglected.

The Inquisitive Complex urges one to inquire all about things that are the private concern of others. If a person is bitten hard by this Complex it causes the victim to snoop and sniff around to get something "on" somebody. It's a very busy Complex.

**ABOVE: Inquisitive Complex**
*The Saturday Evening* Post, November 1, 1924
12" x 14"

**RIGHT: Fear Complex**
*The Saturday Evening Post*, November 15, 1924
11.5" x 14"

The Fear Complex not only jumps at his own shadow but at all kinds of shadows. It anticipates all disasters, from a national panic to ptomaine poisoning, long before they actually happen. Most things it anticipates, however, never happen.

This Complex usually stays right where he is, because he doesn't know which way to jump. He is the sworn enemy of that positive, Go-Get Complex which is sometimes as destructive to the human conduct as his rival.

ABOVE: **Indecision Complex**
*The Saturday Evening Post*, September 6, 1924
13.75" x 12.5"

RIGHT: **The Hurry-Up Complex**
*The Saturday Evening Post*, October 4, 1924
13.25" x 12"

The Hurry-Up Complex runs ahead of his victim, urging him to catch him if he can. Another runs behind shouting "Think of all your expenses! Taxes, rent and everything! Faster!" A Hurry-Up Complex insists that you keep going, even though the cause for hurry has subsided.

**Revenge Complex**
*The Saturday Evening Post*, October 8, 1924
12.5" x 13.75"
Collection of Charles Schneider

The revenge complex can't sleep. He hisses through his teeth and waits his chance to get even with somebody. This complex is the favorite mascot in scenarios and melodramas generally. In real life he is a very undesirable pet.

**A Complex Procession**
*On My Way* cover
1928
29.5″ x 10.75″
Collection of Cameron Jamie

# GOOD MORNING

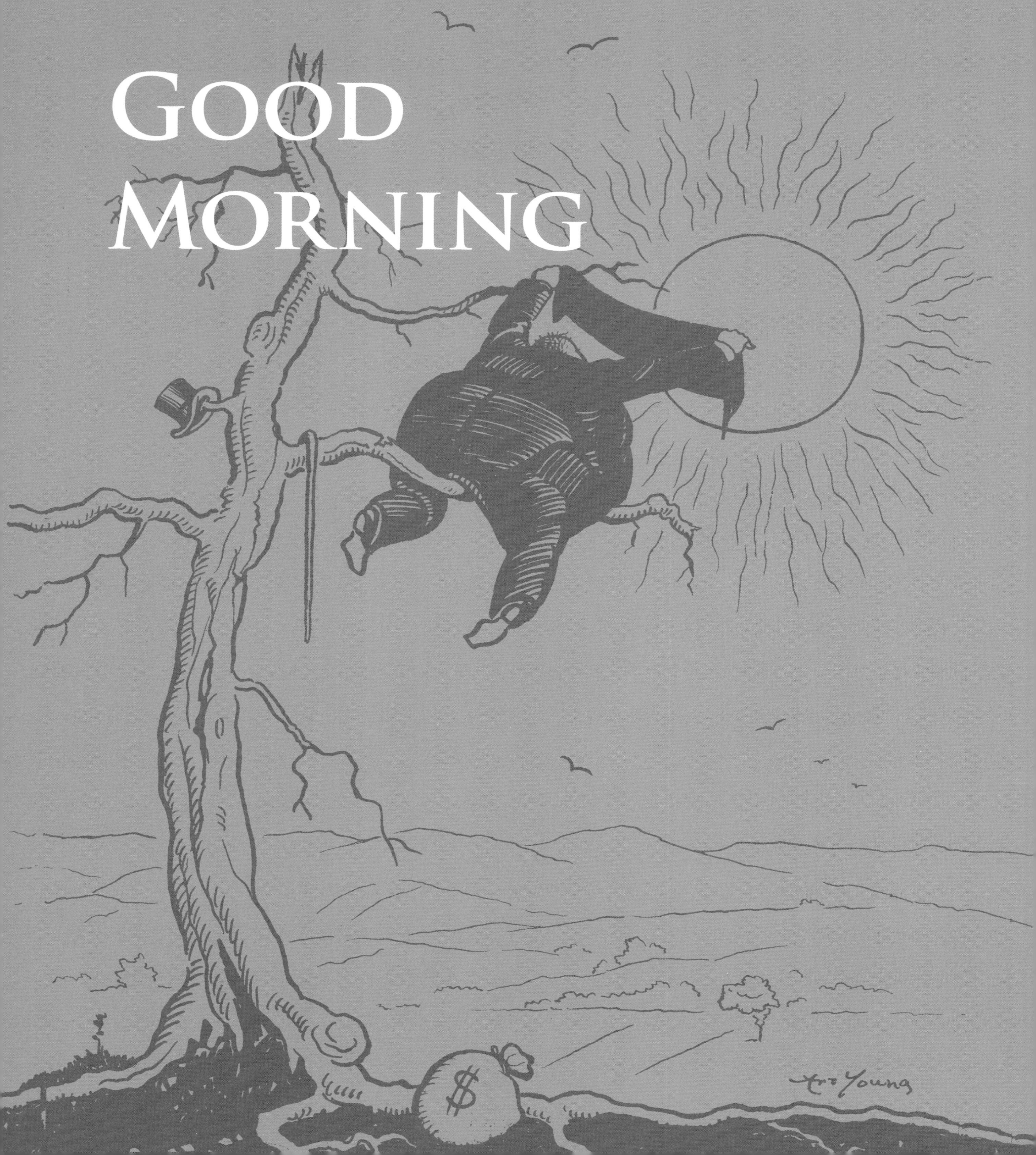
Art Young

# 09

## As so many amazing ideas are born out of necessity, so too was Art Young's *Good Morning* (1919–1922).

Frustrated at not being paid by *The Liberator*, and with nearly three decades of magazine and newspaper work behind him, Young felt it was time to start his own publication. *Good Morning* awoke out of the encouragement of friends and a conversation between Young and Ellis O. Jones, who had been an associate editor at *Life* and would be the literary editor of *Good Morning* for its first few months.

In his autobiography, *Art Young: His Life and Times*, Young recounts the magazine's founding and naming:

> Then I said, "Why not call it by some familiar name, some name that we hear everyday?"

> Ellis chimed in with: "Like 'Good morning, have you used Pear's Soap?" which was an advertisement long familiar to the public.

> "That's it," I said, "Let's make it *Good Morning*."

The weekly's first issue, dated May 8, 1919, billed itself as "The New Humorous Weekly." Sold at 10 cents a copy ($3.00 for a year's subscription), the contents included illustrations by Al Frueh and William Gropper, but most of the work was from Young's hand. Printed in that first issue were letters wishing the new venture good luck from luminaries such as Hendrik Van Loon and Horace Traubel.

Other contributors over the years included Boardman Robinson, Howard Brubaker, Edna St. Vincent Millay, Louise Bryant, Robert Minor, Samuel DeWitt, John Nicholas Beffel, Peggy Bacon, Maurice Becker, Reginald Marsh, and many other notables of the day whose names are less well-known now.

It is in the pages of *Good Morning* that we meet the character who is the perfect embodiment of Young's take on the world: the Poor Fish, "a classic, genuine contribution to the scene and civilization," according to Carl Van Doren, literary editor of *The Century* magazine. It is through the lens of Poor Fish that we can best understand *Good Morning*.

The Poor Fish is the person whose belief is so solid in something so absurd that the reader simply has no response and is thus almost obliged to agree. Young referred to the language of the Poor Fish as the "naive language of common street talk which I used as the true Fish idiom."

**ABOVE:** *Good Morning*, October 20, 1919

**RIGHT:** Original cover art for the first issue of *Good Morning*,
May 8, 1919
11.5″ x 16.5″

The Poor Fish appeared in each issue, his hand upturned or his sullen features resigned to whatever fate might be on his mind that week. Poor Fish observations included: "The Poor Fish says he knows that many of our leading citizens got their wealth dishonestly, but we ought to let bygones be bygones"; "If people would work harder we would not have so much unrest"; "Progress is all right, but it ought to stop sometime"; and "The Poor Fish says agitators just stir up trouble, and what with his two sons crippled in the War for Democracy, and the High Cost of Living, we have enough trouble as it is."

As time went on, the contents of *Good Morning* became more and more the sole creation of Young, and not just because of Jones's departure. Each issue was a combination of new work and pieces that had been published in various periodicals from the previous decade. Of all the reprints, easily the most famous is "Capitalism," also known as "The Last Supper" (p. 12). The illustration, which

originally appeared in *Life* magazine, was the first take on the "fat-cat capitalist" for which Young's work would become synonymous. The design eventually included the top hat, cane, and mustache that signified the self-aggrandizing pseudo-dignified big businessman who controlled government, newspapers, workers' rights, the call to war, and more.

Sadly, by October 1921, *Good Morning* — which had gone from a weekly to a bi-monthly to a monthly — was floundering. The early warnings of other editors, who had implored Young to hold off publishing until they had a $10,000 reserve in the bank (Young states they had but $4,000 at launch), would prove to have been good, but unheeded, advice.

Young made one last publishing gasp in early 1922 by releasing one volume of *The Art Young Quarterly*, titled *The Soldier*. The 32-page issue, which went through multiple printings, gathered Young's most stunning work on how poorly soldiers and veterans

*American (parents born in Europe):* "Say, if you Indians don't like our country, why don't you go back where you came from?"
*Good Morning*, October 22, 1919
16.25" x 20"

were treated during and especially after the Great War. Illustrations such as "Bonus or no bonus, Pvt. McGinnes is determined to have a wooden leg" (p. 208) and "Fixing Up the World War Soldiers" (p. 220) are Young at his sharpest and most moving. While *The Soldier* sold more copies than any issue of *Good Morning*, it was not enough to pay off the outstanding debts, and *Good Morning* ceased publication.

*Good Morning* was financed by donations, the proceeds from numerous benefit dances and masquerades (at which luminaries such as Helen Keller gave rousing speeches to the artists and activists of Greenwich Village), and the small amount of money brought in by subscriptions and single-copy newsstand sales.

Its short, three-year run was not due to any lack of enthusiasm among readers. Instead, the initial shortfall of startup capital, Young's overall lack of business acumen, and his greater devotion to the editorial rather than the business side of things (something

he had not had to deal with when working on other magazines) combined to keep *Good Morning* from staying afloat.

Over its short life, *Good Morning* published an astonishing range of cartooning — from the aforementioned social and political to the whimsical, such as "Hands We Have Met" (p. 216). It also showcases the often undervalued quality of Young's wit and writing capabilities — more than just a hook for a caption.

*Good Morning* stands as a testament not just to Young's daily nightmare but also to his hopeful vision of how life could be better. Perhaps the statement at the top of the masthead sums it up best — "To Laugh That We May Not Weep." Art Young was always seeking to find and point out a light in the darkness — and with *Good Morning* he became a rooster crowing to wake up the world and greet each new sunrise with a smile.

Bonus or no bonus — Pvt. McGinnis is going to have a wooden-leg, if he has to grow one
*Good Morning,* August 1921
**ABOVE:** Published cover
**RIGHT:** Original art
13" x 12"

Home, Sweet Home!
*Good Morning,* September 1921
**ABOVE:** Published cover
**RIGHT:** Original art
16.75" x 15.75"

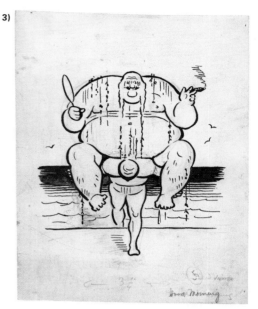

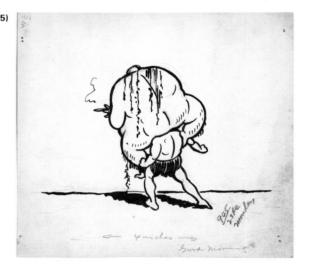

**Sindbad and the Old Man of the Sea**
"The Time Is Not Ripe"
A muscular Worker carries a fat, defecating
Capitalist as they carry on a dialogue concerning
when the time would be ripe for the Worker to
throw the Capitalist off his back. These pieces
appeared in various issues of *Good Morning.*

**1)** 1919, 8.5″ x 11″

**2)** 10″ x 7.5″

**3)** 8.5″ x 11″

**4)** 9.5″ x 9″

**5)** 8″ x 10.25″

**Anti-Superstition Ball Poster**
Friday, January 13, 1922
18" x 22.25"

## INHERITED

My father many times removed
And many times removed from that,
Went wandering through the verdant wood.
He wore no shoes nor any hat.

Across his hairy chest was hung
A leopard skin — or maybe not —
And weather made no never mind
Whether cold or whether hot.

He wandered round in ev'ry clime,
His bed was in a walnut tree,
His feed was raw red lion steak,
The blood he drank instead of tea.

His wife, an equal suffragette,
He wooed and won right daintily,
He cracked her skull with his war club
And dragged her off to slavery.

So when I'm told that I am bad
And ornery and awful tough
I always think of my old dad
And say "I'm not half rough enough."

— George Thomson

Inherited
*Good Morning*, January 1, 1921
**ABOVE:** Original art
6" x 8"
**LEFT:** Original accompanying poem

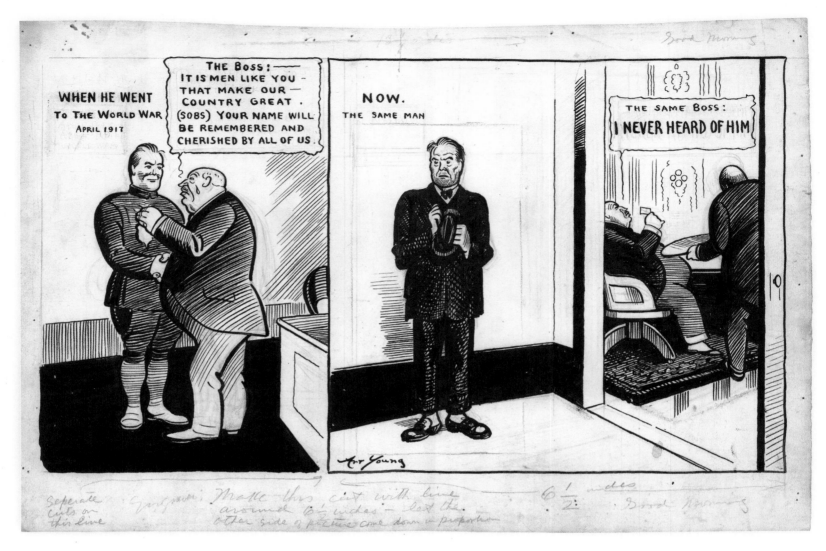

**ABOVE:** When He Came Back
21" x 13.875"

**RIGHT:** If We All Went Back Where We Came From
*Good Morning*, October 29, 1919
7.5" x 8.25"

If you shuddered when you heard that the German imperialists were using poison gas in an effort to win the war, let's see if you shudder when our American imperialists use super-poison, improved to cause more torture than the German brand, to do the job on a larger scale, and to make it the poisonest annihilator of masses of people known to man.

We suggest a statue to modern science (especially American science) for its services in the cause of destruction. We simply must be prepared to hate any nation or people the imperialists tell us to hate and be ready to annihilate them.

ABOVE: **Suggestion For A Statue**
*Good Morning*, April 1, 1921
6.75" x 9"

RIGHT: *Dining Car Waiter:* "Look out foh yoh face boss — we're goin round a curve"
*Good Morning*, September 15-October 1, 1920
9.25" x 9.25"

**Hunting Down the Profiteers**
*Good Morning,* October 8, 1919
**ABOVE:** Published cover
**RIGHT:** Original art
18.25" x 16.75"

**At the Pearly Gates**
*Good Morning,* April 15, 1921
**ABOVE:** Published cover
**RIGHT:** Original art
16" x 13.25"

**It Is**
*Infant: "Is this where I check my brains?"*
*Good Morning*, v.3 #3, February 1, 1921
**ABOVE:** Published cover
**ABOVE LEFT:** Original art
12.25" x 9.25"

**It's the Early Subscriber That Has the Complete File**
A subscription ad in *Good Morning* #2,
May 15, 1919
**ABOVE:** Published ad
**ABOVE LEFT:** Original art
11.75" x 9"

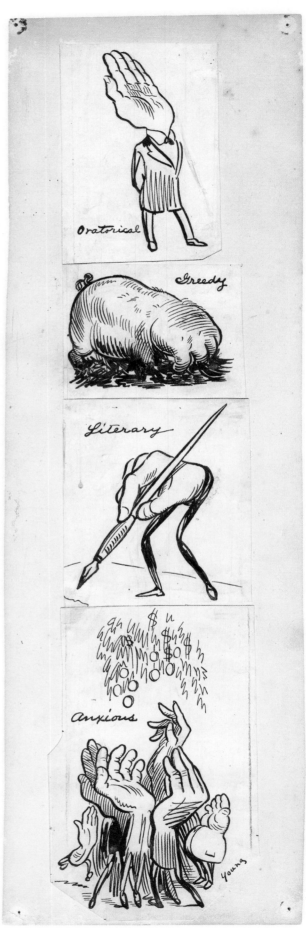

**ABOVE: Hands We Have Met**
*Puck*, March 1-15, 1921
Printed page in color
10.5" x 14"
**RIGHT:** Four individual cartoons mounted on board
6.75" x 21"

**Music — the Cure for Unrest**
We have had many solutions offered, but it takes a two-hundred-thousand-a-year-brain to go to the root of the matter.
*Good Morning,* May 1, 1920
22" x 13.5"

The following verse proves the author, Levi B. Snitzhoofer, one of the foremost writers of that essential product, the poetry of abandonment. No magazine is alert to the tendency in art that does not print a back-to-the-hills poem in every issue. He saw the hills once — when he went to camp. He is now back at his job collecting the wash for a small laundry.

**The Uplifting Lute**
Stuck to the asphalt.
I write in dreams.
I see the lillied field,
The Pulsing knoll, the ecstasy of life,
Free to do, free to be —
And answering back
With zephyred feet
The Free soul of my love.
Wine of daring winds
Arouse my soul
Stuck to the asphalt!

**ABOVE: Back To The Hills**
*Good Morning*, May 15, 1919
Original cover art, also used for a *Good Morning* flyer, 1919
8.5" x 9.5"

**RIGHT:** *The Soldier* #1, First Quarter 1922, cover
15.75" x 20.75"

After *Good Morning* ceased publication, Art Young published *The Soldier*. It lasted only one issue.

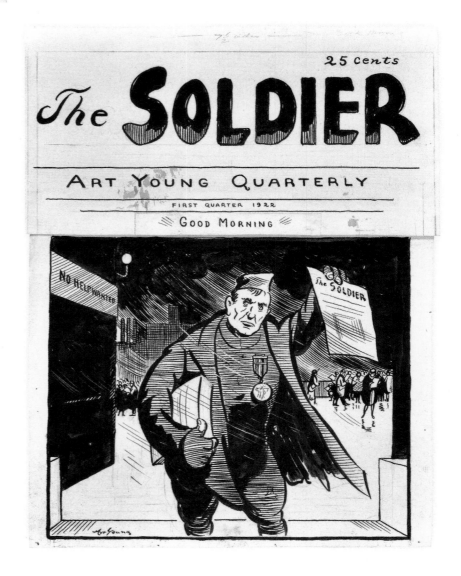

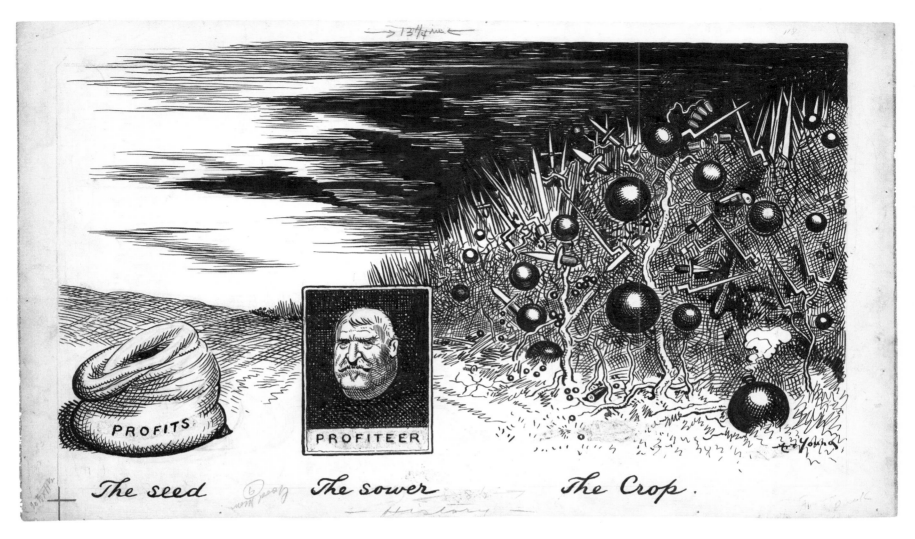

The seed     The sower     The Crop.

**The Seed — The Sower — The Crop**
*Good Morning*, June 12, 1919
23.25" x 14"

TOP: **Fixing Up the World War Soldiers**
Make 'em over as good as new,
with wood and rivet, bolt and screw.
Sodder them, tire them, ready to go
To another victory — say, Mexico
*Good Morning* #2, 1919
14.5" x 8"

BOTTOM: **Educated**
"Ex soldier kills prominent citizen and takes all of his money" — newspaper
*Good Morning*, January 15, 1921
19.25" x 10.5"

Modern Tendencies in Education
*Good Morning*, April 1, 1921
15.25" x 9.5"

## PLUMES DE CONQUEST
### SYNOPSIS OF THE OPERA

*(Note: All of the star performers wear their plumes of conquest and carry squirt-guns, each containing enough poison gas to kill themselves and everybody else.)*

In the first act, President Harding stands at a table trying to look like a combination of Uncle Sam, G. Washington and Old Man Normalcy. To the tune of *Hail Columbia*, he sings: "It Must Not Occur Again."

Secretary of State Hughes, Senator Lodge, and the White House Dog join him in the chorus: "It Must Not Occur Again."

A loud explosion is heard and La Belle France makes a crazy leap from a war-plane to the stage waving the tricolor and Napoleon's hat. She sings: "It Is Ze Limit, Oo La La."

Another explosion, a rattle of machine guns, the stage illuminated by a flare of gas. Enter Britannia and her Paramour, The Jap. They prance across the stage singing: "We're here because we're here."

Italy in the meantime has bolted to the front of the stage and sings a Fascisti song of warning — to the effect that no limit is to be put on his "ambish". While he sings, France kicks Japan's hat off, punches Britannia in the stomach and tickles Harding's chin.

In the final scene of the opera each actor signs a document called "The Pledge of Limitation", prepared with great care by Elihu Root. It reads, "We solemnly swear to limit armaments as soon as possible".

GRAND CHORUS AND CURTAIN.

*Good Morning*, October 1921
26» x 16»

**Dreaming**
*Good Morning,* July 15–August 1, 1920
7.75" x 19"

## TRUTH DRAWS THE CURTAIN
#### Between eighteen and twenty thousand American ex-soldiers are insane as a result of the war

(See editorial

**Truth Draws the Curtain**
Between eighteen and twenty thousand American ex-soldiers are insane as a
result of the war.
*Good Morning*, May 1-15, 1921
Also published as the centerspread of *The Soldier* #1, First Quarter 1922
16" x 11"

ABOVE: *Business:* "Help — Hell"
*Good Morning*, v.3 #11, September 1921
18.5" x 10.5"

RIGHT: **The Prohibition Question**
*Speaker:* "Wassa use of tryin' to do anything — for the (hic) working-man? When the working-man gets a little money — he spends it for liquor. I have no (hic) hesitation in saying that liquor is the curse of the working-man." (Applause)
*Puck,* January 25, 1910
Reprinted in *Good Morning* #3, May 22, 1919
23.5" x 16.625"

# POOR FISH

Original art for spot illustrations from various issues of *Good Morning*

← 1½ inches →
Good Morning

HEP!
← 2½ inches →
Good Morning

← 1½ inches →
Good Morning

← 2¾ inches →
Good Morning

← 1½ inches →

← 1¾ inches →
Good Morning

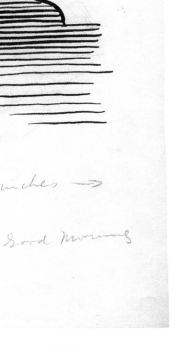

ABOVE: **Out Again**
*Good Morning*, May 1920
17" x 9.25"

RIGHT: **The Ancient Honorable and Independent Order of Poor Fish Certificate**
*The Soldier* #1, First Quarter 1922
13.75" x 12.75"

OPPOSITE: *Judge:* "Miss Striker, this is the third time you've been arrested for picketing. Why, a girl of your fine appearance and brains ought to associate with the best people."
*Miss Striker:* "I do"
*Good Morning* #1, May 8, 1919
14.75" x 18"

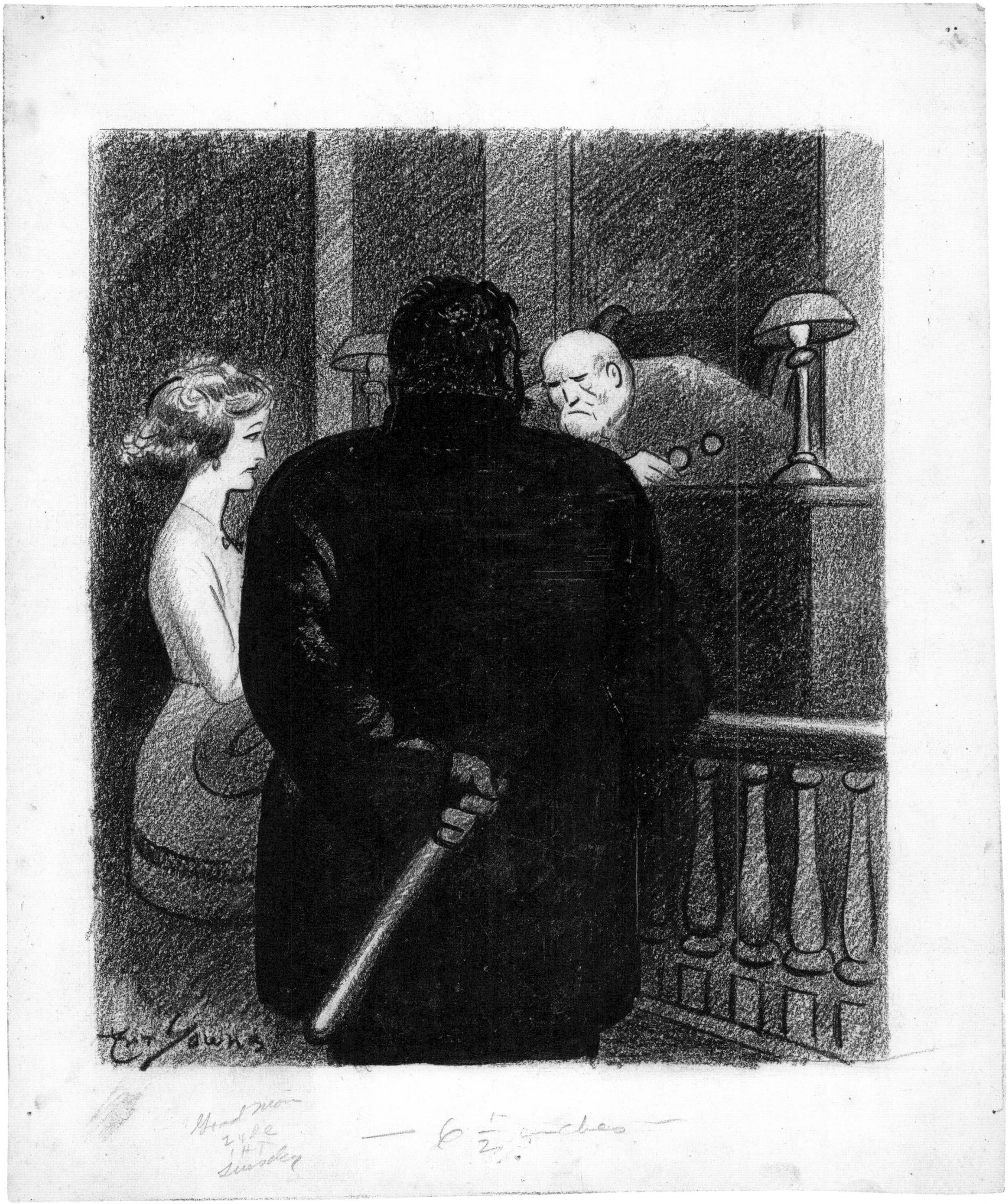
— 6 1/2 inches —

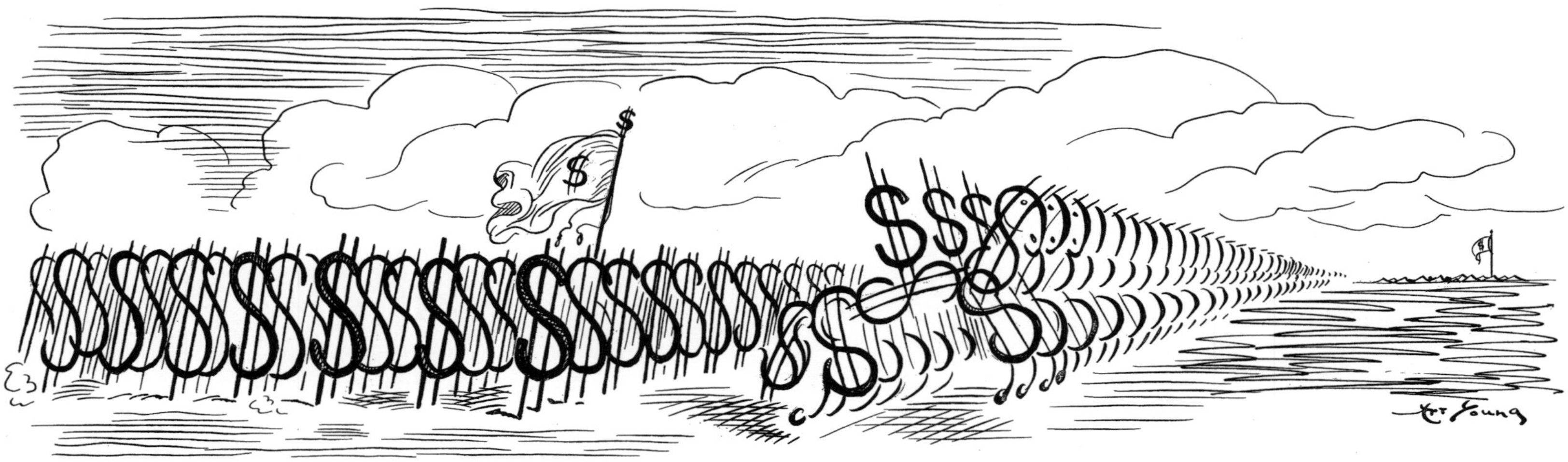

**ABOVE:** The Grand Army of the Republic
*Good Morning*, August 1, 1920
19"x 7"

**RIGHT:** Good Morning
Original art for an advertising insert in *Good Morning*, 1919
7.5"x 10.5"

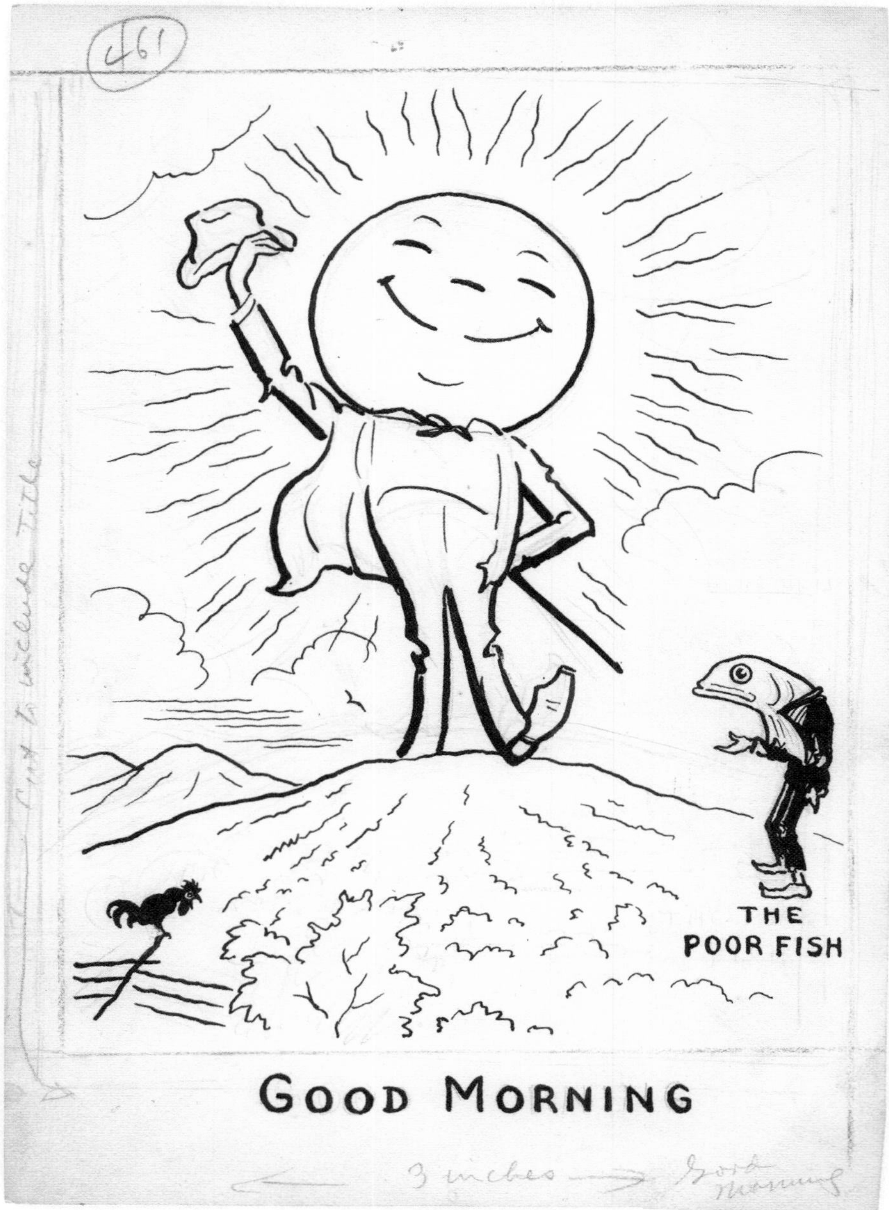
THE
POOR FISH
GOOD MORNING

If you are sane, you will be interested in *Good Morning's* new venture to build an asylum for sane people. For four long years our cities and towns have been seething with the insane. People that you thought sensible have leaped into the air, cavorted and danced with wild enthusiasm for hating and killing. We have seen calm college professors, sensitive poets, harmless ministers, and even professional humorists gnawing their finger-nails looking at us google-eyed and whispering confidentially that the Kaiser was sneaking up behind them. We have seen motherly mothers, the kind that say: "Don't tease the cat, Willie," and "Love your enemies, Pa," — read the newspaper headlines and then go out to the kitchen, get a butcher knife and come back snorting that she'd "like to kill something, no matter what." We have seen almost everyone coaxing everybody else to get on the bandwagon of insanity. The country was one big mad house and sane people were lonely.

TOP: *Good Morning's* Asylum for
Sane People
*Good Morning* #7, June 19, 1919
11.5" x 9"

RIGHT: **When We Woke Up**
*Good Morning*, May 15, 1920
16" x 13"

After *Good Morning* tried so hard not to violate the Prohibition Law by intoxicating our readers with too much mirth, what do you think? We were thrown out of the U.S. Mail for violating the Anti-Lottery Law. Our offense was that we used the word "must" instead of "may" and that is why page 7 of the last issue was stamped cancel-led. You will find the corrected statement of the contest on page 13.

Dear Reader, don't be surprised if the next issue of *Good Morning* is also delayed. There are only eighty thousand laws to obey and we may get held up for violating the smoke ordinance, trespass, blocking traffic, sneezing in public or wearing a straw hat before the official date.

The Poor Fish says we got just what we deserved.

# Quotation Cartoons

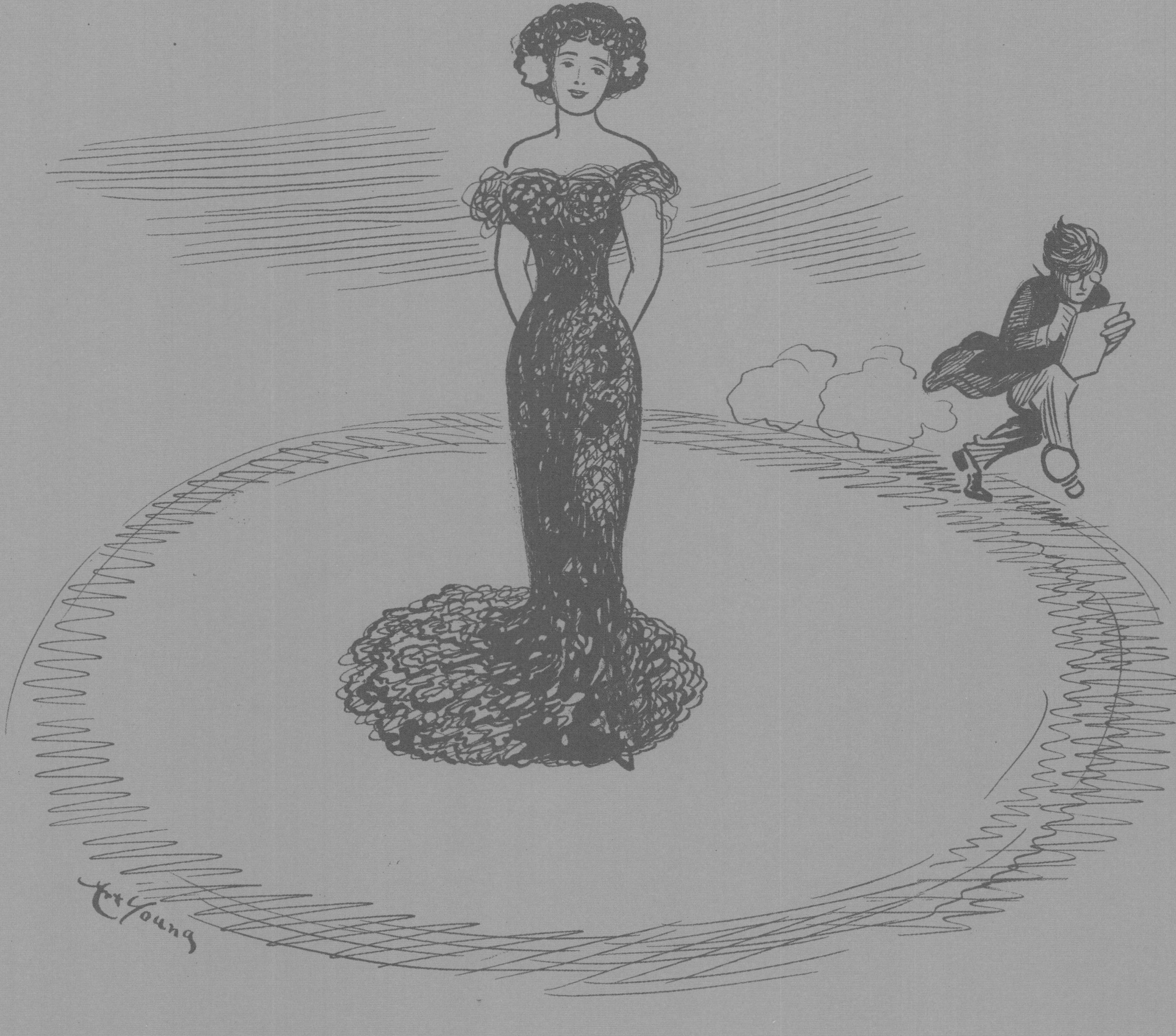
Art Young

**Verbal Fireworks**
"That grand old party whose valorous deeds flare like a beacon light on the pages of immortal hi-s-s-s-tor-e-e-e."
6.375″ x 11″

"Thou hast seen a farmer's dog bark at a beggar, and the
creature run from the cur: There, There, thou might'st behold
the great image of authority; a dog's obeyed — in office"
— *King Lear* [by Shakespeare]
10.75" x 12.5"

"Fear follows crime and is its punishment"
— Voltaire
*10" x 10.25"*

*To be keyed high intellectually, is to have great sympathy for sadness and a keen appreciation of the droll and ludicrous.*

KILLING TIME

**TOP:** **The Comic Tragedy**
"To be keyed high, intellectually, is to have great sympathy for sadness and a keen appreciation of the droll and ludicrous."
— Abraham Lincoln
*Life,* February 11, 1909
15″ x 7″

**LEFT:** **Killing Time**
9.5″ x 11.5″

**ABOVE RIGHT:** "That is the bitterest of all — to wear the yoke of our own wrong-doing."
— Geo. Eliot
11″ x 10″

TO LAUGH THAT WE MAY NOT WEEP

ABOVE: **Taking it Easy**
9.75" x 9.25"

RIGHT: **Air "Craft"**
8.75" x 11.5"

— A LOOSE NUT —

**ABOVE: A Loose Nut**
12" x 7.5"

**LEFT: Theories Explode Every Day**
Still the Search Goes On
*Life*, October 1910
6.75" x 5.75"

**Poverty and Talent**
"It is difficult to rise if your poverty is greater than your talent."— Juvenal
*Good Morning*, September 15–October 1, 1920
11" x 10.5"

ABOVE: "If our inward griefs were seen written on our brows, how many would be pitied who are now envied"— Metastasio
10.5" x 13.5"

RIGHT: Self-Advertising
11" x 14.25"

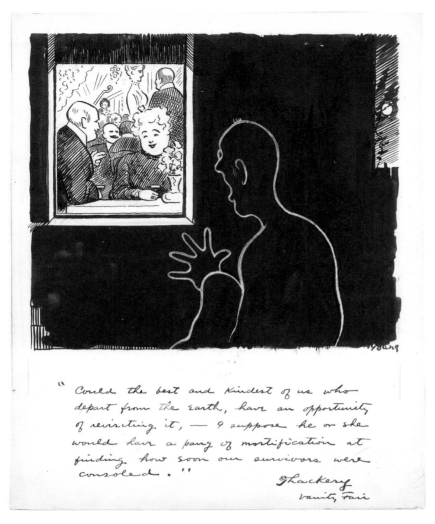

"Could the best and kindest of us who depart from the Earth, have an opportunity of revisiting it, — I suppose he or she would have a pang of mortification at finding how soon our survivors were consoled."

Thackeray
Vanity Fair

ABOVE: "Could the best and kindest of us who depart from the Earth have an opportunity of revisiting it, I suppose he or she [...] would have a pang of mortification at finding how soon our survivors were consoled."
Thackeray, *Vanity Fair*
10.5" x 13"

RIGHT: **The Bone is Knitting Nicely**
For *Life,* date and publication status unknown
9.75" x 12.5"

**ABOVE: Weather Note**
A backward spring
16" x 11.5"

**LEFT: Unlimited Possibilities — Moral and Intellectual**
22.25" x 14"

In the Twentieth Century war will be dead, the scaffold will be dead,
animosity will be dead, royalty will be dead, and dogmas will be dead;
but man will live — for all there will be but one country — that country, the
whole earth; for all there will be but one hope — that hope the whole heaven.

— Victor Hugo

**ABOVE:** Fame Follows the Base Drum
11" x 8"

**RIGHT:** Writing a Play Around Her
*Life*, March 19, 1910
16.25" x 15.75"

*— writing a play around her —*

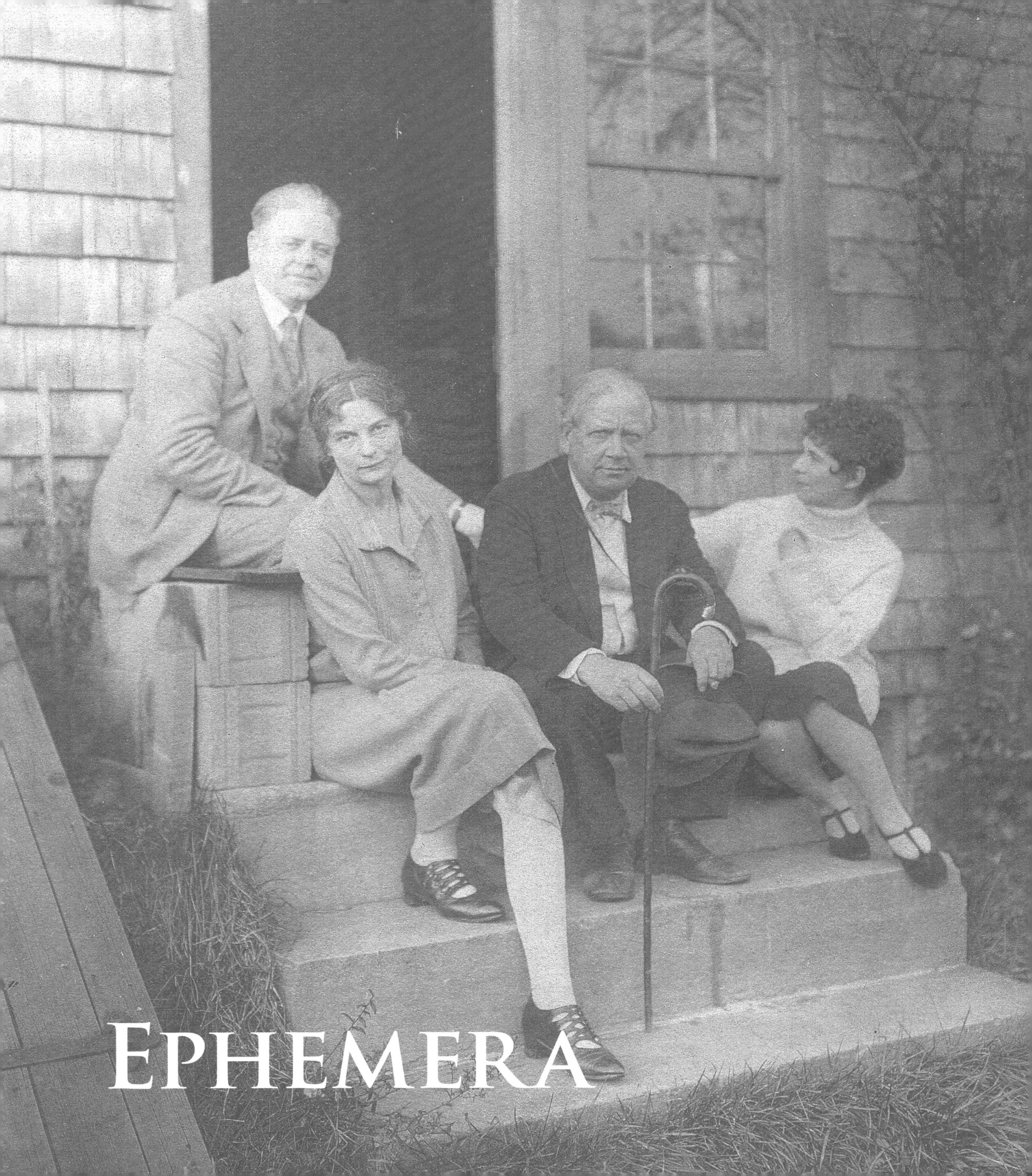

# EPHEMERA

FOR SENATOR OF NEW YORK STATE

THIRTEENTH SENATORIAL DISTRICT

ART YOUNG

Art Young is well known through his cartoons and political writings. He was a Washington correspondent for four years and knows politics and the machinery of legislation from every angle.

He was born fifty-two years ago. Back in his boyhood he took an interest in public affairs. At eighteen years of age he drew cartoons of the public officials in the town where he was raised, Monroe, Wis., that influenced the thought of the town. At twenty-one he drew cartoons for Chicago newspapers, that created interest throughout the country for their artistic quality and direct human appeal.

For many years in his writing, cartoons and speeches he has worked for woman suffrage, abolition of child labor, the right of workers to organize and strike and all measures that make for industrial democracy. His political cartoons are notable for their humor, simplicity, and strength, and have appeared in leading magazines and daily papers of New York. In recent years he has been indicted twice for cartoons that were too true to find favor with the powers that be.

The latest indictment for which he was tried, was the result of a cartoon called "Having Their Fling." Young on the witness stand testified that he drew it "to express the frenzy, and chaotic thinking that accompanies the war spirit," and that he wanted it printed "for the public good." Is it not obvious that in war time more than ever there is need of clear thinking and calm judgment? This is the time to get at true causes and reconstruct society on a basis of real honest democracy.

A man of common sense sees the practical important facts of life. From the complexities and horrors that result from the private ownership of publicly necessary land and industries he disentangles the truth. Such a man is Art Young. A man with a social conscience, who concerns himself with fundamental causes of unrest, poverty, and injustice. Young is known for his integrity and his honest uncompromising position on public questions. He has lived in New York City twenty years.

Art Young was nominated by unanimous vote of the Socialist Party for State Senator of New York from the 13th district and if elected can be relied upon to further the interests of the rank and file of this district and the State at large. The Socialist Party stands and works for a better world for the toilers. Art Young is one of its representatives.

*Do you want to live in a better world?*

*If so vote for it.*

LEARNING — CO-OPERATION — PEACE — LIBERTY

GRAPHIC PRESS, NEW YORK

ABOVE: **For Senator of New York State**
Campaign flyer, 1918
9" x 11.75"

RIGHT: A sticker that Art Young used to identify his artwork
Undated

The Art Young Gallery

NOW OPEN

*Exhibition of Original Drawings
by* ART YOUNG

SATURDAYS *and* SUNDAYS
10 a. m. *to* 7 p. m.

↑ ↑ ↑

One mile south of Bethel, Conn. on the Chestnut
Ridge Road

(*Bethel is near Danbury*)

ADMISSION FREE

**ABOVE: The Art Young Gallery Now Open**
Art Young gallery card
c. 1915
3.25″ x 5.5″

**RIGHT:** *Art Young's Political Primer,* cover
1918

# ART YOUNG'S
## FIRST AND LAST EXHIBITION

DRAWINGS        1910-1934

*Art Young*

## January 2nd to January 14th
### 1   9   3   4

## DELPHIC STUDIOS
9 East 57th Street      New York

1. THE COMING DAY.
2. THE FITTEST TO SURVIVE
3. BIRD IN THE RAIN.
4. HEAVEN.
5. PILLOW FIGHT.
   *(Presidential Campaign, 1928)*
6. RUSSIA.
7. SELF PORTRAIT.
   *(For a Spring Dance)*
8. CHARLES EVANS HUGHES.
9. INFERIORITY COMPLEX.
10. FEAR COMPLEX.
11. SUPERIORITY COMPLEX.
12. STORM BOY.
13. LA FOLLETTE.
14. THE LAST MAN.
15. POWER.
16. "NICE COOL SEWER."
    *(Loaned by Amos R. E. Pinchot)*
17. "I THINK I'LL TAKE THE MURDER."
18. EDWIN MARKHAM.
19. WILLIAM JENNINGS BRYAN.
20. PENITENT INDIVIDUALISM.
    *(Loaned by Vincent Astor)*
21. OVERTHROWING THE GOVERNMENT.
22. HENRY CABOT LODGE.
23. THE VILLAGE BACHELOR.
24. THE TOWN LAMP-LIGHTER.
25. SACCO-VANZETTI CARTOON.
26. USEFUL LABOR.
27. THE VILLAGE GROUCH.
28. BEAST AND MAN.
    *(Loaned by R. T. Trowbridge)*
29. MARKET DAY.
30. SHE GOES TO ALL THE FUNERALS.
31. HAVING THEIR FLING.
    *(Art Young's criminal offence during the World War)*

### TREES AT NIGHT
32. THE PENALTY OF PROMINENCE.
    *(Loaned by Constant Eakin)*
33. CARAVAN.
34. THE WIDOW.
35. PANIC.
36. DEFEAT.
37. CATHEDRAL.
38. GOODBYE SUMMER.
39. WEARY AND HEAVY LADEN.
40. LIKE BIRDS IN THEIR FLIGHT.
41. LAST APPEAL.
42. END OF THE WOODS.
43. THE PATRIARCH.

44. GATEWAY TO LIVING.
45. "NOW, ALTOGETHER, THREE CHEERS."
    *(Presidential Campaign, 1928)*
46. BIG AND LITTLE BEGGARS.
47. FROM JUNGLE TO CIVILIZATION.
48. THE IDIOT GIANT WAR.
    *(From Art Young's Inferno, Delphic Studios, 1934)*
49. LETHE.
    *(From Art Young's Inferno, Delphic Studios, 1934)*
50. THE FINISH.

Art Young's First and Last Exhibition
Flyer, 1934
8.5" x 11"

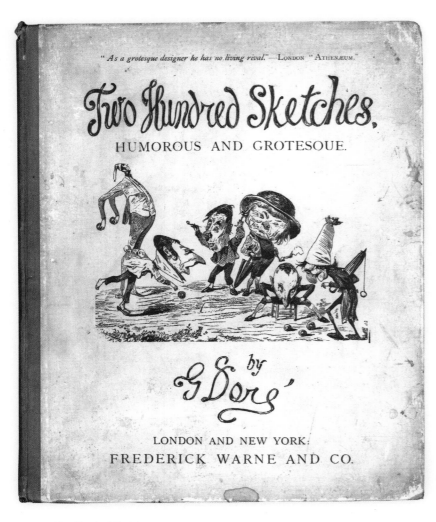

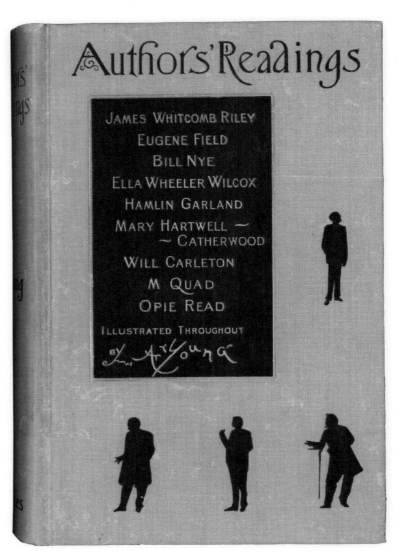

**ABOVE:** *Two Hundred Sketches*
by G. Doré
An inspirational book from the 1880s that Young saved on his library shelf

**RIGHT:** *Authors' Readings*
1897
Young's compilation of favorite stories by favorite authors

The casual autobiography in comment and anecdote, cartoon and confession of America's trenchant social caricaturist—a well known and well loved figure in American life.

ART YOUNG is a rare human being. Had he wanted it he might have made a fortune. He chose to cast in his lot with the underdog and his cartoonist's brush has been one of the most powerful weapons of liberalism in this country.

Still rarer, he has been a radical who never lost his love for humanity. He has exposed shams, hypocrisies, injustices, but he has never hated human beings; he has won the esteem and affection of all with whom he has had contact.

ON MY WAY is the record of his rich and vivid life. It contains memories of such notable figures as Jack London, O. Henry, Thomas Nast, Joseph Keppler, John Reed, "Bob" Ingersoll, P. T. Barnum, Lew Wallace, W. T. Stead, Mark Twain, "Bill Nye", James Whitcomb Riley, Eugene Field, Robert LaFollette, Bouguerreau, Randolph Bourne, George Bellows, and many others who have passed into history, including one or two presidents. He tells anecdotes, and comments on many notables still living.

Especially interesting are his story of the Anarchist trial in Chicago, Student Days in Paris, meetings with earlier American humorists, impressions of past Congresses, the better days of Greenwich Village before realtors chased out the real artists; the story of his candidacy for the New York State Senate, the trial of "The Masses" editors, including himself, and his experience as an editor—a long, full, fascinating life of drawing cartoons, writing, speaking, making friends, working for causes, playing a part in the drama of American life.

Its geniality, its wit, its calm philosophy, its charm of narrative in which he makes words as pungent and revealing of character as the many drawings that fill the book, give it a quality rare in the egotistical and strutting autobiographical literature of our time—and all times.

HORACE LIVERIGHT

ABOVE: *On My Way*, dustjacket, 1928

RIGHT: *Hawaii — A Snap Shot*
Illustrated book, 1893

FAR RIGHT: A Baby Carriage
for the Poor
First deck — Kindling
Second deck — The wash
Hurricane deck — For baby
Sketch on *Good Morning* notepaper
Undated
5.5″ x 8.5″

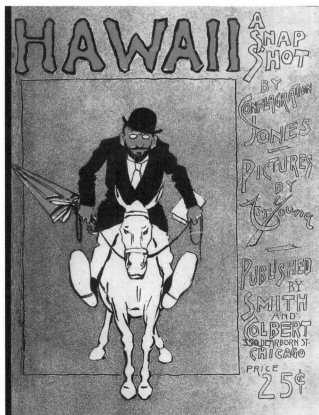

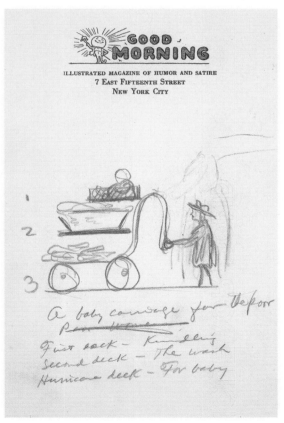

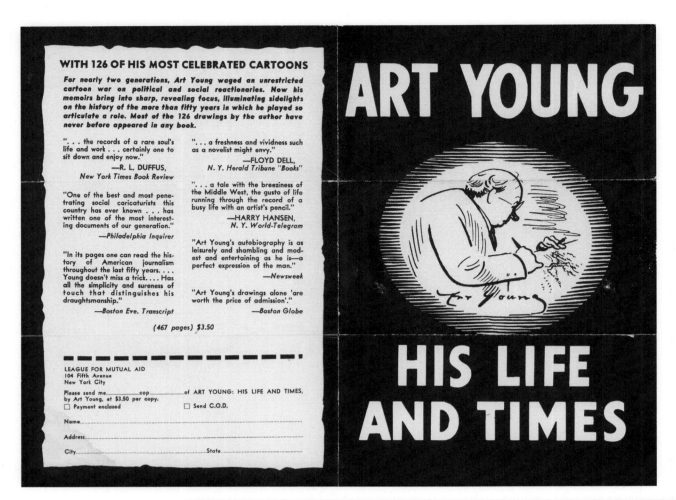

RIGHT & ABOVE: Unfolded
advertising flyer for *Art Young:
His Life and Times*
Obverse and reverse
1939
11.5″ x 8.5″

TO LAUGH THAT WE MAY NOT WEEP

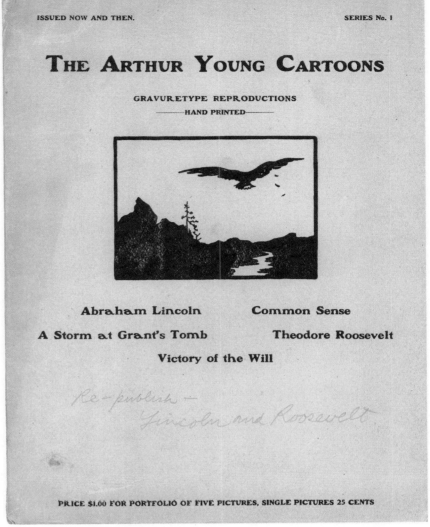

ABOVE: *The Socialist Primer* cover, 1930
(Original art, p. 63)
9.5″ x 12.5″

ABOVE RIGHT: **The Arthur Young Cartoons**
Print portfolio cover, 1904
10″ x 13″

ABOVE: **This 1928 Campaign in Cartoons**
Cover to printed booklet
14" x 10.5"

RIGHT: *New Masses*, February 1, 1944
(Announcing Art Young's death)
9.5" x 12.5"

*The Big Stick* (New York)
April 28, 1922, front page
Newspaper, published in Hebrew
15.25″ x 25.5″

ART YOUNG

STUDIO: 9 EAST 17TH STREET, NEW YORK CITY

TELEPHONE ALGONQUIN 4191

HOME ADDRESS —— BETHEL, CONN.

SUMMERTIME

Green Hotel Danbury Conn
Feb. 12 1932

Dear Mr Carroll
    In your interesting letter you ask
a question of me that I ought to
answer — But, just to say now
that I have already had something
to say on the subject of your
inquiry in my book " On My Way "
The book may be in your local library.
    I thank you for your letter
            Yours sincerely
                Art Young

P. S. Speaking only for my own soul
I am glad that not many years out of my life
were wasted doing pictorial comment
on affairs that were merely topical —
                            Y.

Art Young letter to Mr. Carroll
Dated February 12, 1932
7.75" x 10"

**1-2)** Art Young, age 45

**3)** Art Young, 1910, matted and signed
6" x 9"

**4)** Art Young, age 49

**5)** Copeland studio portrait of Art Young,
Monroe, Wisconsin
Undated

ART YOUNG

4571-14

**ABOVE:** Art Young at one of the two *The Masses* trials in 1918

**ABOVE RIGHT:** Art Young standing by carriage
Undated

**Standing in Front of the Frog Sculpture at the Entrance
to Art Young's Gallery**

ABOVE: Art Young with Jeanne Duval, unknown woman,
and Harry Weinberger
Undated

RIGHT: Art Young with Harry Weinberger
Undated
(Harry Weinberger (1888–1944) was the producer of the play
*God of Vengeance* (p. 286), but was best known as an attorney
for Emma Goldman and as a champion of civil liberties.)

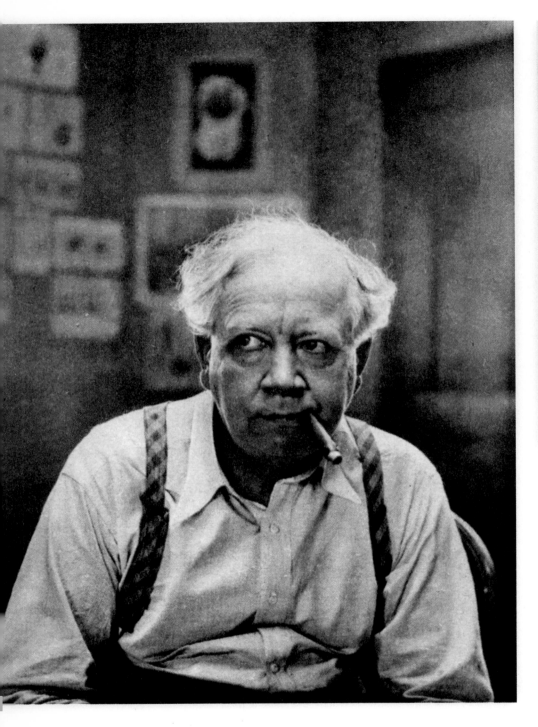

**RIGHT:** Photo of Art Young by Frederick Hier
*Heroes I Have Known* by Max Eastman, 1942

**ABOVE:** Photo portrait of Art Young by Harry Godfrey
Undated

**1)**

**3)**

**2)**

**4)**

**1)** Dan Young's general store
(First store on left. Sign reads
"D.B. YOUNG & CO.")
Monroe, Wisconsin
late 1800s

**2)** Printed caption reads "Art among his
originals in the Bethel Gallery"
Undated

**3)** Art Young's house c. 2014
Photo by Marc Moorash

**4)** Art Young and others on the front steps
of his house in Bethel, Connecticut
Undated

**1) Portrait of Art Young**
by Lynd Ward
Undated
4.0625″ x 6.0625″
Collection of Marc Moorash

**2)** Bust of Art Young by Louis Keila
Undated

**3)** Art Young by Al Frueh
Undated
11.5″ x 10.5″

**4)** Postcard portrait of Art Young
by Ray Walters
*Good Morning* #3, May 22, 1919
5.5″ x 4″

**1)** Clay figure of Art Young
by Jack Sears
Original caption: "A Caricature in Clay
of Art Young by Jack Sears, an ardent
friend and admirer. Mr. Sears had in mind
the militant Cartoons and Comment on
Congress in the Metropolitan when he
modeled this statuette."
Undated

**2)** Art Young — the 20th Century
Socrates
by Willis Birchman
1938
8"x 10"

**3)** Art Young double portrait
by Willis Birchman, also signed by Art
Young
Dated November 7, 1939
9.875"x 14"

**4)** Care of Woe
by Fred Lewis
c. 1920
Ink & watercolor
11"x 8"

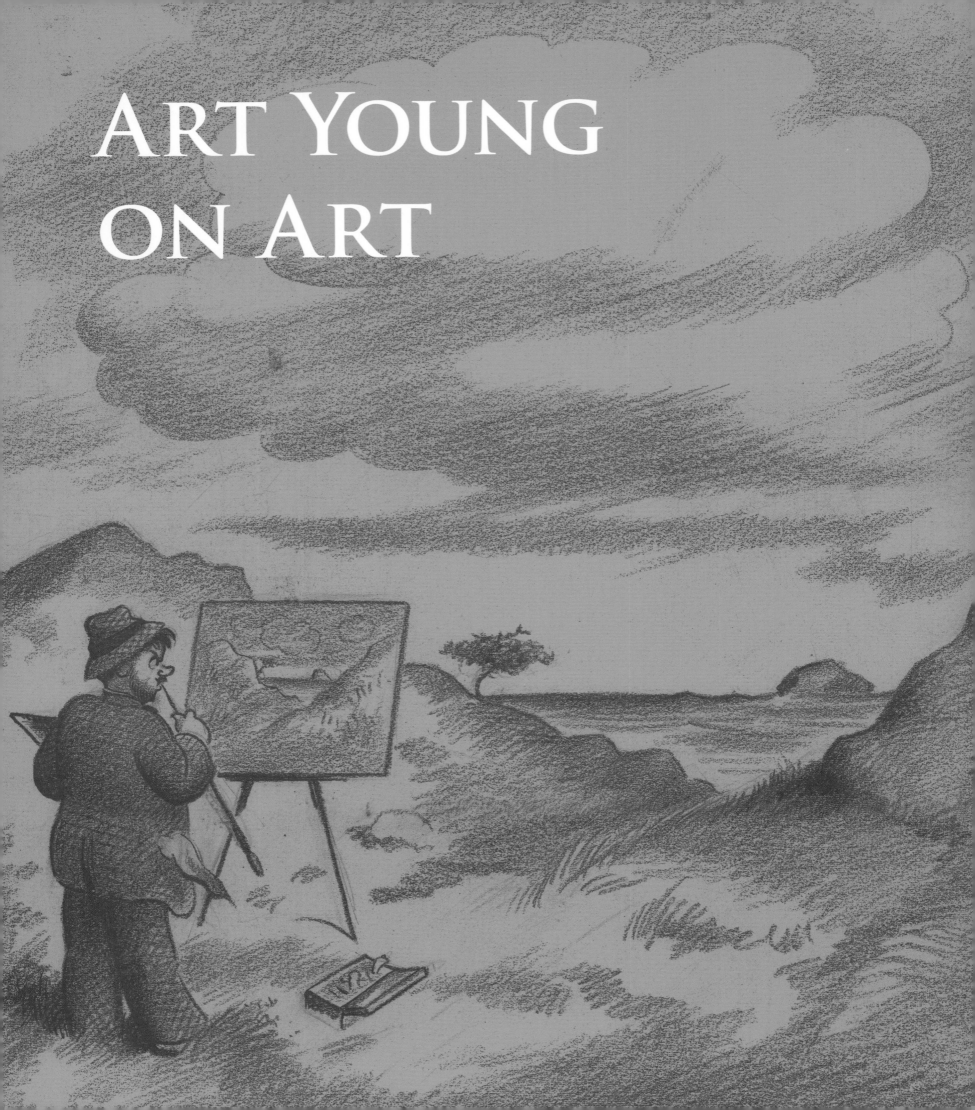

# ART YOUNG
# ON ART

# 12

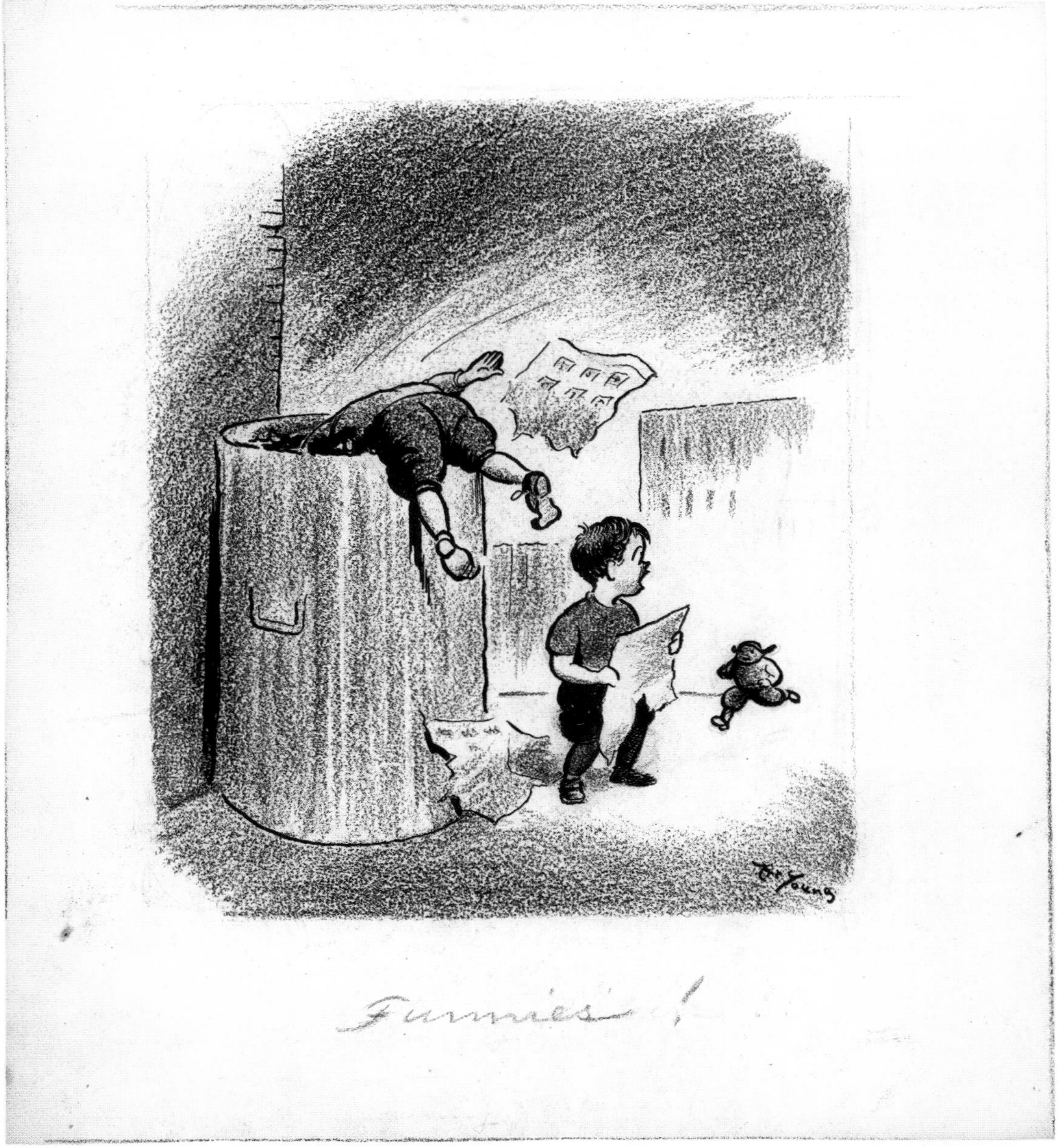
Funnies!

**Funnies!**
Undated
9.75" x 10.75"

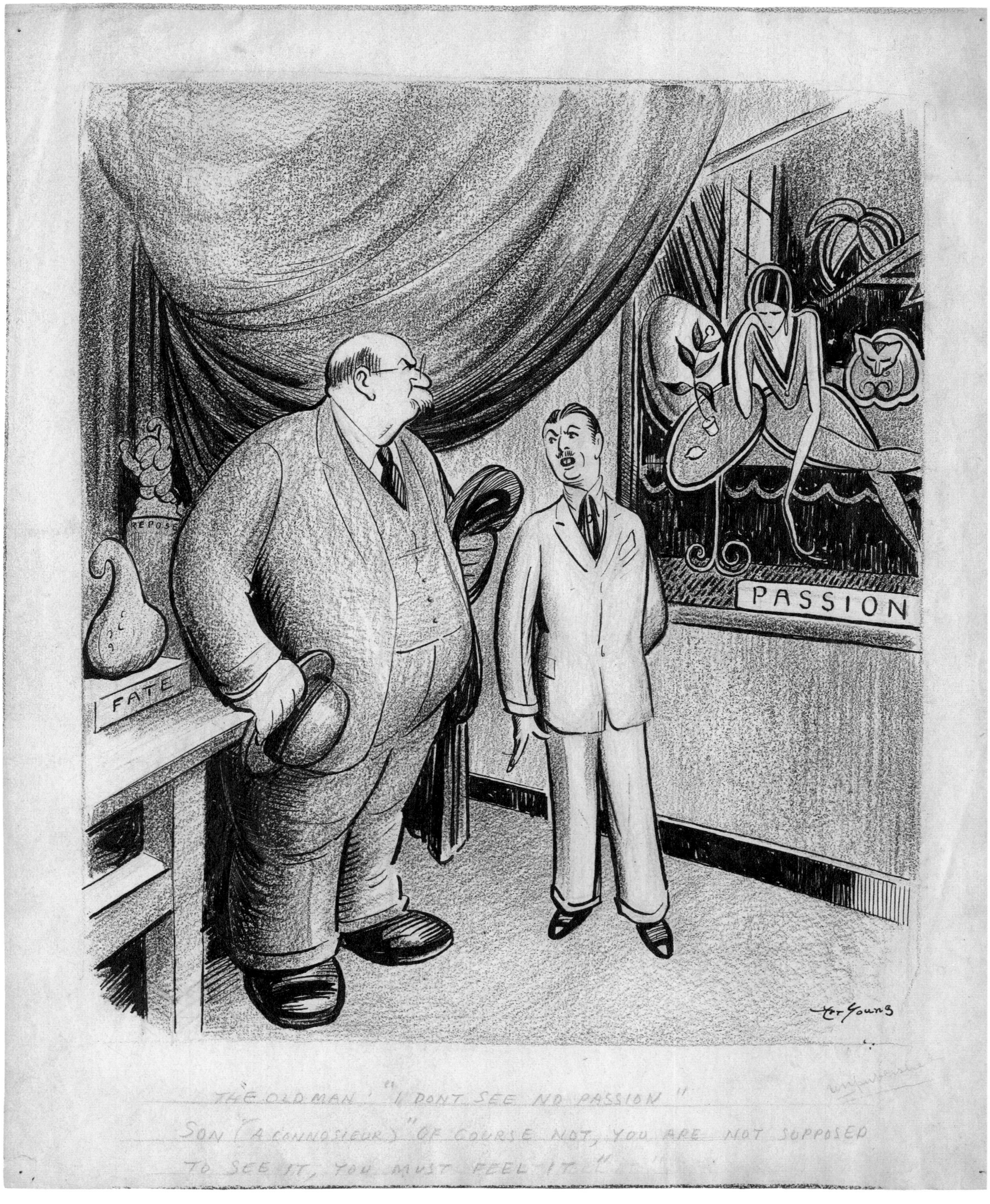
REPOSE
FATE
PASSION
Art Young
THE OLD MAN: "I DONT SEE NO PASSION"
SON (A CONNOSIEUR) "OF COURSE NOT, YOU ARE NOT SUPPOSED
TO SEE IT, YOU MUST FEEL IT."

OPPOSITE: *The Old Man:* "I don't see no passion."
*Son (a connoisseur):* "Of course not. You are not supposed to see it. You must feel it."
Undated
14.75" x 18"

ABOVE: "That's a wonderful view."
"O yes — that is, if you like views."
Undated
15" x 9"

RIGHT: *Artist:* "Thought I'd do a little landscape painting around here."
*Joshua Backwoods:* "Don't think ye'll find much fer picters, mister. There was a photograph-feller up here last year, and he tuk about everything."
Undated
10" x 12.25"

ABOVE: "No use, I've got to eliminate the ocean, make the left hill higher, and change the sunset to sunrise."
Undated
14" x 18.75"

RIGHT: "Can Anybody Get In?"
*The New Yorker*, March 1931
15" x 17.5"

**Fagged Out**
Cover to *The Inter Ocean Illustrated Supplement* (Chicago), May 31, 1893
(Original art, next page)

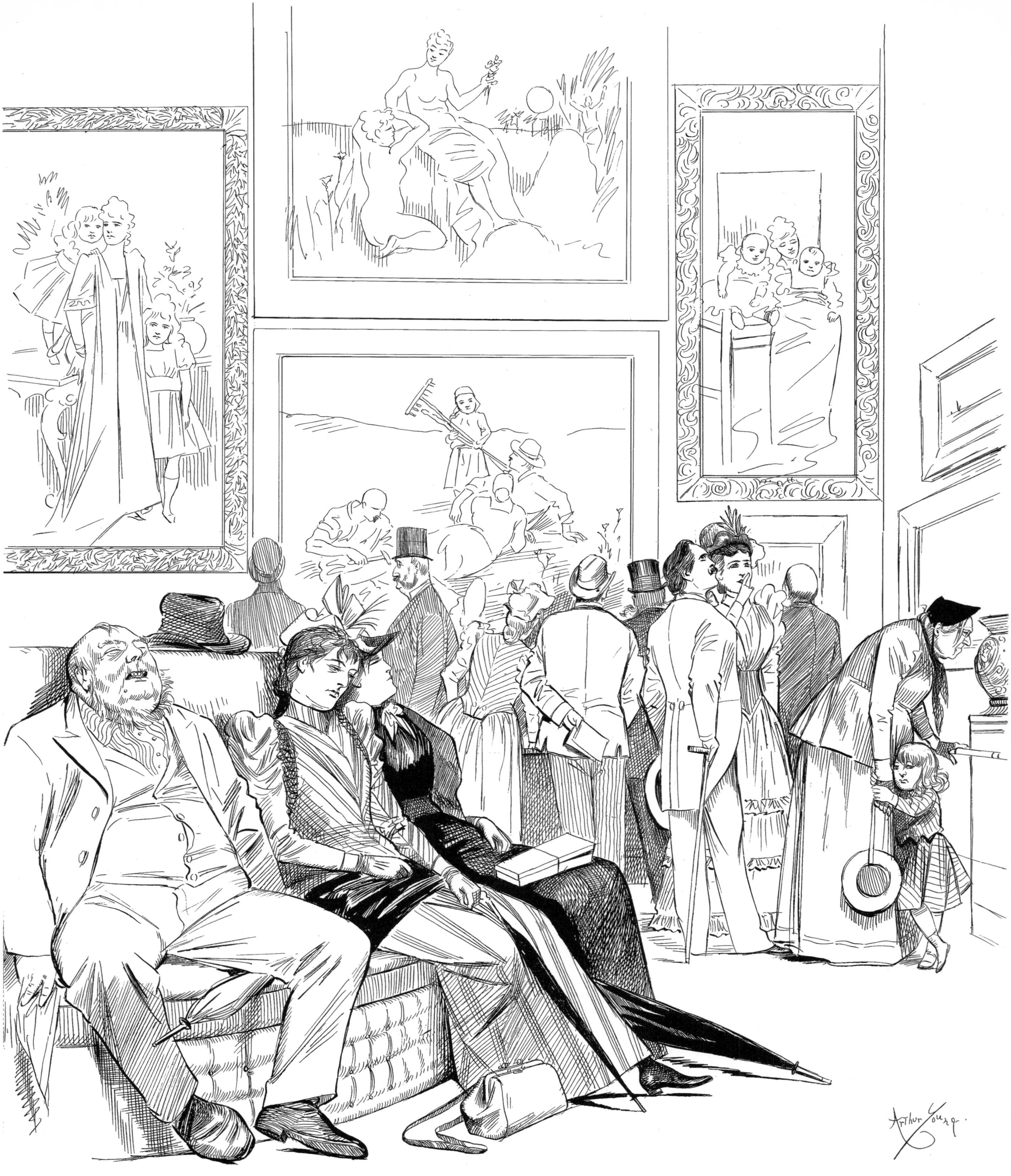
Arthur Young

| NO. | |
|---|---|
| 22 | WOMAN LOOKING AT PARROT |
| 23 | MAN SITTING DOWN |
| 24 | A LADY. |
| 25 | STILL LIFE-COPPER KETTLE AND CABBAGE |
| 26 | GIRL IN PINK KIMONA |
| 27 | MISS W.- STANDING |
| 28 | A COSY CORNER |
| 29 | ARRANGEMENT IN YELLOW AND PRUSSIAN BLUE |
| 30 | AFTER THE BALL |
| 31 | AFTER THE BATH |
| 32 | COW EATING |
| 33 | STILL LIFE — FISH AND POTATOES |

OPPOSITE: **Fagged Out**
*The Inter Ocean Illustrated Supplement*
(Chicago), May 31, 1893
18.25" x 22"
(Printed version, previous page)

ABOVE: **Art for Art's Sake**
Undated
21.5" x 10"

RIGHT: *Farmer: "Do You Have to Do That?"*
*Life*, February 25, 1915
Reprinted in *Good Morning*,
September 15-October 1, 1920
11.75" x 12"

# RELIGION

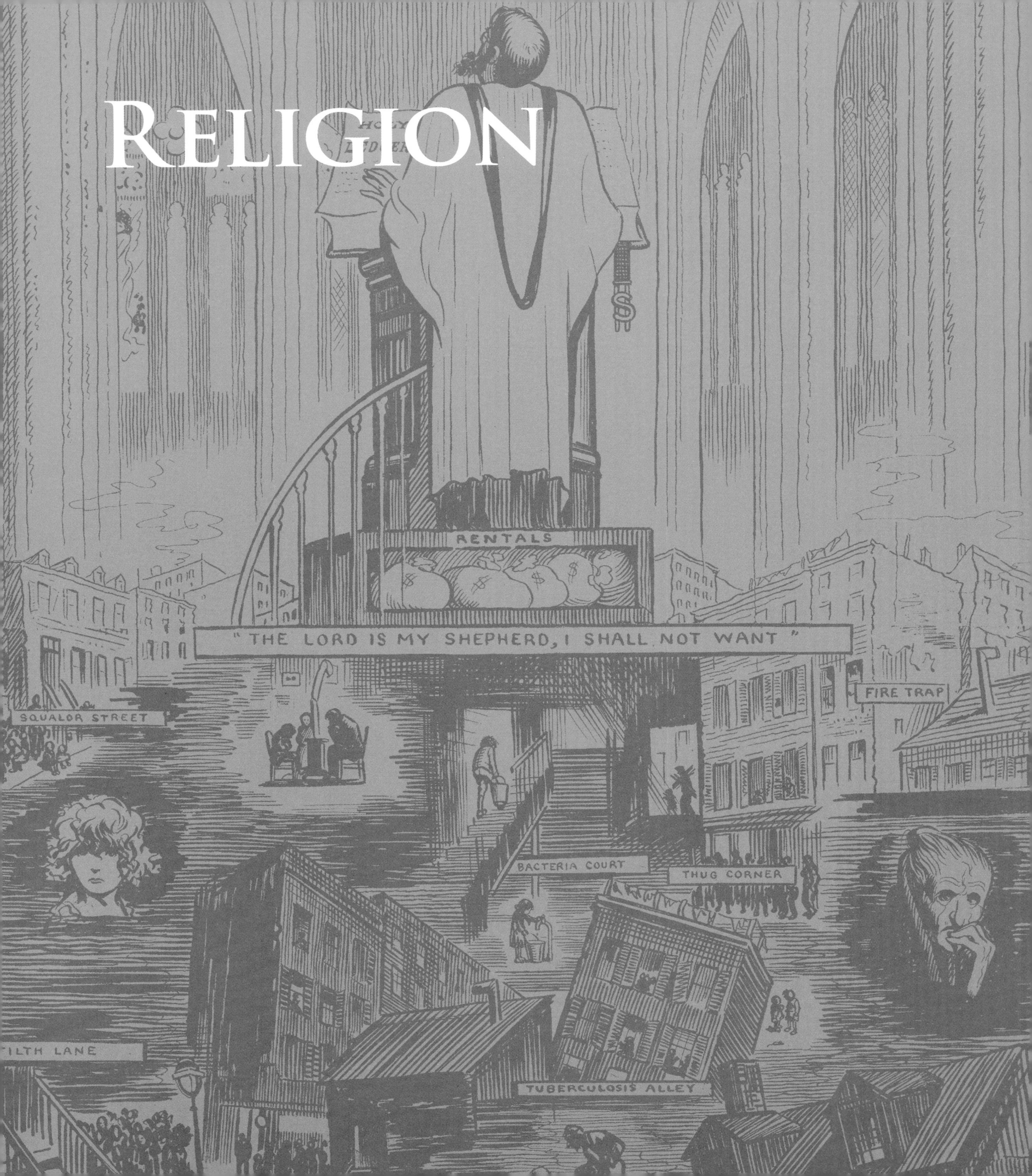
RENTALS
"THE LORD IS MY SHEPHERD, I SHALL NOT WANT"
SQUALOR STREET
FIRE TRAP
BACTERIA COURT
THUG CORNER
ILTH LANE
TUBERCULOSIS ALLEY

## 13

**ABOVE: A Trip to the Holy Land**
*Life*, April 20, 1922
9.75" x 6.125"

**RIGHT:** "No thank you. There's a lot of trouble coming, and I'll be blamed for it."
*The Masses*, November 1914
11" x 11.75"

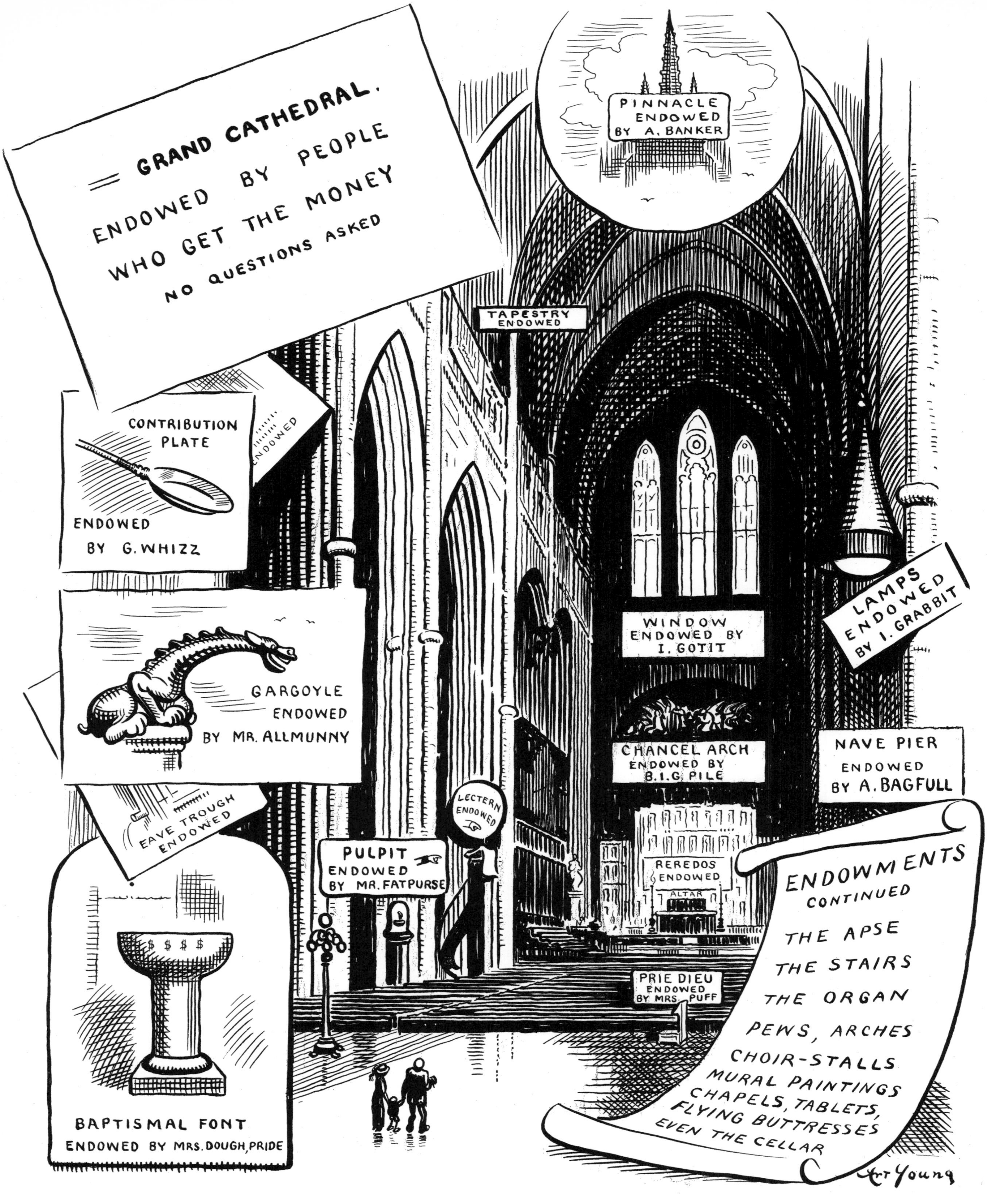
GRAND CATHEDRAL.
ENDOWED BY PEOPLE WHO GET THE MONEY
NO QUESTIONS ASKED
PINNACLE ENDOWED BY A. BANKER
TAPESTRY ENDOWED
CONTRIBUTION PLATE
ENDOWED BY G. WHIZZ
ENDOWED
GARGOYLE ENDOWED BY MR. ALLMUNNY
EAVE TROUGH ENDOWED
WINDOW ENDOWED BY I. GOTIT
LAMPS ENDOWED BY I. GRABBIT
CHANCEL ARCH ENDOWED BY B.I.G PILE
NAVE PIER ENDOWED BY A. BAGFULL
LECTERN ENDOWED
PULPIT ENDOWED BY MR. FATPURSE
REREDOS ENDOWED
ALTAR
PRIE DIEU ENDOWED BY MRS. PUFF
BAPTISMAL FONT ENDOWED BY MRS. DOUGH, PRIDE
ENDOWMENTS CONTINUED
THE APSE
THE STAIRS
THE ORGAN
PEWS, ARCHES
CHOIR-STALLS
MURAL PAINTINGS
CHAPELS, TABLETS,
FLYING BUTTRESSES
EVEN THE CELLAR
Art Young

**OPPOSITE: Who Said It Was God's House?**
*Puck*, May 10, 1911
Reprinted in *Good Morning*, April 15, 1921
16.75" x 20.5"

**Jesus With Sayings**
*Good Morning*, April 1, 1921
**ABOVE:** Original art
10" x 11"
**RIGHT:** As published with accompanying text

## Friend J. C. and Propertee

(This is the story of Zach and Nick
And Jesus Christ of the Communist clique,
Zach—the Publican and the sinner
And Nick—the Republican and the skinner.)

Friend J. C. and you and me
And all of us
Don't make no fuss
About the rights of propertee,
Because we aint got any.  See?

Friend Jesus told one Zachee-us
That he might be better and couldn't be wuss
If he gave away his propertee;
And danged if Zach did not agree
To clothe the naked and feed the poor
And call the hoboes to his door,
But Zachee-us was an exception
Like a communist at election.

One night there came—on a spirichool spree—
A whiskered guy named Nicodec
Who told J. C. he liked his line
And thought the parable was fine
And hoped the gang would up and jine.
Old Nicode the Pharisee,
Lousy with rank and propertee,
Liked the line but couldn't agree
To amputate his propertee.

But Friend J. C. and you and me
And all of us
 Don't make no fuss
About the rights of propertee,
Because we aint got any.  See?

*Art Shields.*

Most of our readers are aware that during the war, the Constitution of the United States and the Declaration of Independence were under ban of the law; that is to say, persons who circulated reprints from these documents were brought before the courts and convicted of seditious conduct. This seemed rather remarkable; but an even more remarkable fact has now come to light. The Association to Abolish War is reprinting and circulating the Sermon on the Mount in a four-page leaflet. This is headed by the caption "Now It Can Be Printed"; and an explanatory note is added, stating that late in 1917, a member of the Association proposed to print the Sermon on the Mount, without note or comment, for free distribution. The secretary of the Association, Mr. Wilbur K. Thomas, was officially informed that such a procedure would be regarded by the Department of Justice as "pro-German."  How is that for high?

*—The Freeman.*

**Suggestion for a Statue to the Triumph of Practical Christianity**
Why not a statue to the early exponent of the business slogan, "Sell Yourself"?
Undated
10.75" x 14.5"

**Still Waiting After Two Thousand Years**
Undated
11" x 13.75"

— In Heaven —

When one pair of wings is inadequate.

ABOVE: **In Heaven**
When one pair of wings is inadequate
Undated
10.5″ x 10.5″

RIGHT: *The Lady:* "But don't you think, Professor, that sin is
better than it was?"
Undated
8.5″ x 10.5″

| TO LAUGH THAT WE MAY NOT WEEP

**Talk All You Want To**
For *Life*, date and publication status unknown
13" x 13"

**Reward**
Poster sold in 1960s poster and head shops
(Original art, p. 116)
17.75" x 24.75"

— A Compulsory Religion —

"The trouble with the world is the insane worship of money."

How often we hear this thundered from the pulpit, emphasized in the press and in ordinary conversation.

Yes that's the trouble. But what drives people to this insanity?

In the first place life is a fight for food, shelter and clothing.

No matter how high the price of food soars we must struggle to pay the cost. No matter how high the cost of apparel goes we must pay to keep a degree of comfort and a decent respectable appearance. No matter how exhorbitant far the landlord advances his rent, we must struggle to pay for shelter.

We must fight to get these things or die, and the average man does die fighting for them between 48 and 50 years of age.

You might truthfully write over the tombstones of four-fifths of the human race: 'Died fighting for food shelter and clothing' — In a world of plenty.

The fear that they will not get the necessities of life and that their children will suffer for them — drives the restless spirits on.

It is this kind of a civilization that breeds an insane worship of money. That some men want more, after they have been assured a life of comfort merely emphasizes the tragic baseness of this mad movement.

In a world that is running amuck, individuals cannot stop, even if they would, for back of it all is the original cause:

A stampede of cattle carries all with it. even if one of the herd is ready to stop.

So, bend your back to the lash. cringe, crawl. prostitute yourselves mentally and physically. bribe, graft. do anything to get money. Get it, says father to son, marry for money says mother to daughter. Can there be anything else but worshippers of maximum under these circumstances? Socialism is the only creed the only party that denies the right of this capitalistic political system to thus ruin its men women and children.

Arthur Young

**A Compulsory Religion**
Two handwritten pages
Undated
(Accompanying cartoon and typeset text, p. 120)
8" x 10" each

**Holy Trinity**
*The Wealthy Church and Its Real Estate Holdings*
*Puck*, January 6, 1909, centerfold
16" x 24.5"
(Printed version, p. 27)
Collection of Rick Marschall

ABOVE: "All I say is — things wouldn't go on as they do, if there wasn't a supernatural being"
Undated
14" x 11"

RIGHT: **Thou Shalt Have No Other God But ME**
Pencil rough, unsigned
Undated
19" x 19"

# TYPES

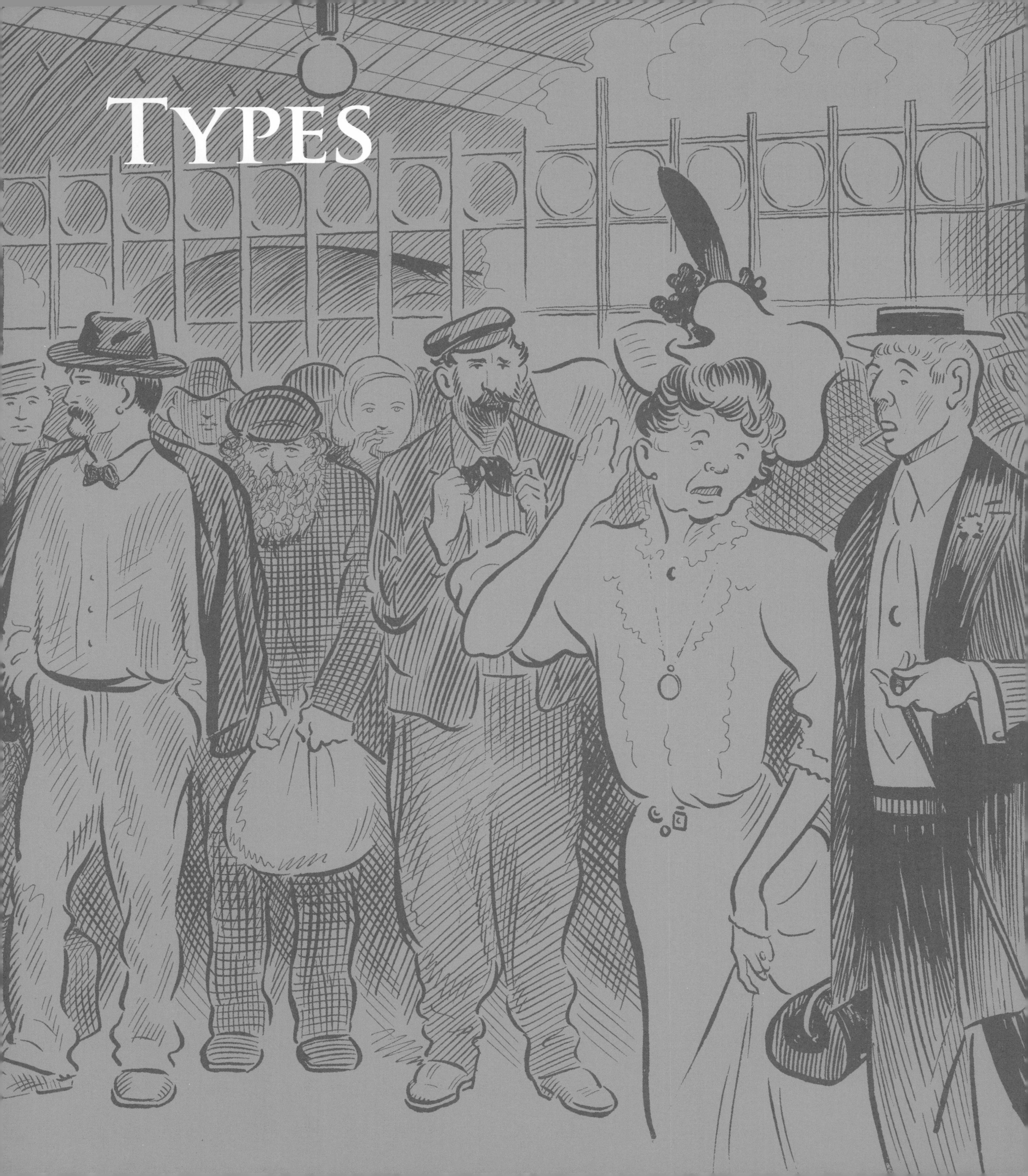

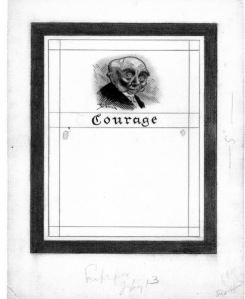

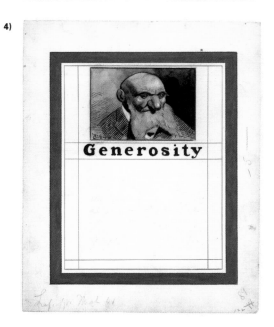

## 14

**1) Character Study: Forgiveness**
Original art for a feature in *Life*, 1902
Dated February 26, 1902 on reverse
10.75" x 8"

**2) Character Study: Courage**
Original art for a feature in *Life*, 1902
9.25" x 12.25"

**3) Character Study: Work**
Original art for a feature in *Life*, 1902
9.5" x 12.25"

**4) Character Study: Generosity**
"Give freely — if the public is looking —
otherwise it won't pay."
— Joseph Graball Purcher
Original art for a feature in *Life*, 1902
9.25" x 11.75"

*Now that everybody is becoming almost as familiar with the human figure as an art student, we wish to raise the question once more — is woman more beautiful than man?*

**ABOVE: Strength or Grace — Which?**
*Good Morning*, August 1921
8.5″ x 7.5″

**RIGHT: Radio Photographs of Our Ancestors**
Undated
12.75″ x 17″

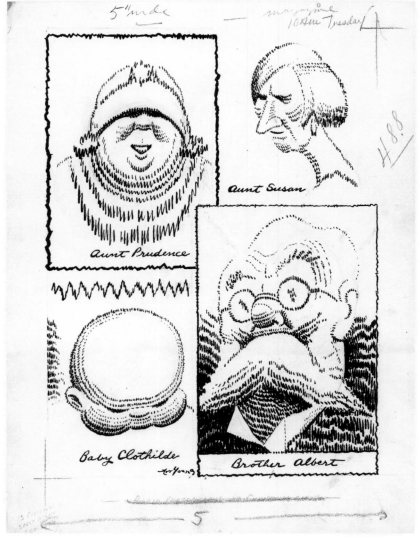

ABOVE: Jo Davidson (March 30, 1883–January 2, 1952) was an American sculptor. Although he specialized in realistic, intense portrait busts, Davidson did not require his subjects to formally pose for him; rather, he observed them and spoke with them. He worked primarily with clay, and the final products were typically cast in terra cotta, marble, or bronze.

LEFT: *The Masses* was founded in 1911 in New York City by the Dutch immigrant Piet Vlag. His goal was to educate the working people of America about art, literature, and socialist theory, but he and the magazine's first editor quit within 18 months. In 1912, Max Eastman became editor.

TOP LEFT: Jo Davidson, 1928

TOP RIGHT: **Jo Davidson by Art Young**
1928
6.75" x 10"

BELOW: **Piet Vlag by Art Young**
Undated
5.5" x 8.5"

ABOVE: **Rudolph Schildkraut in** *The God of*
*Vengeance* **by Art Young**
*The Nation,* 1923
7.75" x 10.75"

RIGHT: **Actor Rudolph Schildkraut**
1923

## Rudolph Schildkraut in *The God of Vengeance*

Rudolph Schildkraut (March 22, 1896–January 21, 1964) was an Austrian-American stage and film actor.

The Broadway run of *The God of Vengeance* lasted 133 performances, from December 20, 1922 to April 1923.

Because of its portrayal of prostitution and lesbian life, the play was shut down, and its producer and actors were prosecuted. The producer, Harry Weinberger (photo, p. 257), and Schildkraut were convicted of giving an immoral performance and fined. Although the play was closed on Broadway, it re-opened at the Prospect Theatre in the Bronx even before the trial reached a verdict.

**ABOVE: Thoughtless**
Undated
7.25" x 9.25"

**RIGHT: Doubtful Compliment**
*Jones (meeting his old friend the Professor for the first time in several years):* "Well — you look just the same."
Undated
10.5" x 15.5"

**ABOVE: Fathers We Have Met**
Marked "PUCK February 9, 1909" on reverse
24.5" x 15"

**RIGHT: At the Museum of Wonders**
Undated
19.75" x 15.5"

**Woman of 1887**
Undated
4.25" x 10"

**ABOVE:** The Stupidity Twins
If the time has come for the State to
tell the rich fool and the poor fool what
mustn't be done — all right.
For *Today Magazine*, date and publication
status unknown
14" x 10"

**RIGHT:** *Miss Puttybrain:* "O, those
ignorant-looking foreigners."
*Puck*, July 2, 1906
21" x 14.5"

**Edison**
(Thomas Alva Edison,
February 11, 1847–
October 18, 1931)
Undated
20" x 25.5"

ABOVE: **By The Way They
Hold Their Skirts — Ye Shall
Know Them**
For *Life*, date and publication
status unknown
14.75" x 5.75"

RIGHT: **The Old Jaw**
Undated
9.75" x 8"

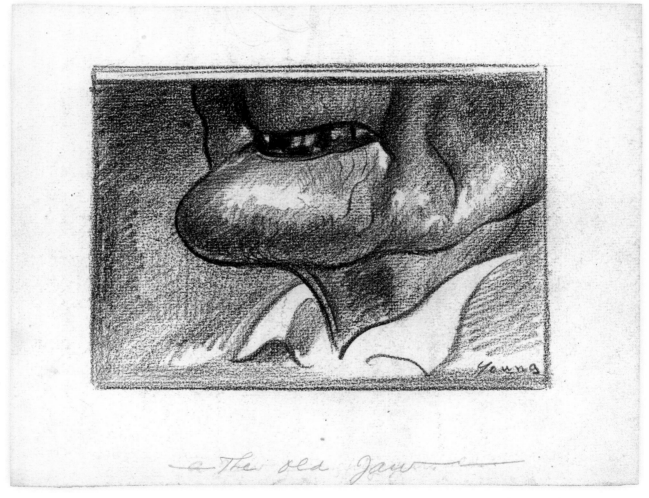

| TO LAUGH THAT WE MAY NOT WEEP

SHE CALLS HIM "A LITTLE SKEEZICKS".

NORTH AND SOUTH UNITED.

DISCUSSING FAMILY CUSTOMS.

KAMEALUT
THE BELLE OF THE
VILLAGE MAKING
HER TOILET.

TO
WHILE AWAY
THE TIME.

FATHER AND SON.

PRINCE POMIUK SINGS TA-RA-RA-BOOM WITH VARIATIONS.

**ABOVE: North and South United**
Sketched from life at the 1893 Columbian
World Exposition
22.75" x 15.5"

**RIGHT: The Athletic Club**
Undated
23.75" x 18.25"

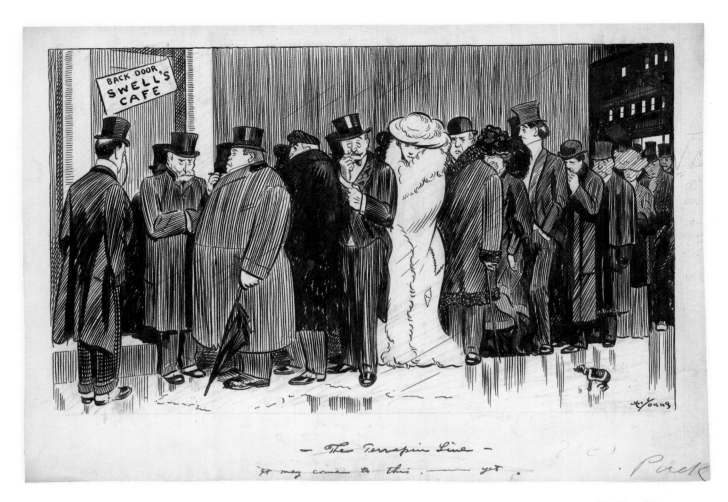

**ABOVE: The Terrapin Line**
It May Come to This Yet
*Puck*, January 20, 1908
24" x 17"

**RIGHT: Improving the Breed**
*Puck*, April 1, 1908
18.875" x 12.25"

ABOVE: **A Scene at the Station**
Undated
21″ x 10″

BELOW: **The Black Delegation**
Undated
9.75″ x 6.5″

**Our Discussion Club**
Undated
11.5" x 14.5"

*Gerald B. Smart (our best talker):* "Science will yet discover a synthetic process by which all power of thought will be reduced to a maximum quota per capita, equalizing, but at the same time raising the individual standard.

Once this is accomplished there will be such an impact of collective wisdom as to penetrate far out and beyond the vast void of the unknowable."

*Dr. Sneezinski (our radical member in the foreground says in rebuttal):* "The previous speaker is all right as far as he goes —"

**Two Old Codgers**
*Puck*, August 22, 1911
12.5" x 12.25"

**All is Vanity**

*Wife reading local paper:* "Ezra Whitcomb was seen yesterday driving his new rubber-tired carriage."
(Note the "Well, I guess" wriggle of that leg)
*Puck*, July 12, 1910
18" x 13.5"

ABOVE: **Five Members**
Undated
14.5″ x 10.5″

RIGHT: **Captains of Industry**
*The Masses*, January 1915
9.25″ x 7″

*Where Are The Captains of Yesteryear?*
But a short time ago the magazines were filled with pictures of captains of industry — can it be that captains of industry are becoming unpopular?

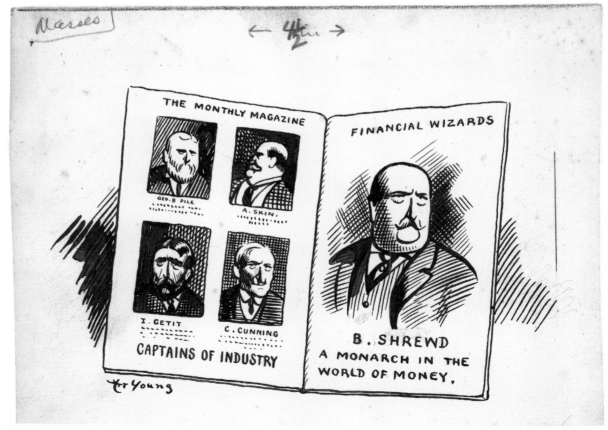

## CHOCTAW JIM — THE MEDICINE MAN

Every year the town was visited by a "Choctaw Jim" or a "Kickapoo Charley," who would sell us Indian Medicine, made the roots of wild cabbage, and liniment from the bark of the snake tree.

On a platform near the Court House, he would cure farmers of their rheumatism right before our eyes. Them were the happy days.

Could the best and Kindest of us who depart from the earth, have an opportunity of revisiting it, — I suppose he or she would have a pang of mortification at finding how soon our environs were consoled.

## HOMELY FRED BEASLEY

At the M.E. sociable Saturday night, Margy Hinkle took the first prize in the beauty contest, receiving sixty-two out of seventy-nine votes cast. Fred Beasley got the most votes for the homeliest man. But Fred said he had proof that the ballot box was stuffed, he having received six more votes than there were people at the party.

**TOP: Choctaw Jim**
Original art and accompanying caption
Undated
14.75" x 18.5"

**BOTTOM: Homely Fred**
Original art and accompanying caption
Undated
11" x 12.25"

## THE VILLAGE GROUCH

Our village grouch never talked very much. If a passer-by said: "How do ye do, Mr. Wickem?" he would sometimes turn his head to see who had interrupted his dark blue thoughts and say "How are ye?" But it was an effort. As one of the original early settlers he had come to the conclusion that: "Hangin's too good for some folks in this town."

## OUR ELOCUTIONIST

No social function in the Old Town was complete without a recitation from our elocutionist. Some thought she was at her best with *The Wreck of the Hesperus*. Others enjoyed *Curfew Must Not Ring Tonight* or a poem accompanied with a song refrain, *Polly, The Cows Are In The Corn. How Salvatore Won* was perhaps her most artistic triumph. She was a bit heavy to impersonate a jockey; but we overlooked that, and could only feel her emotional intensity as she cracked an imaginary whip and won the race gasping for breath. Fred Smith, who worked in the livery stable, said "She done well."

TOP: **The Village Grouch**
Original art and accompanying caption
Undated
14"x 18.5"

BOTTOM: **Our Elocutionist**
Original art and accompanying caption
Undated
14"x 15.75"

## THE EDITOR OF THE GAZETTE

The Editor of the Gazette, "A Journal of Civilization," didn't have to bother much about moulding political opinion. Except for Doc Wright, the veterinary surgeon, and one or two others, our town was habitually Republican. As for news: if Ernie Blunt "was seen out riding with his best girl" or "Stella Bentley went to Elm Grove to visit her aunt," that was the kind of news that appealed to the folks of the old town. And we liked the genial Editor's style when he wrote of the town something like this: "Cradled in the spacious valley of Thunder River, Pikeville is destined to a future unparalleled in the westward of civilization toward a climatic and commercial ideal."

## THE FORTUNE TELLER

In the old stone house out near the edge of the village lived Mrs. Tibbetts. She was our fortune teller. It was fun for the girls to be warned that they must beware of a "dark complected man," and for the boys to be told that they were going on a long journey. Also that there was a "great surprise coming to you." An agreeable prediction, because the surprise element in everyday life in the Old Home Town was not equal to the demand.

TOP: **Editor of the Gazette**
Original art and accompanying caption
Undated
14" x 15.5"

BOTTOM: **The Fortune Teller**
Original art and accompanying caption
Undated
14" x 16"

## OUR OLDEST INHABITANT

He had fought the Indians — and had been in the Mexican and Civil Wars. Some folks said he had been a drummer boy in the War of 1812, but that was laying it on pretty thick. Anyway, he built the first log-cabin in our county, struggled with the "unyielding soil," wolves, panthers, grasshoppers, crows, gophers, chinch bugs, frosts, floods, installment agents, mortgages, a large family, and had scars enough to prove anything. What's more, at ninety-four, he could dance the Virginia Reel "with the best on 'em."

## THE VILLAGE DRUNKARD

'Us boys' would gang up on the village drunkard and follow him with shrill whistlings and teasing. Then — our fun was running away in breathless fear that he might not be so uncertain on his legs as he appeared and would run us down.

This was sport that made our parents scold us for having fun with the unfortunate man who couldn't or just wouldn't stop the liquor habit.

TOP: **Our Oldest Inhabitant**
Original art and accompanying caption
Undated
13.25" x 14.5"

BOTTOM: **The Village Drunk**
Original art and accompanying caption
Undated
12.75" x 15"

## How to cure World-Unrest

### No. 1

*Doctor O. U. Woosy*

Columbus, Ohio. — Doctor O. U. Woosy, D.D.B.O.D.F., professor of entomology in the Seidlitz College of Pharmacy of this city, delivered a scholarly discourse yesterday before the Cosmos Club, on "the way to combat the pernicious propaganda of unrest."

The Doctor would sprinkle all books that advocate organizations of labor, strikes for higher wages, or any theory of government not exactly like that of the United States, with a snuff that he has patented, war-ranted to prevent reading of the diabolical literature.

## How to cure World-Unrest

### No. 2

*The Reverend A. Jawbunk.*

Denver, Colo.—The Reverend A. Jawbunk, a local minister of prominence, preached an eloquent sermon yesterday on "Social Unrest, the Peril of the Twentieth Century."

Mr. Jawbunk says, "Parlor-socialists should be imprisoned for life and communists who advocate the rule of labor should be tarred and feathered daily until cured." .Mr. Jawbunk announced that his sermon next week would answer his critics— "Was Jesus really poor and opposed to aristocracy?" The Reverend Jawbunk has proof that Jesus was an aristocrat and wanted the poor to stay where they belong.

## How to cure World-Unrest

### No. 3

*John B. Grab.*

Salt Lake City, Utah.—John B. Grab, a well-known financier of this city, has given out an interview on labor problems and the cure for wide-spread discontent.

Mr. Grab advocates "labor at homes" one day in the week, when the workers can visit the homes of "the best people" and look at the carpets, chairs, chandeliers, wood-work and all the other beautiful things which they have produced.

## How to cure World-Unrest

### No. 4

*Karl Muddlechump.*

Helsingfors, Finland.—Karl Muddlechump, head of the Foreign News Service of this city, says that the way to cure the Bolshevistic unrest the world over is, to spread the news at least every six weeks that the Russian Soviet Government has fallen. He says, "It keeps the monarchists and capitalists of the world hopeful, and the Russian people may believe it themselves if the newspapers keep diligently at it."

## How to cure World-Unrest

### No. 5

*Henry Sniff Hound.*

Portland, Ore.—Henry Snniff Hound, a leading corporation lawyer of the north-west, says that he has made a thorough study of the movements in Europe against the existing governments. He says without hesitation that "they are all pernicious and unsound in principle." Mr. Hound says further that "the intellectual, moral, and material force of the world should be exerted against the spreading of such communist doctrines as the abolition of the "noble, dignified profession of law." "None of us will feel at ease if such doctrines prevail," said the distinguished lawyer.

## How to cure World-Unrest

### No. 6

*Mrs. Price Bulge.*

Rochester, N. Y.—Mrs. Price Bulge, a wealthy society woman of this city, has announced that she intends to devote much of her time and money to further the movement against the radical teachings that cause so much world unrest.
To a reporter she said: "Communism and all the other radical "isms" will destroy the family." Mrs. Bulge has been divorced four times.

How to Cure World-Unrest
12 postcards, each 4.5"x 5.5" to 5.5"x 5.25"
Undated

## How to cure World-Unrest

### No. 7

*Giovanni Pileuppi.*

San Francisco, Cal.—In a public statement Giovanni Pileuppi, a billionaire broker of this city, says he favors absolute restriction of all immigration from Europe, as the first step toward quieting the unrest that has become such a menace to profitable business. Mr. Pileuppi came to this country thirty years ago and claims that we have been getting nothing but the scum of Europe since his arrival.

## How to cure World-Unrest

### No. 8

*Clarence Lily Pinkputty*

Philadelphia, Pa.—Clarence Lily Pinkputty dilettante, perfume expert, and social light son of George Pinkputty, the billionaire, writes a comprehensive and learned essay on "The Errors of Radical Thought" for this month's Vanity Bag Magazine.

He says "it would be unspeakable cruelty to deprive the best people of the leisure to indulge that discriminating taste and subtle perceptibility that is the exclusive birthright of those who are born in the soul-zone of refinement." He defies the leading radical thinkers to answer his arguments, and asserts that "the only cure for unrest is to teach the common people to rear their children in a highly perfumed atmosphere of luxury and refinement."

## How to cure World-Unrest

### No. 9

*Henry B. Allmine.*

St. Louis, Mo.—Henry B. Allmine, leading Capitalist of this city, says, "The cure for discontent is hunger." Mr. Allmine has closed down his extensive manufacturing plant, throwing out of employment two thousand men and women. He says that when his workers come pleading for their old jobs at reduced wages—"they will bring with them the spirit of love and gratitude and will be cured of their discontent."

## How to cure World-Unrest

### No. 10

*Darius B. Dewlap.*

New Haven, Conn.—Darius B. Dewlap, Professor of Physics in Pale University, says the spirit of unrest is a disease of the glands. If a man complains of the so-called struggle for food, shelter, and clothing, and will not face realities cheerfully—his alogophlectic gland should be taken out and varnished.

## How to cure World-Unrest

### No. 11

*Marcus Cohngilt.*

New York.—In an interview with Marcus Cohngilt, motion picture magnate, this authority on public welfare says that social unrest can be cured by the presentation of wholesome movies. Mr. Cohngilt's masterpiece is "Veda the Vamp" in five parts, a million dollar revel with a thrill in every foot of film. The moral of which is "Seek not riches."

Mr. Congilt says he hopes to make two million dollars out of this play, and is satisfied that it will influence the masses to be content with their humble savings.

## How to cure World-Unrest

### No. 12

*Musha Sagbrain.*

Chicago, Ill.—Professor Musha Sagbrain, head of the scientific laboratories of the Wiggle-Gum factory, says there is no theory of government that will cure the existing causes of unrest. Prof. Sagbrain has made a special study of the principles of Socialism. He had them printed on litmus paper and after a chemical test they dissolved.

The Professor is convinced that "faith in scientific conclusions" alone points the way to a cure for world unrest.

# APPROACHING YOUNG'S TREESCAPES

**JUSTIN GREEN**

## 15

These remarkable images, devoid of the overt political content that drove much of Young's work, are still expressive of our human nature, which is the root cause of those social struggles and aspirations. In this series, begun in 1922 and published in 1927, he makes these intangible forces explicit.

Though most *Saturday Evening Post* readers (a few of the drawings also appeared in *Life* and *Collier's*) were not card-carrying members of the socially conscious sector that had followed the artist in his firebrand Socialist days, they were certainly aware he was a controversial figure. His sensational trials for violating the Espionage Act (by his virulent anti-war cartoons) had only ended a few years earlier. These middle-of-the-road publications doubtless had an editorial staff that would reject any controversial political idea before its ink was dry.

Knowing this, Young looked elsewhere for inspiration. Lucky for us, one night he saw trees across the Hudson River that strongly resembled loping camels. And so began the series of guided hallucinations that materialized into lasting art. Forbidden by the powers that be to provoke the moral sensibilities of his gentle readers — not quite "the teeming masses" that were his kindred spirits — he entered their unsuspecting minds through the side door of their hearts.

The practice of accidental vision as the basis for creating imagery is a phenomenon that has persisted through the centuries. Da Vinci mentions in his notebooks that he was able to create landscapes by squinting at the cracks of a garden wall. Even while Young produced his tree series, the surrealist Max Ernst was busy working on his "frottage" (rubbings) that turned texture into figurative art with a few deft lines.

It is a human trait to extract imagery from nature. Children and drunks can spot dragons in clouds. It is only the gifted human hand that can turn these ethereal visions into tangible imagery through the manipulation of the picture plane. Young, a masterful draftsman then at the zenith of his career, was able to stage natural and architectural environments that became the foundation of the drama for each vignette.

Illustration for the index page of *Trees at Night*
1927
8" x 5.75"

Brilliant use of composition, lighting, and emphasis on detail are consistently employed. Rare is the cartoonist with a painter's eye, but Young was that hybrid bird. The original function of the cartoon was to serve as the preliminary outline on canvas for embellishment by paint. His subtle and bold strokes in wash, litho crayon, charcoal, and chalk are more often the tools of a painter rather than the traditional pen and ink favored by most cartoonists.

He was, in fact, personal friends with the circle of New York artists known as the "Ashcan School," in which all of the above mediums were commonly used. In these whimsical trees, the great artist seems less constricted by the direct cartooning process, which demands a simple graven black line flowing into the channels of underlying pencil work. With the trees, he is less a yeoman craftsman and more a purely expressive artist.

His gift for representing the human form in all its expressiveness, including an uncanny knack for caricature, shapes the anthropomorphic traits of the trees. Whether in supplication, despair, or wild abandon, they are closer to theater than landscape. Keenly aware of visual clarity and focus, he avoids those ambiguous details that are so abundant in nature.

The *Trees at Night* seem to be caught in a netherworld between what is first perceived and then trapped. General readers will be unaware of the freedom of Young's execution in these little gems. Yet because of today's new digital standards, any artist working within the wide parameters of realism will spot countless imperfections and glitches that they seldom permit themselves. Somewhere along the transition from hand craftsmanship to Photoshop, we have lost a sense of the unabashed grappling with an image arising and also

Penalty of Prominence
1927
12" x 16"

the courage to show our tracks, too. Yet any image shown at high resolution reveals that the idea of perfection is a joke.

Each artist must accept his or her own tolerance, or relative crudeness, as their unique stylistic signature. Many spend a lifetime trying to achieve the fluidity and assurance that is in ample evidence here and in countless other great cartoons and illustrations Young produced while still a young man. Yet his mastery is never ostentatious, because its function is to serve each panel's content.

This series is as close to immortality as popular art can achieve. Yet they were never presented as having the gravitas and pretension of fine art. You may be seeing them for the first time in this "art book," but imagine them printed on much flimsier paper with ample ads nearby. Though some elements may be evocative of lapsed eras, Young's botanical specimens still sway.

Beyond showing many facets of human existence, they also have a poignancy that he never intended: as our planet literally faces extinction, we are in collusion with all living things against the very forces of global dominance that were just getting started back in the Roaring '20s.

As much as I am enthralled and intrigued by his trees, I still see the forest: I feel solidarity with Young the social observer. His courage, wit, and artistry are ideals that would serve any cartoonist who is "yet quick." We may lack the print venues so common just yesterday, but we have plenty of other showcases to provoke and surprise the populace.

**ABOVE:** Cathedral
1927
10.5" x 14.5"

**RIGHT:** Orator
1927
7" x 10"

ABOVE: Like Birds in Their Flight
1927
9.5" x 13"

RIGHT: Dead Love
1927
10.5" x 14.5"

ABOVE: **Miss Hawthorne Entertains a Group
of Scrub Oaks and Old Sycamores**
1927
8" x 10.5"
Collection of Cameron Jamie

RIGHT: **Patriarch**
*The Saturday Evening Post*, November 8, 1924
9.5" x 11.5"
Collection of Cameron Jamie

ABOVE: Good Bye Summer
1927
8.5" x 11"

RIGHT: They Were Lonesome
1927
8.5" x 10.5"

**ABOVE:** Spring
1927
8.25" x 11.25"

**RIGHT:** Defeat
1927
9" x 12"

**ABOVE:** Uprooted
1927
9" x 9.75"

**RIGHT:** Battle Prehistoric
1927
10.5" x 13"

**ABOVE:** An Old Braggart
10.75" x 14"

**RIGHT:** Naked Truth
1927
10" x 13"

Within the image: ORCHARD REVEL — From Trees at Night

**Orchard Revel**
*The Saturday Evening Post*, June 28, 1924
12" x 15"

**ABOVE:** Stubborn Cypress
1927
8.75" x 11.5"

**RIGHT:** Mother Earth
1927
8.75" x 12.375"

**ABOVE:** A Winter Palace
1927
8.5" x 11"

**RIGHT:** Panic
1927
9.25" x 12"

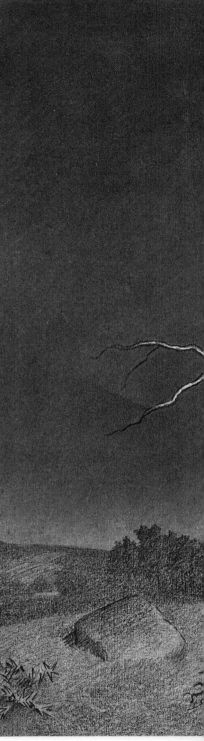

LEFT: **Why?**
1927
16″ x 24″

RIGHT: **Hope**
*Life,* May 6, 1915
24″ x 16″

TO LAUGH THAT WE MAY NOT WEEP

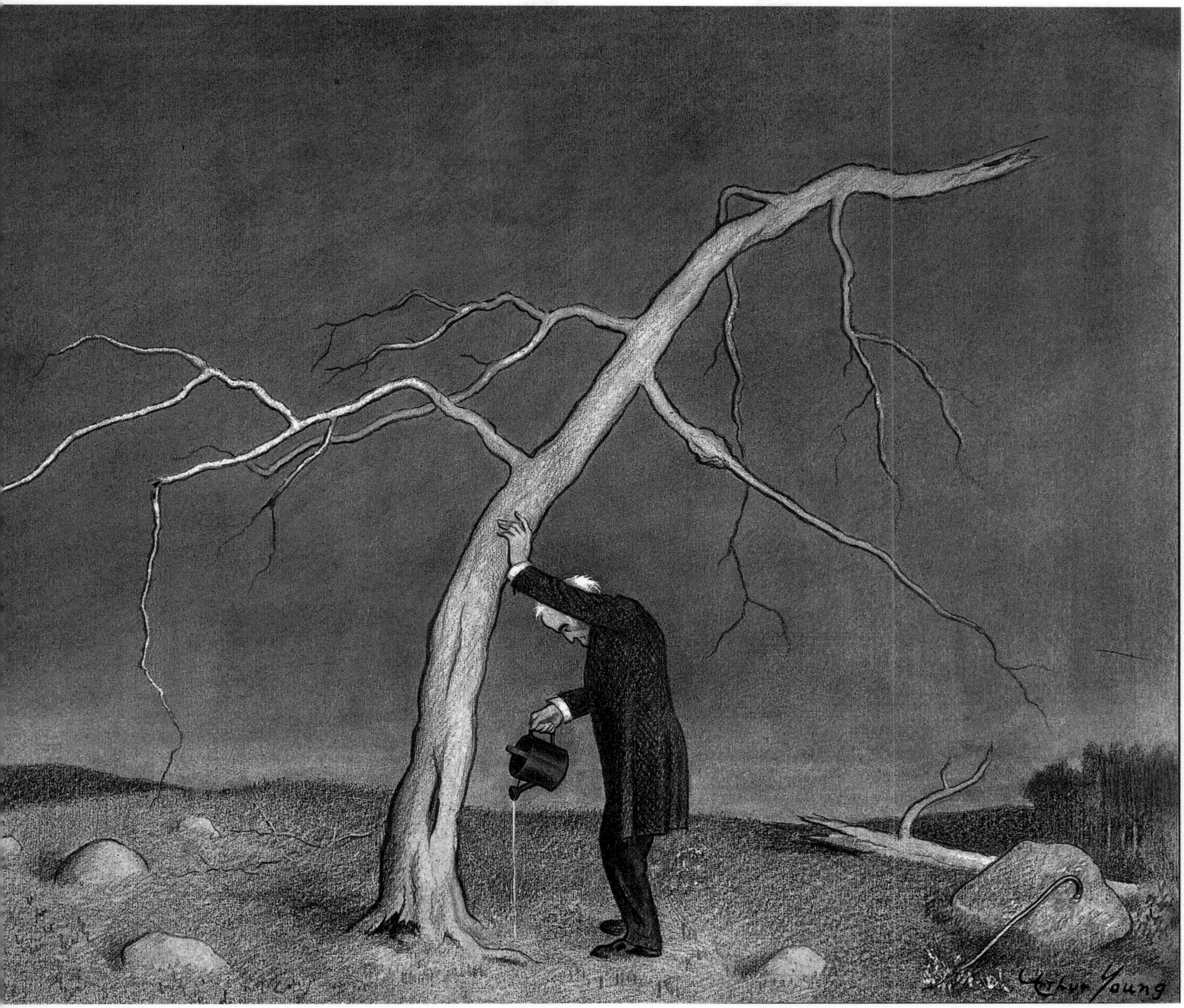
Arthur Young

| TO LAUGH THAT WE MAY NOT WEEP

*October 6:* On my table lie two letters just received from strangers who write me to say that they like my drawings "Trees at Night," which are published from time to time in the *Saturday Evening Post.* I have received a great many such letters. Some of the writers enclose suggestions and photographs for other drawings on the subject, some wrote poems about them, others were anxious to know if they would be published in book form.

In common with most people of artistic perception, I like trees. While looking out of my window toward the wooded hills one summer night, a caravan of camels seemed to be humping along the sky. They were trees of course but enough like camels to key my imagination up to discover other pictures in the formation of foliage. The rest of the summer nights I enjoyed hunting for tree pictures against the light of the sky or thrown into relief by the glare of automobiles, and drawing them next day. It seemed to me that this silhouette handling of trees at night had never before been done by any artist. I felt that I had discovered something.

After the caravan, I saw "a woman and a fan" and other subjects followed. Any night I could walk or ride along the road and see interesting silhouettes made by tree forms, many of them so clearly defined as to need no improvement on my part. But aside from the appearance of a tree by day or night, is it not kin of the human family with its roots in the earth and its arms stretching toward the sky as if to seek and to know the great mystery?

*From* ART YOUNG'S DIARY

OPPOSITE: **Peace**
1927
14.25″ x 20.5″

ABOVE: *Trees at Night*, dustjacket, 1927

RIGHT: **The Devil's Orchestra**
1927
12″ x 15″

# Art Young's Infernos

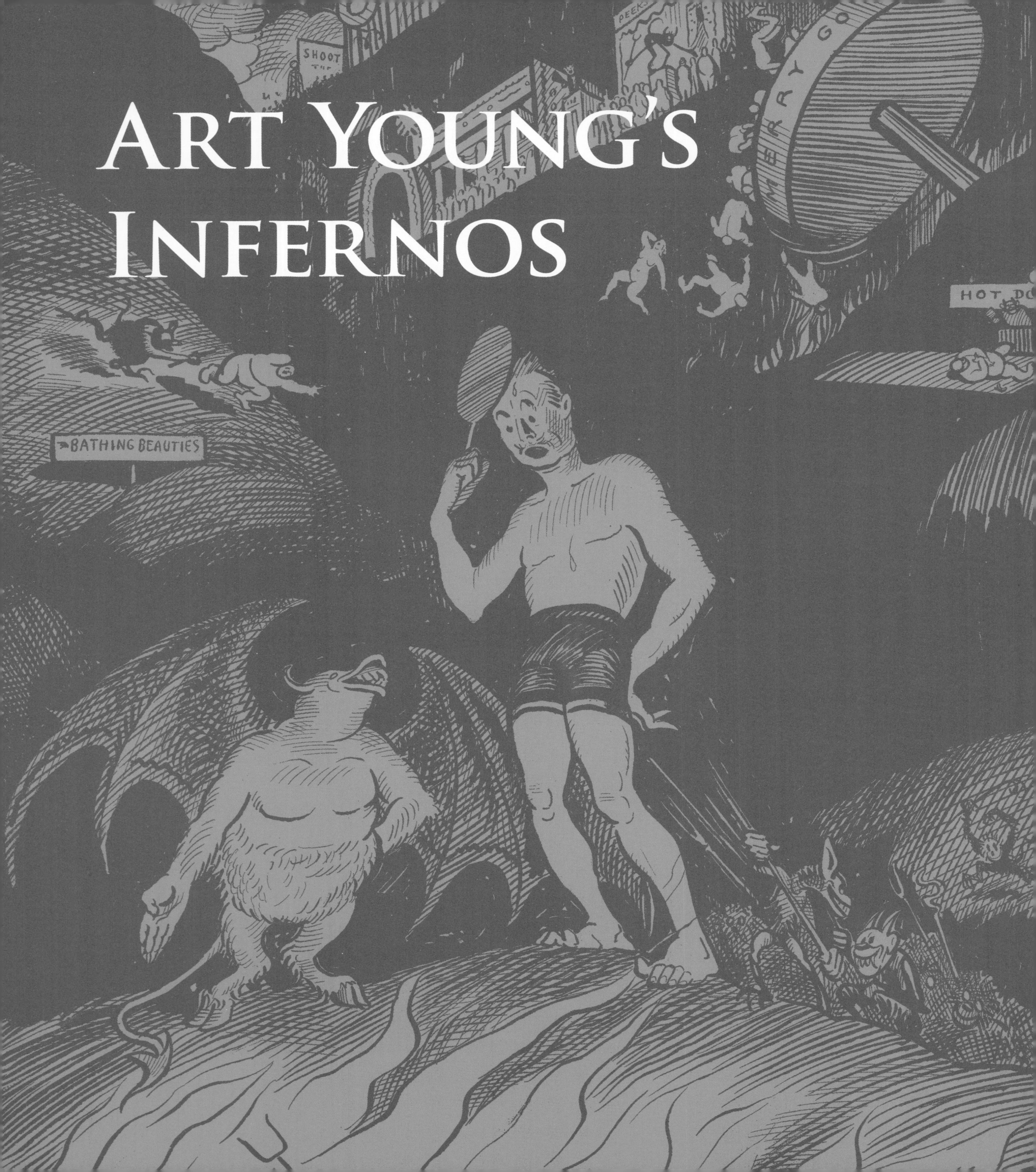
SHOOT
PEEKS
MERRY GO
HOT DO
BATHING BEAUTIES

GLENN BRAY

# 16

**"The author has gone to Hell three times, twice in-cognito" reads the caption to one of the introductory drawings in *Art Young's Inferno* (1934). That single image illustrates the history of Young's three separate publications regarding these "adventures."**

*Hell Up to Date* (1892), *Through Hell With Hiprah Hunt* (1901), and *Art Young's Inferno* (1934) encompass half of the author's foray into illustrated, standalone books.

What caused this hellish obsession with the Darker Region? Around 1882, when he was 16, Young's father gave him a copy of an illustrated edition of *Dante's Inferno* by Gustave Doré (1832–1883). The one pictured here is possibly the same edition he first saw.

At age 26, Art Young got his first full book published; it was one he had completely written and illustrated by himself. He uses the imaginary character of R. Palasco Drant (who looks like a cartoon version of Art Young at that age) as a stand-in for Dante. At age 35, Young updated the original book with a new traveler, Hiprah Hunt (who bears no resemblance to Young's physical appearance). At age 68, Young returned to the Netherworld, this time undisguised, for the last time.

The differences among the three journeys are easy to spot. In 1892's *Hell Up to Date*, his targets of ridicule are mostly human foibles — it's that guy who climbs up the ladder of prosperity and forgets his friends. He also does a take on Doré's version of Judge Minos, the judge of the dead in the Underworld of Greek mythology. Some of the earliest drawings are stiffly overworked and more reminiscent of A.B. Frost crossed with Charles Dana Gibson from the late 1800s. The mature work that would thrust Young into the class of an Honoré Daumier was still ahead.

The 1901 publication of *Through Hell With Hiprah Hunt* apparently sold many thousands of copies in different editions. Here, Young flexes his now more mature illustrating muscles and provides the reader with large-scale drawings of devil crowds, banquets, parades, and Hellish landscapes.

LEFT: Cover to c. 1882 edition of *Inferno* by Dante Alighieri (c. 1265–September 13/14, 1321) illustrated by Gustave Doré (January 6, 1832–January 23, 1883)

OPPOSITE: **The Author Has Gone to Hell Three Times, Twice Incognito**
*Art Young's Inferno*, 1934
11"x 13.5"

Although his third Hell book wasn't published for another 33 years, during that time Young was constantly drawing Hell images for several publications — *Life* and *The Saturday Evening Post* among them. It's difficult to say at this point in time just how many uncollected Hell drawings Young produced — published or unpublished. His archives saved well over 100 images that have never been collected into book form. Jonathan Barli of Rosebud Archives and I are currently working on a book collating these pieces, along with more samples from the three published books, which are harder and harder to locate as time passes.

Many agree that 1934's *Art Young's Inferno* is the cartoonist's best effort. Drawn while well into his senior years, the line work is looser, livelier, and more comical, and the wit is more focused on his lifelong targets: capitalism and the failings of the system. Young never preaches; he makes his point with humor. And he is still, after all these years, giving a nod to Gustave Doré in redrawing some of the Canto scenes (see "Devil and Art Young" vs. "Devil and Dante").

The illustration of "Graft" is one of the more chilling images from the book: little piggies squealing at the cloven feet of a bulbous Satan and gobbling up the favors he feeds them. The drawing is clear and understated through the economical joy of his pen.

To follow the work of Art Young from the 1890s into the 1930s and beyond is to witness the full scope of a master of the pen, ever evolving into his own, honing his craft of humor and art — a genius of Light and Dark.

1892

1933

1901

R. PALASCO DRANT

HIPRAH HUNT

**ABOVE: Everybody Knows This Fellow — He Climbed Up in the World and Forgot His Friends**
*Hell Up To Date,* 1892
12.5" x 17"

**RIGHT: The Monopolists**
*Hell Up To Date,* 1892
19" x 14.5"

ABOVE: Looney Island
*Art Young's Inferno*, 1934
13" x 17.5"

RIGHT: Broadcasting
(Station WINCE)
*Art Young's Inferno*, 1934
14.5" x 19"

ABOVE: **Falling Souls**
As reproduced in *Cosmopolitan*, July 1900

**Satan Receives a Delegation**
*Art Young's Inferno,* 1934
14.5" x 19"

**ABOVE: Hell Hole**
Publication unknown
14.5˝ x 14˝

**RIGHT: Graft**
*Art Young's Inferno*, 1934
9.25˝ x 14˝

ABOVE: **The Devil And Art Young**
*Art Young's Inferno*, 1934
13.5" x 10"

RIGHT: **Dante and the Devil**
By Gustave Doré
As published in the c. 1882 edition of *Inferno*

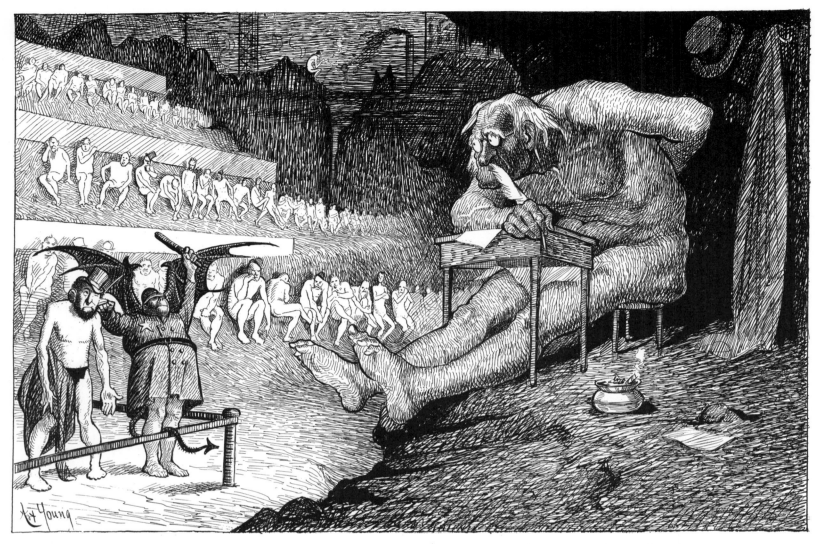

ABOVE: **The Court of Judge Minos Where He Has Sat for Centuries Judging Malefactors**
Also published as "Judge Minos' Court Room"
*Hell Up To Date*, 1892
15.5" x 11.5"

BELOW: Doré's version as published in the c. 1882 edition of *Inferno*

**ABOVE: Hiprah Hunt Reviews the Annual Parade of Sinners**
*Through Hell With Hiprah Hunt*, 1901
21.5" x 15"

**RIGHT: The Man Who Was Too Suspicious**
*Hell Up To Date*, 1892
13.25" x 9.5"

**ABOVE:** A Farewell Banquet in Honor of
Hiprah Hunt
*Through Hell With Hiprah Hunt,* 1901
19.5" x 13"

**RIGHT:** Hiprah Hunt Speaks With Pig-Devil
*Through Hell With Hiprah Hunt,* 1901
8" x 12"

**ABOVE:** Hiprah Hunt Meets the Devil
*Through Hell With Hiprah Hunt*, 1901
20" x 14.25"

**RIGHT:** Hiprah Hunt Running From Demon
*Through Hell With Hiprah Hunt*, 1901
8" x 12.5"

# MISCELLANEOUS POLITICAL CARTOONS

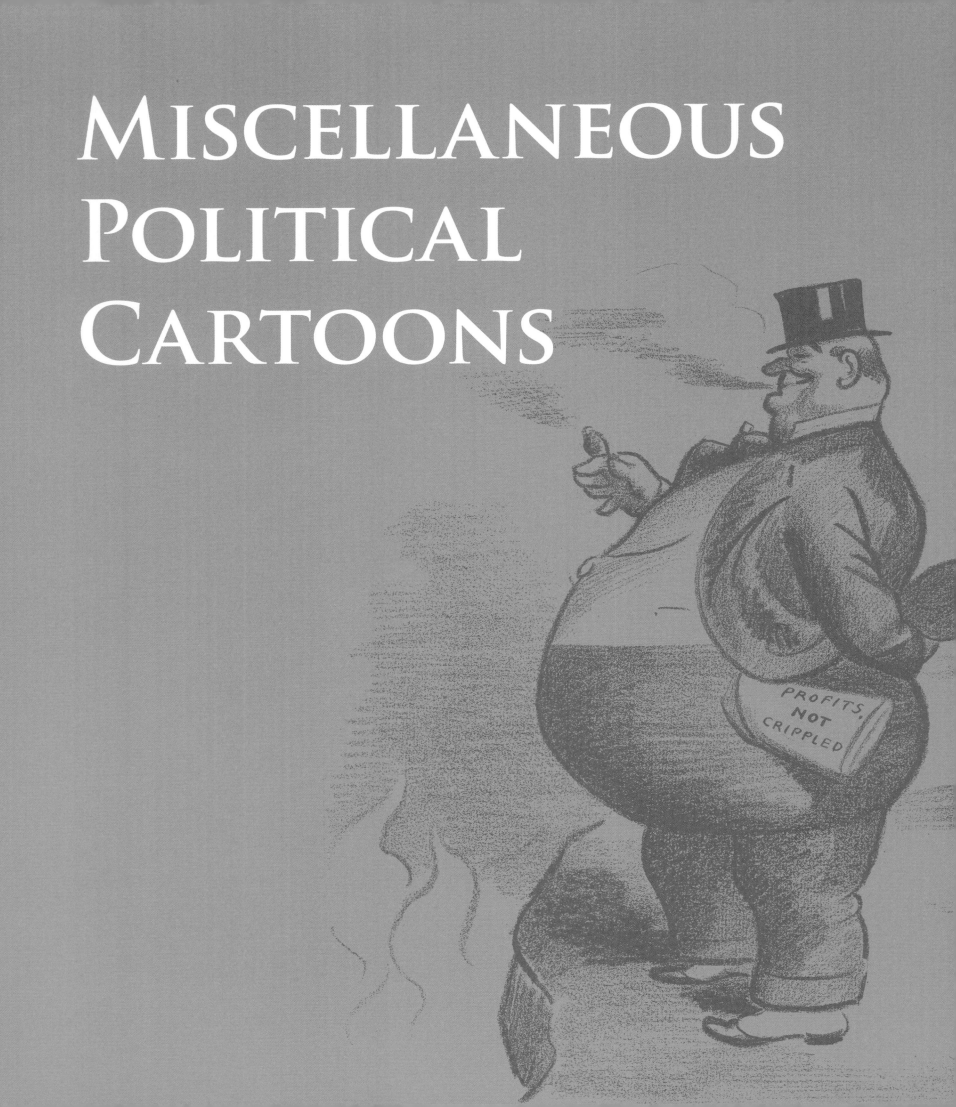

The Monster's Instinct —
Favor a Few of the Hated
Ones and Use Them as
Decoys
Undated
11.5" x 14.5"

## 17

**TWELVE THOUSAND YOUNG MEN KILLED**

**FOUR YARDS OF DIRT GAINED**

**ABOVE:** Four Yards of Dirt Gained —
Twelve Thousand Young Men Killed
For *The Dawn*, date and publication
status unknown
11" x 8"

**RIGHT:** Reviewing Their Troops
Undated
11" x 8.5"

**ABOVE: Made in America**
How the bosom of the American soldier must swell with
pride when he finds that the bayonet of the enemy was
"Made in America"!
Undated
11" x 7.25"

**RIGHT: To the Last Man**
*The New Masses,* November 1926
11.75" x 15"

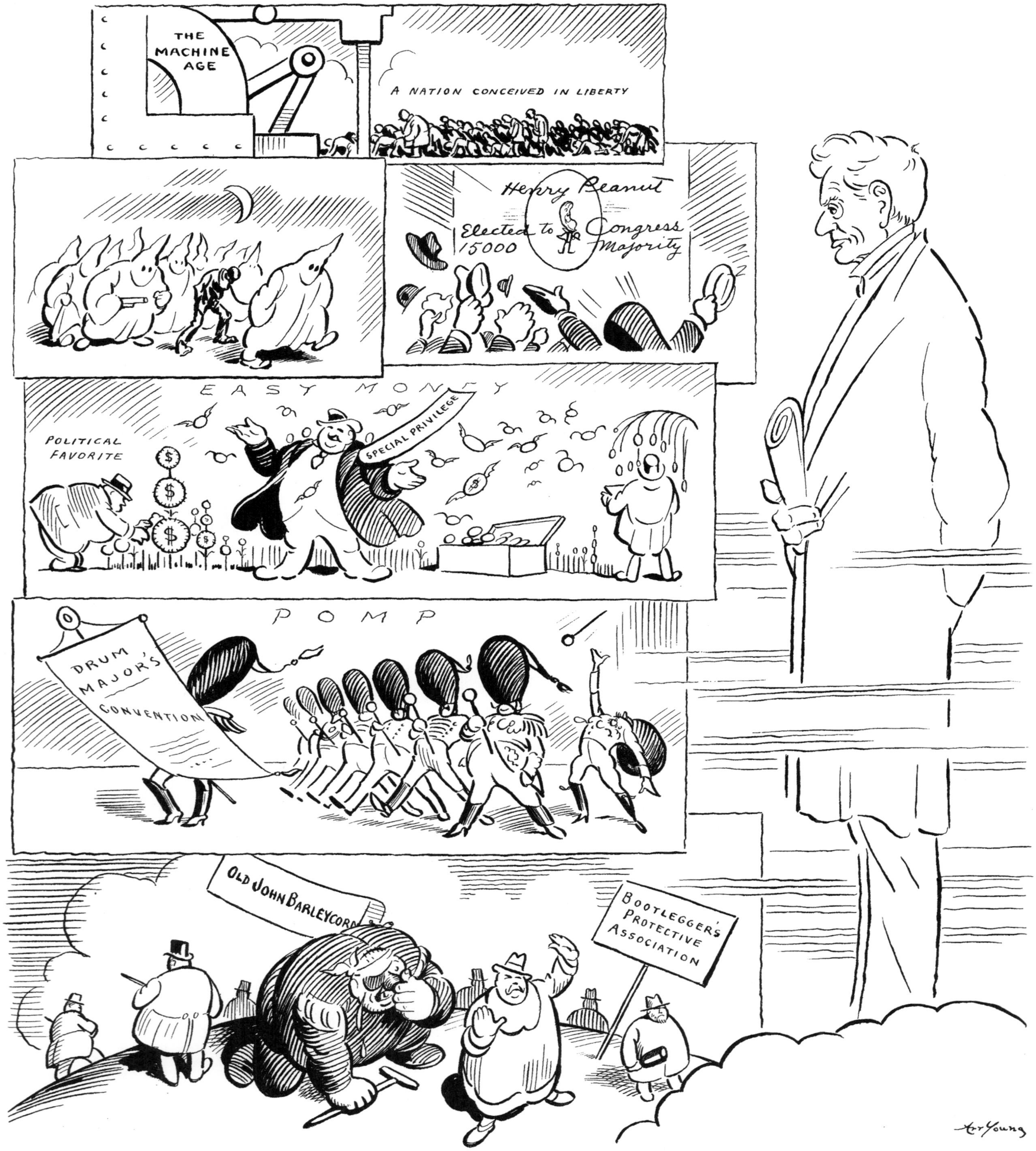
THE MACHINE AGE
A NATION CONCEIVED IN LIBERTY
Henry Peanut
Elected to Congress
15000 Majority
EASY MONEY
POLITICAL FAVORITE
SPECIAL PRIVILEGE
POMP
DRUM MAJOR'S CONVENTION
OLD JOHN BARLEYCORN
BOOTLEGGER'S PROTECTIVE ASSOCIATION
Art Young

Appease! — To quiet, pacify, conciliate — Webster

Published, New Masses.

OPPOSITE: **A Nation Conceived in Liberty ~ Abraham Lincoln**
For *Life*, date and publication status unknown
15.75" x 18.25"

ABOVE: **Appease: — To Quiet, Pacify, Conciliate — Webster**
*New Masses,* May 5, 1942
11.5" x 7.5"

RIGHT: **The Maniac's Last Spasm**
Undated
10.75" x 12.5"

ABOVE: *Uncle Sam:* "Anyway, I'm getting advice enough!"
Undated
14" x 11.75"

RIGHT: **The Outlook for 1921**
*The Liberator*, December 1920
22" x 12"

| TO LAUGH THAT WE MAY NOT WEEP

**ABOVE: The Harvest**
Anniversary of the World War, August 3
For *The Nation*, publication status unknown
19" x 9"

**RIGHT:** *Editor:* "Keep this old file on atrocities alive. We'll need them as soon as the next war begins."
Undated
10.5" x 8.75"

| TO LAUGH THAT WE MAY NOT WEEP

OPPOSITE: The Land of the Free
Undated
8.75" x 10.5"

ABOVE: A Trinity That Is Pretty Sure To Beat Justice
Undated
15.5" x 15.5"

RIGHT: Lapping Up the Cream as Usual
1943
10.25" x 13.25"

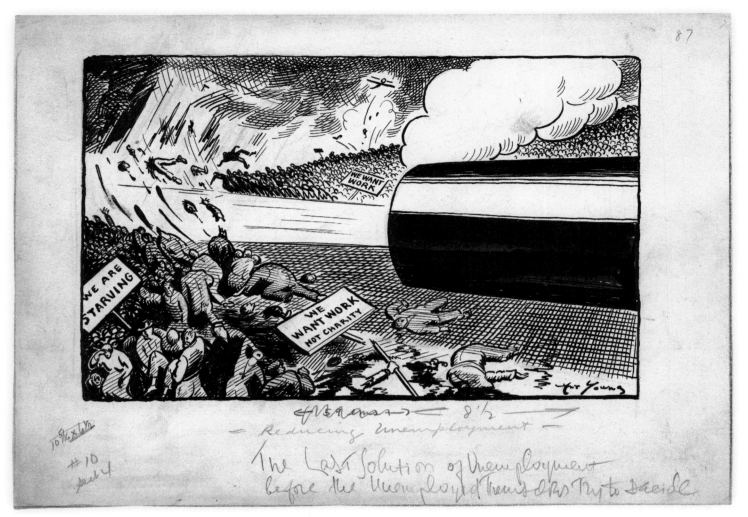

**ABOVE:** Reducing Unemployment
Undated
13.25" x 9.5"

**RIGHT:** Madam Capitalism
*The Masses,* Valentine number, February 1935
13.5" x 14"

*The rose is red, the violet blue*
*Madam Capitalism — I love you*
*I love your form, I love your face*
*and your old heart's in the right place*

**OPPOSITE:** The Road Show Entering Houston
*This 1928 Campaign In Cartoons* folio
1928
14.75" x 19.75"

**OPPOSITE:** It was a motley crew that marched on the Democratic convention in Houston.

Everybody anticipated a riot, but the eight lean years suffered by the Democratic politicians under G.O.P. rule led them to rally to Smith who, with the aid of Big Business, held out hopes of victory.

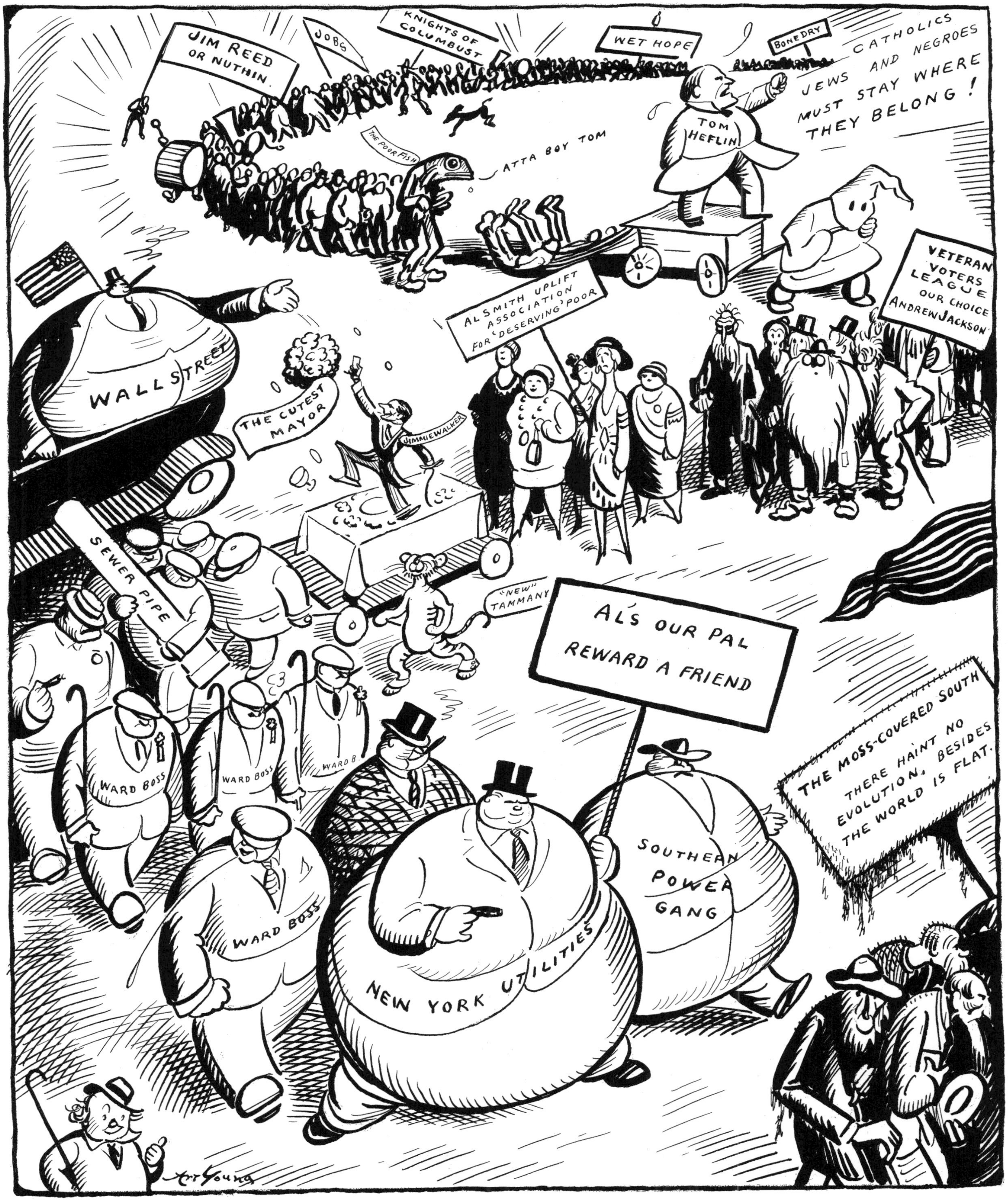
JIM REED OR NUTHIN.
JOBS
KNIGHTS OF COLUMBUST
WET HOPE
BONE DRY
CATHOLICS JEWS AND NEGROES MUST STAY WHERE THEY BELONG!
TOM HEFLIN
THE POOR FISH
ATTA BOY TOM
WALL STREET
AL SMITH UPLIFT ASSOCIATION FOR 'DESERVING' POOR
VETERAN VOTERS LEAGUE OUR CHOICE ANDREW JACKSON
THE CUTEST MAYOR
JIMMIE WALKER
SEWER PIPE
"NEW" TAMMANY
AL'S OUR PAL REWARD A FRIEND
THE MOSS-COVERED SOUTH THERE HAINT NO EVOLUTION, BESIDES THE WORLD IS FLAT.
WARD BOSS
WARD BOSS
WARD B
WARD BOSS
SOUTHERN POWER GANG
NEW YORK UTILITIES
Art Young

The United States of America — The Greatest Show on Earth
Undated
37" x 21.5"

# GREATEST SHOW ON EARTH

**YMNASTIC WRITERS**
MBLING OVER THEMSELVES
ALL SIDES OF A QUESTION

OPLE WHO GO 'ROUND AND
ND' BUT NEVER GET ANYWHERE

DVERTISERS
ST

FLIP FLOP POLITICIANS

BUNCOMBE

WILD LEAP
FROM FASHION
TO FASHION

CAPITALISM

AFRAID TO CALL THEIR SOULS THEIR OWN

THE WORLD RENOWNED MRS. GRUNDY
AND HER JUMPING MONKEYS.

RT VULTURE AND PART MAN

HIGHEST BUILDINGS IN THE WORLD

MOST DARING FEAT ON RECORD
CROSSING BROADWAY

COVERS
3,625,574
SQUARE MILES

LAND OF
THE BIG
CIRCUS

ALL
NATIONALITIES
UNDER
ONE FLAG.

GORGEOUS
GARGANTUAN
GRAFTERS.

SOCIETY QUEENS
SANCTIMONIOUS
SYCOPHANTS
CONFUSION!
DELUSION!

ADMISSION
FREE

ABOVE: **After One War — They Start Raising Babies for the Next**
Undated
24" x 11.5"

RIGHT: **Big and Little Beggars**
Undated
23.25" x 14.5"

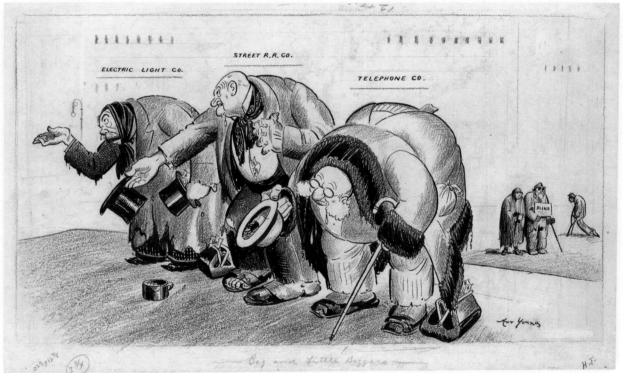

RIGHT: **Millions For Defense**
*The Masses,* January 1916
21.5" x 22.5"

BELOW: **The Next War**
Undated
27.5" x 11"

**ABOVE: Cheer Up Uncle, Otherwise You're All Right**
*Life*
Undated
28.5" x 17.25"

**RIGHT: The Mouth of War** (in Hebrew)
*Giant:* Mars (god of war)
*On teeth:* "New World Holocaust"
*Soldier:* France
*Woman:* Emaciated Europe
Intended for *The Big Stick*, a Yiddish newspaper
Undated
15.75" x 11.5"

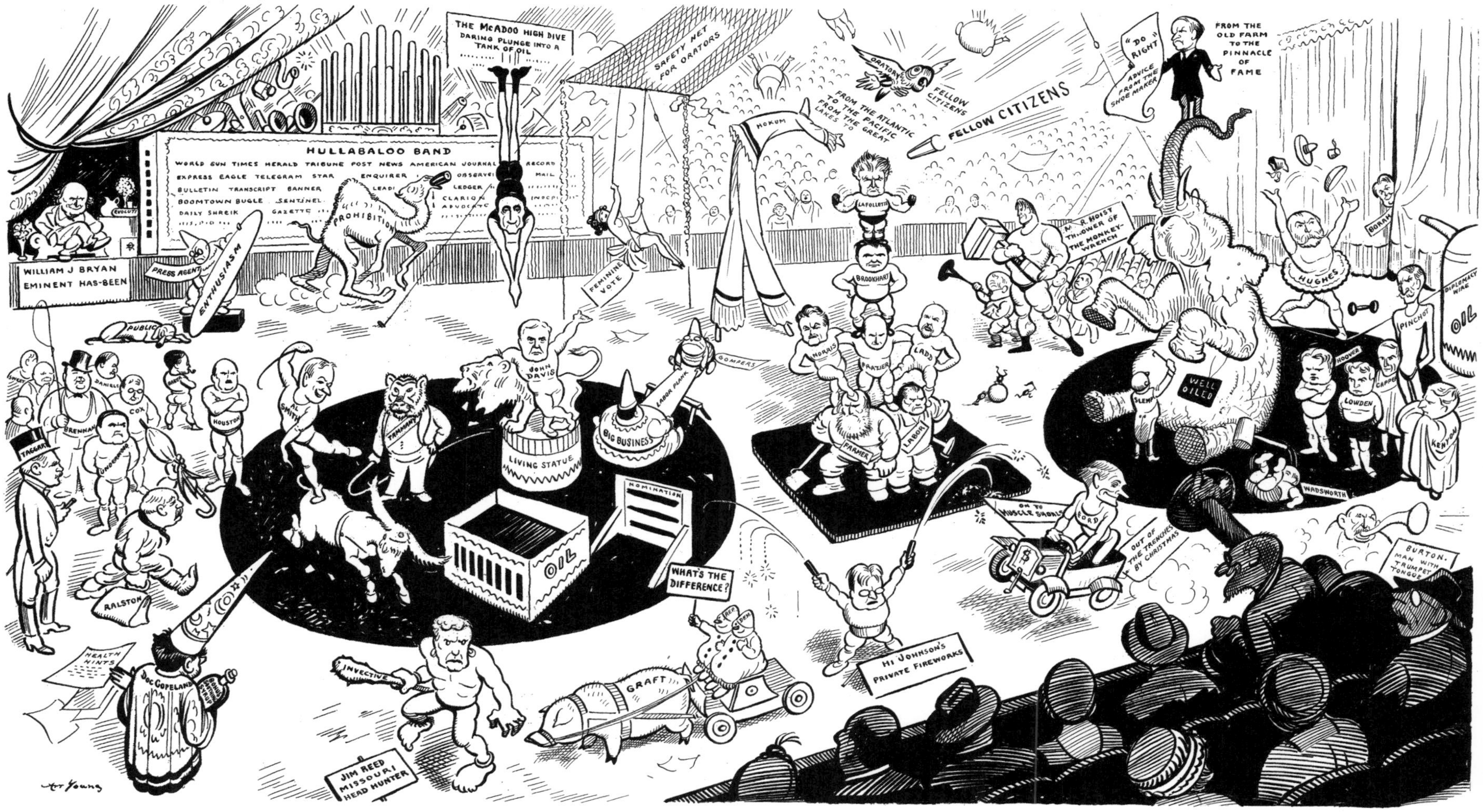
THE McADOO HIGH DIVE
DARING PLUNGE INTO A TANK OF OIL
SAFETY NET FOR ORATORS
HULLABALOO BAND
WORLD SUN TIMES HERALD TRIBUNE POST NEWS AMERICAN JOURNAL RECORD
EXPRESS EAGLE TELEGRAM STAR ENQUIRER MAIL
BULLETIN TRANSCRIPT BANNER LEDGER
BOOMTOWN BUGLE SENTINEL CLARION
DAILY SHREIK GAZETTE
WILLIAM J BRYAN
EMINENT HAS-BEEN
PRESS AGENT
ENTHUSIASM
PROHIBITION
PUBLIC
FEMININE VOTE
HOKUM
ORATORY
FELLOW CITIZENS
FROM THE ATLANTIC TO THE PACIFIC FROM THE LAKES TO GREAT
FELLOW CITIZENS
"DO RIGHT"
ADVICE FROM THE SHOEMAKER
FROM THE OLD FARM TO THE PINNACLE OF FAME
LAFOLLETTE
BROOKHART
M. R. HOIST THROWER OF THE MONKEY-WRENCH
HUGHES
BORAH
DIPLOMACY WIRE
OIL
PINCHOT
NORRIS
FRAZIER
LADD
FARMER
LABOR
GOMPERS
WELL OILED
SLEMP
HOOVER
LOWDEN
CAPPER
KENYON
WADSWORTH
DANIELS
COX
BRENNAN
HOUSTON
UNDERWOOD
TAGGART
RALSTON
AL SMITH
TAMMANY
JOHN DAVIS
LIVING STATUE
BIG BUSINESS
LABOR PLANK
NOMINATION
OIL
WHAT'S THE DIFFERENCE?
REP.
DEM.
HEALTH HINTS
DOC COPELAND
BONUS SOOTHING SYRUP
INVECTIVE
GRAFT
JIM REED MISSOURI HEAD HUNTER
HI JOHNSON'S PRIVATE FIREWORKS
ON TO MUSCLE SHOALS
FORD
OUT OF THE TRENCHES BY CHRISTMAS
BURTON. MAN WITH TRUMPET TONGUE
Art Young

**The Big Show**
*Life*, June 19, 1924
29" x 17.25"

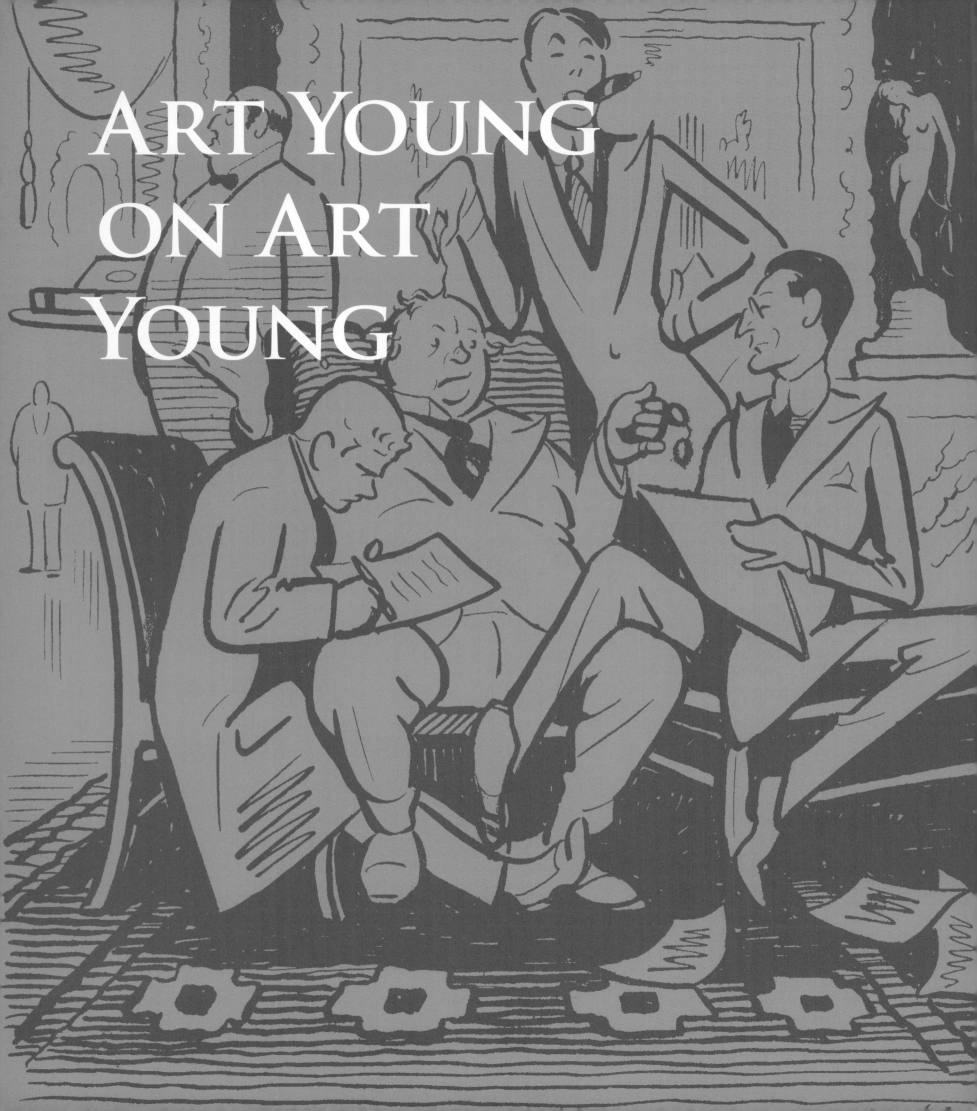

# ART YOUNG
# ON ART
# YOUNG

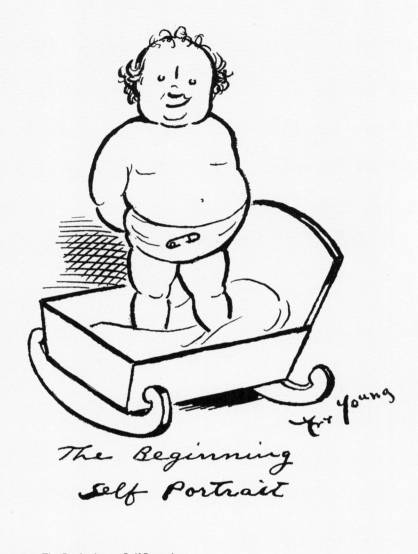

The Beginning
Self Portrait

**ABOVE: The Beginning — Self Portrait**
Dated January 1937
7.5" x 10"

**RIGHT:** *Art Young: His Life and Times,* cover portrait
Original art on New Union Square Hotel (New York City) stationery
6" x 9.5"

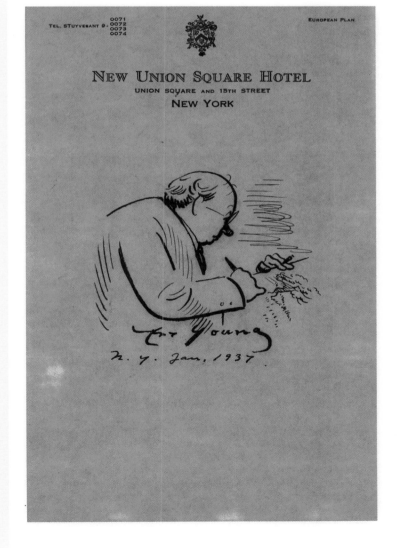

ABOVE: **Flopping Around**
Original pencil art
7" x 4.5"

RIGHT: **Alfred Stieglitz and Art Young**
In Animated Discussion After It's All Over
*The Forum*, April 1929
11" x 10"

61

*Duty to self versus duty to others*

(On my way)

**ABOVE** Duty to Self Versus
Duty to Others
*On My Way,* 1928
13.25" x 9.5"

**RIGHT:** The Thought Tree
Dated 1910
11" x 8"

THE THOUGHT TREE

1910

**ABOVE** **That Always Happens**
An Interview on the Unemployment Situation After the
World War
For *The Nation*, date and publication status unknown
8″ x 6″

**RIGHT: Mr. Young Is Interviewed**
*Good Morning* #16, January 1, 1920
8.5″ x 9″

**OPPOSITE: Trying to Smoke Out an Official of the
State Department**
For *Metropolitan Magazine*, date and publication status
unknown
8″ x 8″

**ABOVE** Graduation Night at Cooper Union, 1906
Class in oratory and debate. I rise to the occasion.
*Art Young: His Life and Times*, 1939
11" x 8.25"

**RIGHT:** It's Still There
New Year's Card 1941
9.5" x 6.5"

**Through This Whirld of Woe**
New Year's Card 1942
11.5" x 7.5"

Out With the Old, In With the New
New Year's Card 1943
6.5" x 10"

Young's Annual
1918
Vintage print
8.5" x 10.75"

**Reversing the Situation**
*The Masses*, September 1915
9.75" x 7.5"

ABOVE: **World's Fairs and Fairs Not So Worldly, Keep Rolling Along**
14.5" x 12"

RIGHT: **Self-portrait (Sleeping)**
Original pencil sketch
8.5" x 11"

**ABOVE** From the Back
Porch
Comments, Scissorings,
and Cartoons by Art
Young
22" x 10.5"

**RIGHT:** Map of My Way
*On My Way,* 1928
Endpapers
18.5" x 22"

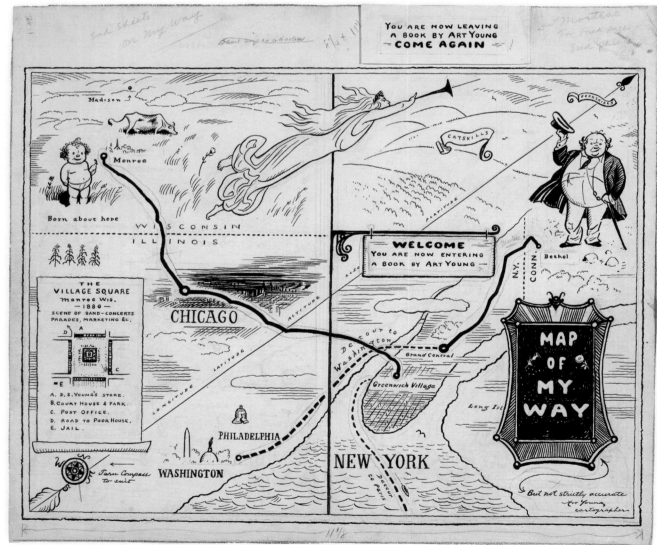

TOP: Art Young's Muse: She Talks for the Metropolitan Bulletin
20.25" x 9.75"

Our Conservative Citizen
*The Coming Nation*, June 15, 1912
ABOVE: Original art
26.5" x 18.5"
ABOVE RIGHT: As published

# ARGOSY

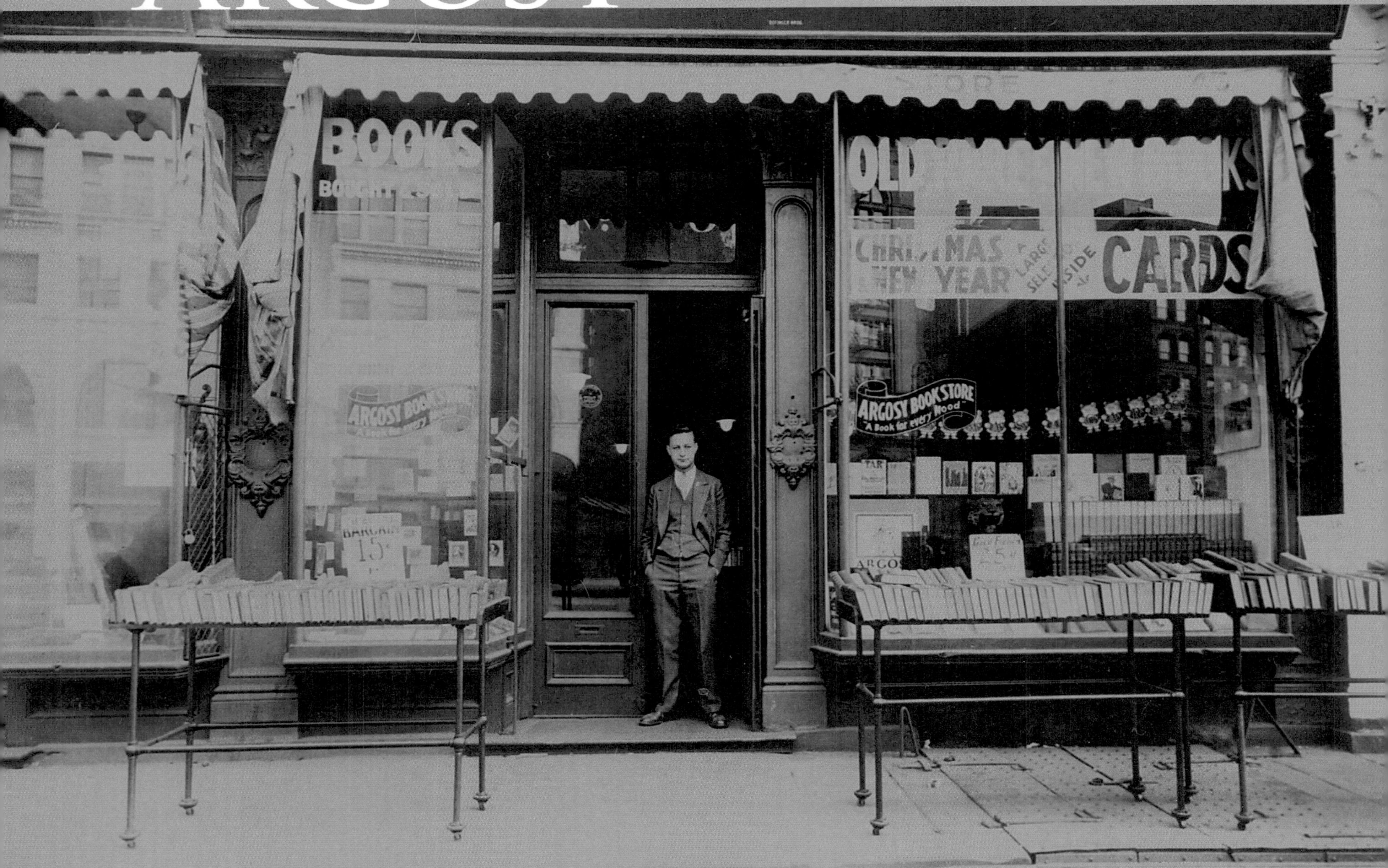
BOOKS
CHRISTMAS
NEW YEAR
CARDS
ARGOSY BOOKSTORE
"A Book for every Mood"
BARGAIN
15¢
25¢

## 19

# A Fortuitous Phone Call

**JUDITH LOWRY**

OPPOSITE: Mr. Cohen in front of the original store on Book Row, 4th Avenue, New York City, c. 1935

**One of the best things about being an antiquarian bookseller is the thrill of the hunt — the continuing opportunity to make new discoveries. On any day, someone might come in with a special book, or a shopping bag full of books, or make a request to come to a home where an uncle has just died and left a collection of rare books.**

In New York City, we've found treasures in all the boroughs, from walk-ups in Harlem to fancy Park Avenue duplexes. I remember a building superintendent who phoned to say a tenant had just moved out and left behind lots of books. It didn't sound very promising, as worthwhile books are seldom left behind, but I asked what sort of books they might be, and he answered that "there must be everything Angie Dickinson ever wrote." I hastened over, and indeed, there were many books that *Emily* Dickinson had written — all first editions and quite valuable.

In the early 1960s I was a beginner, working at the Argosy Bookstore with my father, Louis Cohen, who had founded the business some 40 years earlier, and I was learning by doing, accompanying him as he went on his various "calls" to look at books. We would survey the situation, arrive at an acceptable offer, and later at the shop examine the books individually and price each one. This was before the days of the internet with its many databases, where anyone can look up comparables. It was an arcane process, learned by osmosis after much time, until it became a sixth, or seventh, sense.

One day, a friend of mine, Rebecca — we had been camp counselors together — told me that a relative of hers was the executor of the estate of Art Young and asked me if we might be interested in helping them sell it. I had never heard of Art Young, but my father certainly had and was quite excited. It seems that Art Young — a most prolific artist/illustrator/cartoonist and left-wing activist — had never sold a single original drawing. That is to say, they had been used in various publications, but then returned to him.

Not only had he kept every drawing — from quick pencil sketches to finished pen-and-ink work — but he had hundreds of letters written to him by notables of the day who admired and loved him, books, zinc plates, and other ephemera. It was his entire life, and it was huge in bulk, residing in cartons, albums, folders, and loose stacks.

Overtrowin the Govmunt
8" x 7.5"
Collection of Argosy Bookstore

The family realized its importance and had been trying to sell it to a university library or museum where it could be preserved and kept intact. They had been unsuccessful over quite a long period of time, in part because of the anti-Communist hysteria of the time, stirred up by the Cold War and the spirit of McCarthyism that pervaded the 1950s and early 1960s. Anything left wing was shunned, and no public institution could be found who wanted it at any price.

Added to this liability was the fact that cartoon art was not, at the time, considered worthy of inclusion in "serious" institutions. My father ended up buying it. It was overwhelming in size and content, and despite the fact that he paid less than the original asking price, it was the most expensive purchase he had ever made.

We kept it intact for years, hoping to eventually sell it as a whole, but over time we reluctantly started to sell little bits of it. The letters, being less controversial than the drawings, were easy to sell to autograph collectors. Among the many people who had written warm, friendly letters to Art Young were Helen Keller, H.L. Mencken, Upton Sinclair, John Reed, Lincoln Steffens, James Montgomery Flagg, Booth Tarkington, and Ida Tarbell. Occasionally, we would sell a drawing.

Now, 50 years later, the remainder is still enormous.

*Old friend of family to successful author:* "If I was in your place, Margie, I'd marry some rich fellow — just think! You wouldn't have to write any more of them stories."
Dated February 7, 1911
16″ x 11″
Collection of Adina Cohen

**The March of Civilization**
*Life*, April 19, 1906

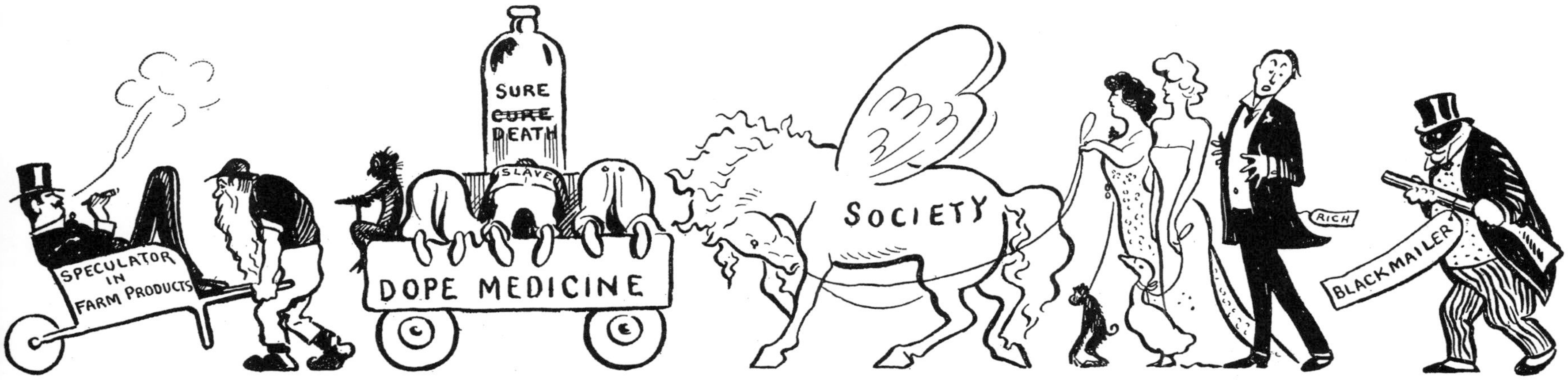
SPECULATOR IN FARM PRODUCTS
SURE CURE DEATH
SLAVE
DOPE MEDICINE
SOCIETY
RICH
BLACKMAILER

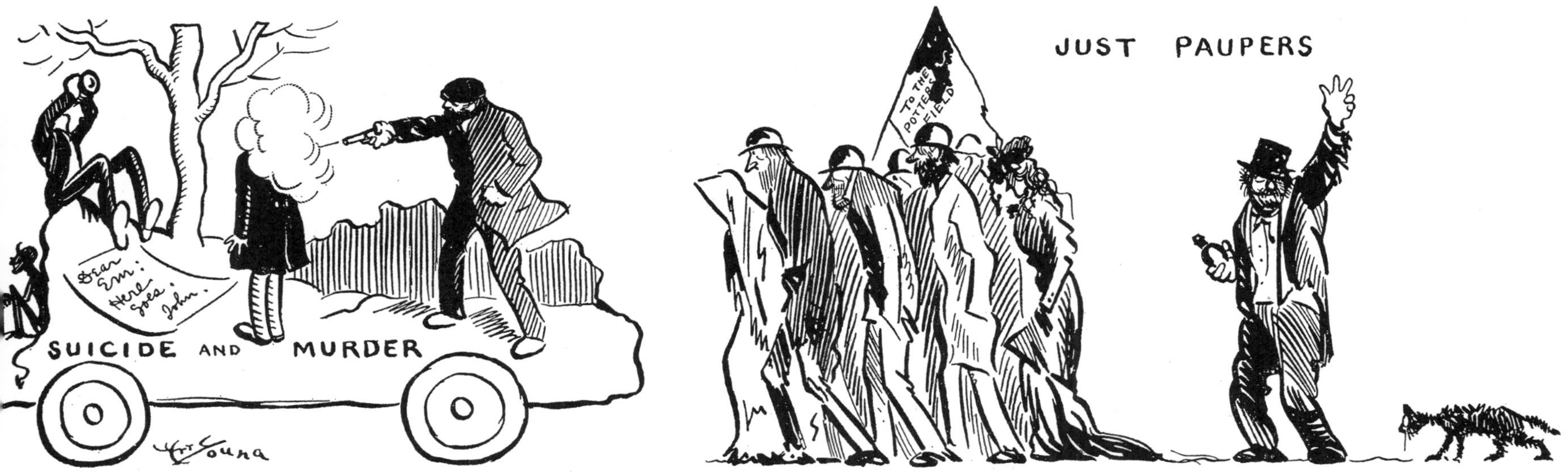
Dear Em: Here goes. John.
SUICIDE AND MURDER
TO THE POTTERS FIELD
JUST PAUPERS

# Epilogue

**LAURA TEN EYCK**

**New York Shadows**
4.75″ x 6.25″
Collection of Laura Ten Eyck

## 20

WHEN I STARTED running the Argosy Gallery, one of my main responsibilities was to "refresh" each of the more than 600 dossiers of antiques maps, prints, and drawings housed in the stacks. Material was obtained from deep storage. By the time I got to Folder Y — Art Young, I was not aware that there were more of his images to find in storage. We had always had an Art Young portfolio of original cartoon drawings available for viewing/purchase since the gallery floor had opened in the 1960s.

By the time I got to the "public" folder, what was left were images of random American political events and lots of portraits of politicians. Although the Internet was beginning to take over our sales transactions, we still had dedicated walk-ins — and the drawings, once pulled by the collector, seemed to come alive. I began to wonder: who was Art Young?

## THAT GUY — SATAN — DEDICATED MYSTERY COLLECTOR

THE PERSON RESPONSIBLE for my discovery of the importance of Art Young was Glenn Bray (whom we affectionately used to call "that Satan guy"). He first emailed requests for devil images by Art Young in 2006 and 2007. As the public folder did not have much of this type of imagery left, I began to roam around in deep storage. I would steal away when there was a quiet moment and search. As soon as I found a few images of Satan to please his request, my search was done — bingo.

The quiet persistence of Glenn's email requests for more images was the impetus behind the ultimate discovery of a treasure trove. Eventually, I fell pretty hard for both the artist and the collector. I began coming early/staying late, squeezing lunch in at the warehouse. It became the activity that I wanted to do more than any of my other responsibilities.

I own two drawings by Art Young. My favorite is called "New York Shadows" which captures perfectly the sensation of walking in New York in early spring or late fall along one of the big avenues. It is not a dazzling light but a raking, dry crisp light that inspires anyone who walks in it. Upon seeing the drawing for the first time, I realized that Art Young was a New Yorker.

**THE EDITORS WISH TO THANK**

Gary Groth, Argosy Book Store: Laura Ten Eyck, Judith Lowry, and the owners of Argosy Book Store, New York (www.argosybooks.com); Marc Moorash, Ava Dawn Heydt, Anthony Mourek, art spiegelman, Justin Green, Lena Zwalve, Monte Beauchamp, Cameron Jamie, Charles Schneider, Rick Marschall, Gabe Bartalos, Carol Lay, Piet Schreuders, Robert Armstrong, Eddie Gorodetsky, Coco Shinomiya, Jonathan Barli, Dean Mullaney, The Kelly Collection of American Illustration, Paul C. Tumey, Joanne and Jennifer Uppendahl, Dan Nadel, Tom Spurgeon, Bob and Lorraine Dietel, Deborah Rouse and the Archives and Special Collections Department of the Savannah College of Art and Design, Calvin, Francis, Gilbert, Toby and Tabitha (cat chums), and Cody Ramlow.

**ARTWORK RESTORATION AND PHOTOGRAPHY**

Frank M. Young, Monte Beauchamp, John Davis, and the staff of Los Angeles Paper Group (www.lapapergroup.com)

**ADDITIONAL PHOTOGRAPHY**

Blue Trimarchi and the staff at Artworks Fine Art (www.fineartpublishing.com)

# CONTRIBUTOR BIOGRAPHIES

## 21

**Anthony J. Mourek,** property manager and political art collector. Fascinated by political cartoons and the use of art in political discourse since the late 1960s. Collects original drawings of political cartoons, prints, oil paintings, sculpture, and related books. Considers Art Young America's best political cartoonist/artist in the period between Teddy and Franklin Roosevelt, though believes Young was often wrong. Author of *Famous, Infamous & Forgotten* (The Grolier Club, New York, 2013), and recently exhibited "It's Hell But Here We Are Again," Art Young drawings from his collection, at Loyola University Chicago (www.lib.luc.edu/specialcollections/exhibits/show/art-young).

Portrait by R. Britto

**Judith Lowry** is a second-generation antiquarian bookseller at Argosy Book Store in New York City. A graduate of Cornell University, she has lectured widely on rare books, first editions, and book collecting. She has taught at Cornell University, The University of Denver, and the University of Florida.

Photo by Ben Lowry

**Justin Green**, best known for his 1972 autobiographical comic, *Binky Brown Meets the Holy Virgin Mary*, has published his cartoons in scores of publications since then. His self-penned titles include *The Sign Game*, reflections on his odyssey into the lettering trade, and *Musical Legends*, a series of cartoon biographies about musicians of all genres. He is an active participant in the growing academic effort to promote comics as a legitimate art form and field of study. He continues to wield brush, pen, and an old-fashioned typewriter on a daily basis.

Self-portrait

**Laura Ten Eyck** was trained as an artist and is a graduate of York University in Toronto, Canada, with an honors BFA in technical print making. She received her MFA from New York University in 1999. Laura is from Mimico, the oldest of the Lakeshore Municipalities of Lake Ontario in Canada. It was her apprenticeship with Ruth Shevin and Adina Cohen in the map trade that informed her decision to emigrate to the United States. When she learned through a client about the nuances of her Dutch heritage (she is a descendant of Coenradt Ten Eyck, one of the Dutch West India company land grant recipients in 1650 New Amsterdam), she knew it was her destiny to stay in New York City. Laura has run the map and print room at the Argosy Book Store in Manhattan since 1999. She currently lives in Brooklyn, New York, with her family.

Photo by Emily Pettigrew

**Marc Moorash** is the editor of Seraphemera Books (www.seraphemera.org), which recently released the previously unpublished and long-lost Art Young manuscript, *Types of the Old Home Town*. He is co-editor (with his wife, Ava Dawn Heydt), of the *Garbanzo Literary Journal*. He has been working diligently with the Bethel Historical Society in Bethel, Connecticut, to reopen and replenish the Art Young Gallery (www.artyounggallery.org), just one mile down the road from where Young had his gallery in the 1920s and 1930s.

Drawing by Dawn Heydt

**Valerie Higgins** received her MLS from Indiana University in 2010. She was an assistant archivist at the Art Institute of Chicago before becoming lab archivist and historian at an Illinois laboratory in 2012. She has been the archivist for Anthony J. Mourek's collections since 2010.

Photo by Lauren Biron

**art spiegelman** is a passionate advocate of the potential of comics. From his early underground comix, which playfully deconstructed clichés of the art form; to *Raw* magazine, co-edited with his spouse, Francois Mouly; to his two-volume Pulitzer Prize–winning *Maus*, which helped to found the concept of the graphic novel; spiegelman has defined the cutting edge of comics' maturation. An accomplished writer and historian, spiegelman recently toured the world with his show Wordless, a multi-media marriage of cartoon images and live music. spiegelman lives and works in the heart of New York City.

Self-portrait

# EDITOR BIOGRAPHIES

### GLENN BRAY

GLENN BRAY, PUBLISHER/EDITOR of books on: Basil Wolverton (*Gjdrkzlxcbwq Comics* 1972, *Foopgoop Frolics*, 1975, *The Original Art of Basil Wolverton*, 2007); Harvey Kurtzman (the first comprehensive study of the *Mad* comics legend, *The Illustrated Harvey Kurtzman Index*, 1975); Stanislav Szukalski (www.szukalski.com), the Polish sculptor (*Troughful of Pearls*, 1980, *Inner Portraits*, 1982, *The Lost Tune*, 1990, *Struggle*, 2000); and the Fantagraphics publication of his personal original art collection, *The Blighted Eye* (2014). He resides in California and keeps his eye tuned toward all things Art Young since finding a copy of *Art Young's Inferno* in the mid-1990s.

Drawing by Dawn Heydt

THINKING OUTSIDE THE BOX

### FRANK M. YOUNG

BORN IN 1963, Young taught himself to read at age three so he could get more out of the comics medium. By the time he became the *Comics Journal*'s managing editor in 1991, he was well-versed in the history and diversity of comics, from classic newspaper strips to the underground revolution. In the 2000s, he gained note for his work in identifying the various works of John Stanley, which he gathered in a three-volume bibliography. In 2013, he won the Eisner award for his work, along with artist David Lasky, as writer/colorist on the graphic novel *The Carter Family: Don't Forget This Song*. He and Lasky have a new graphic novel in the works. As colorist, Young has worked with the cartoons of Rube Goldberg and, most recently, *New Yorker* cartoonist Harry Bliss. He continues to create comics and study the medium's rich history and future, and writes occasionally for the online iteration of the *Comics Journal*. He lives and works in Portland, Oregon.

Portrait by David Lasky

# A SELECTED ART YOUNG BIBLIOGRAPHY 23

**MARC MOORASH**      *Words and illustrations by Art Young unless noted*

## Books and Pamphlets

**1892**: *Hell Up-to-Date*, The Schulte Publishing Company, Chicago

**1892**: *Hades Up-to-Date*, F.J. Schulte & Co., Chicago

**1893**: *Hawaii … A Snap Shot* by Conflagration Jones, illustrations by Art Young and others, Smith & Colbert, Chicago

**1894**: *Hell Up-to-Date*, Ariel Library Series No. 1 (paperback), The Schulte Publishing Company, Chicago

**1897**: *Authors' Readings*, New York, F.A. Stokes Company

**1901**: *Through Hell With Hiprah Hunt*, Zimmerman's, New York

**1904**: *The Arthur Young Cartoons*, Series No. 1, The Patriotic Art Co., New York

**1918**: *Art Young's Political Primer* (for Scott Nearing campaign), Socialist Party of the United States, Chicago

**1920**: *The Campaign Primer*, Socialist Party of the United States, Chicago

**1920** (circa): *Allegories*, Good Morning Publishing Co. (pamphlet)

**1921** (circa): *Art Young Souvenir Pamphlet*, H.S. Reis, New York

**1927**: *Trees at Night*, Boni & Liveright, New York

**1927**: *Heavenly Discourse* by Charles Erskine Wood, illustrations by Art Young, Vanguard Press, New York

**1928**: *On My Way: Being the Book of Art Young in Text and Picture*, Horace Liveright, New York

**1930**: *The Socialist Primer*, Socialist Party of the United States, Chicago

**1930**: *Encyclopedia Britannica*, Fourteenth Edition.

(Young wrote the entry for "Cartoon"; appears with his illustrations)

**1933**: *Art Young's Inferno*, Delphic Studios, New York

**1936**: *The Best of Art Young*, Introduction by Heywood Broun, Vanguard Press, New York

**1938**: *Thomas Rowlandson*, Willey Book Co., New York

**1939**: *Is Plenty Too Much for the Common People* by George R. Kirkpatrick, illustrations by Art Young, Florence H. Kirkpatrick, California

**1939**: *Art Young: His Life and Times*, edited by John Nicholas Beffel, Sheridan House, New York

**1968**: *Good Morning* (Volumes 1–3), Greenwood Reprint Corporation

**2015**: *Types of the Old Home Town*, Seraphemera Books & Bethel Historical Society, Bethel, Connecticut

**2015**: *The Complete Good Morning*, Seraphemera Books & Bethel Historical Society, Bethel, Connecticut.

## Periodicals

*American Field, Americana, Appeal to Reason, The Birth Control Review, Chicago Daily News, Chicago Evening Mail, Chicago Inter-Ocean, Chicago Tribune, Collier's Weekly, The Coming Nation, Cosmopolitan, Denver Times, Der Groyser Kundes (The Big Stick), Direction, Fight, Good Morning (1919–1922, Good Morning Publishing Co., New York), Hello Buddy, Judge, Labor Age, The Labor Journal, The Latin Quarterly, Leslie's Weekly, The Liberator, Life, The Masses, Metropolitan, Milwaukee Free Press, Modern Monthly, The Modernist, The Nation, The New Leader, New Masses, The New Republic, New York Daily Call, New York Evening Journal, New York Herald Tribune, The New York Times, The New Yorker, Nimble Nickel, Pall Mall Budget, Pearson's, Puck, The Saturday Evening Post, Socialist Call, Sons of Veterans, The Survey, Texas Shiftings, Today, Unemployed War Veteran, The Unemployed*

**FOLLOWING:**
**Gateway to Happiness**
Original art exhibited at the New York World's Fair, 1939
21.5» x 13»

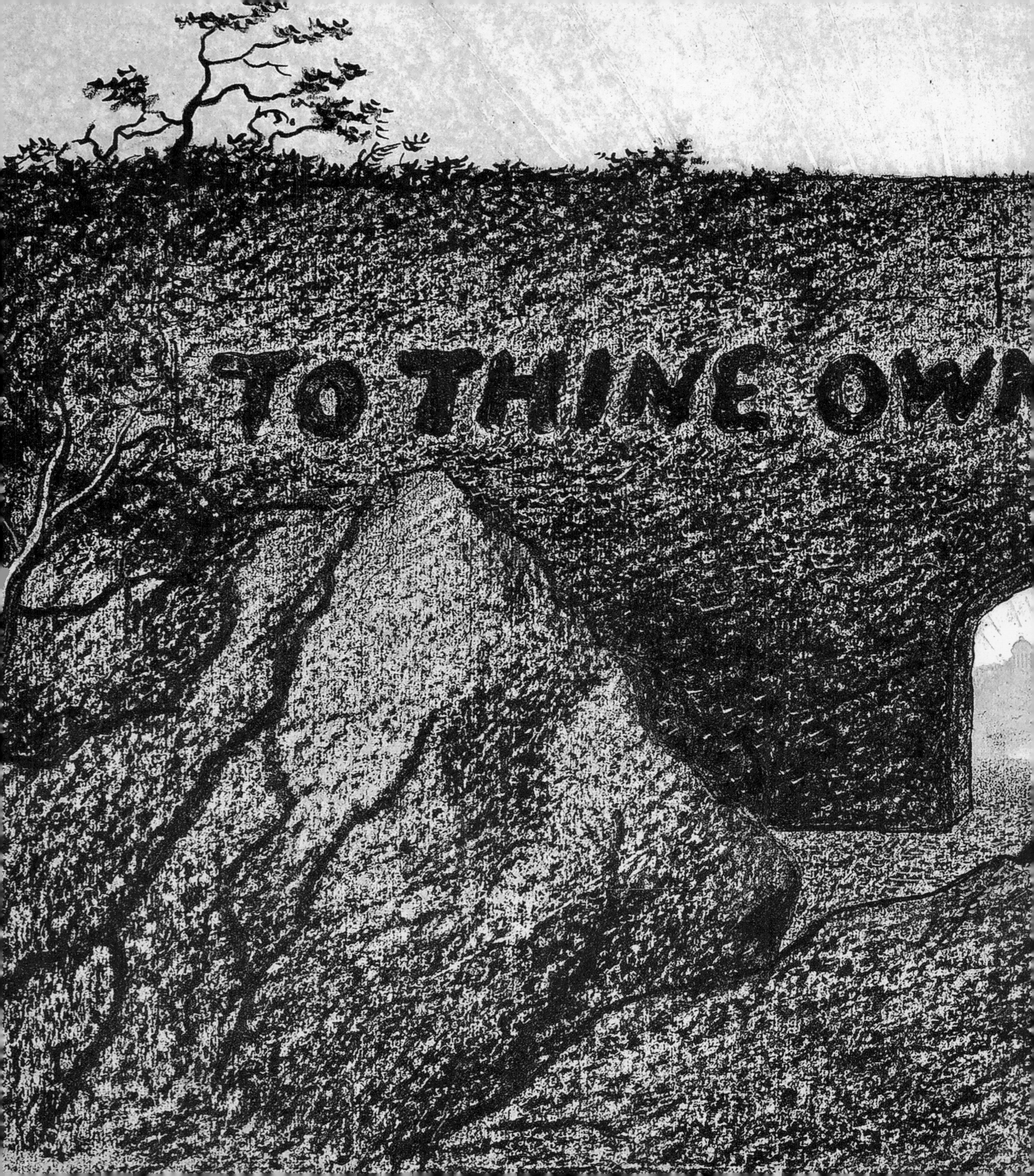
TO THINE OWN

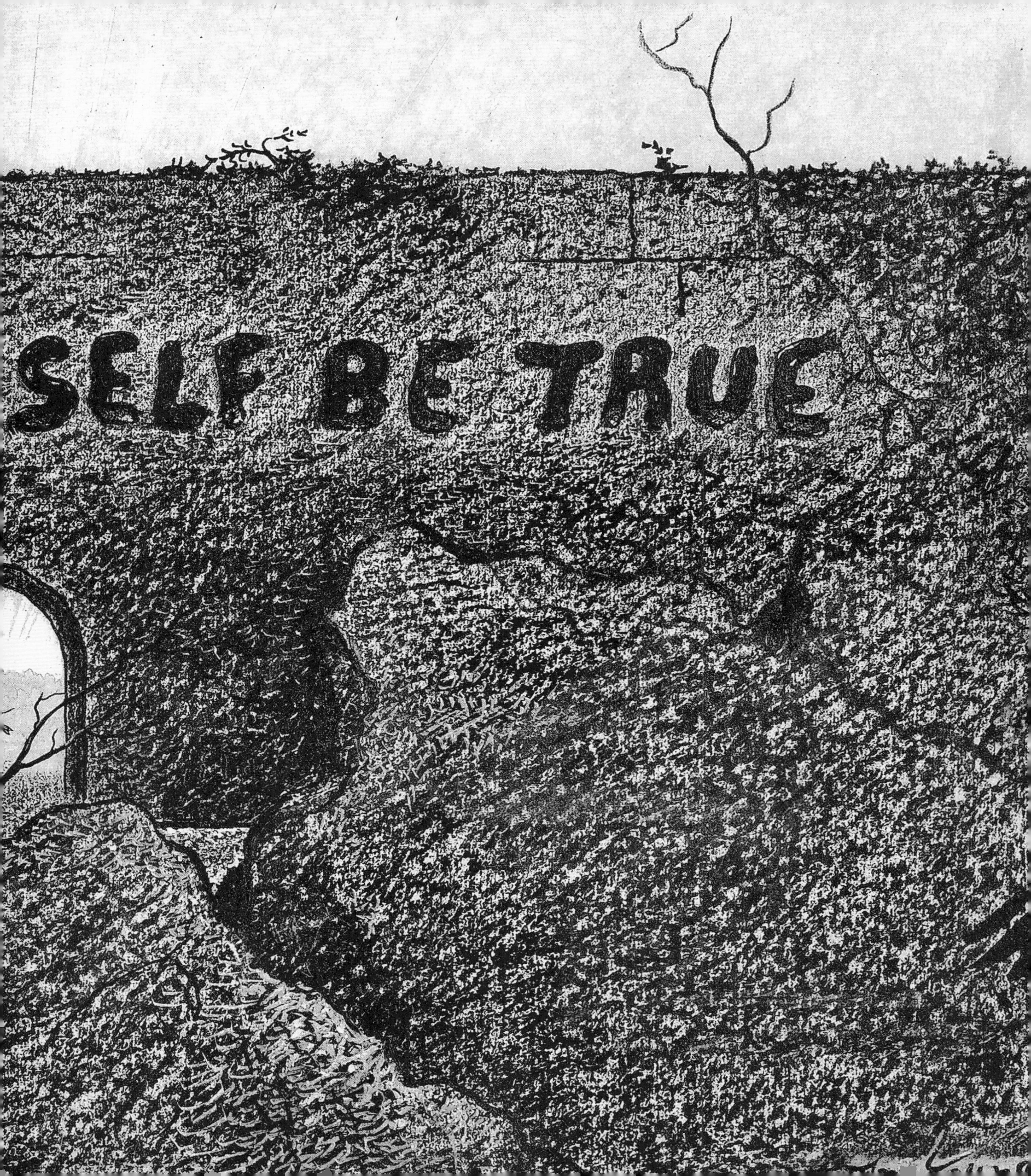
SELF BE TRUE

"THE KIND OF A GIRL THAT MEN FORGET"

IN JAIL AND HE KNOWS IT

STOCKINGS $3⁰⁰ A PAIR

SHOES $9⁰⁰ A PAIR

RENT $30.⁰⁰ A MONTH

WORK HARD

DONT COMPLAIN

SMILE CONTINUALLY AND LOOK PRETTY ON FIFTEEN DOLLARS A WEEK.

DONT ORGANIZE

DONT CALL YOUR SOUL YOUR OWN.

WORK HARD

CAPITALIST SYSTEM

AN AVERAGE CLERK WORKS TEN HOURS A DAY. SUPPORTS A FAMILY. GETS $14⁰⁰ A WEEK. AFRAID OF HIS JOB. WORKED OUT—THEN DISCHARGED

IN JAIL BUT HE DOES'NT KNOW IT

THE SHADOW OF DOUBT

YOUNG CLERGYMAN (REGARDING A GROUP OF MALE BATHERS)—"SO GOD CREATED MAN IN HIS OWN IMAGE; IN THE IMAGE OF GOD CREATED HE HIM!"